STRUCTURING LEARNING ENVIRONMENTS IN TEACHER EDUCATION TO ELICIT DISPOSITIONS AS HABITS OF MIND

*Strategies and Approaches Used
and Lessons Learned*

Edited by
Erskine S. Dottin
Lynne D. Miller
George E. O'Brien

University Press of America,® Inc.
Lanham · Boulder · New York · Toronto · Plymouth, UK

Library of Congress Control Number: 2013930283
ISBN: 978-0-7618-6086-0 (clothbound : alk. paper)
eISBN: 978-0-7618-6087-7

♾™ The paper used in this publication meets the minimum
requirements of American National Standard for Information
Sciences—Permanence of Paper for Printed Library Materials,
ANSI Z39.48-1992

TO

Our mentors, teachers, students, family members, colleagues, and other supporters who have influenced our thinking, teaching, research, and writing during this professional journey

CONTENTS

FOREWORD

Our students are *IN* the 21st century and are waiting for schools to catch up with them. The impact of technology changes the way we think. We are able to think globally and, at the same time, think locally. We are aware instantaneously about the news of events that continuously remind us of our interdependence. Puzzling our senses and conflicting our minds, we are bombarded with an abundance of information from a variety of sources—some reliable and some not.

As Tom Friedman (2005) suggests, "the world is flat". Such noted authors as Tony Wagner (2010, 2012), Andy Hargreaves and Michael Fullan (2012), Daniel Pink (2009), Carol Dweck, (2006), Linda Darling-Hammond (2012), Diane Ravitch (*2010*) and others, join a chorus of affinity groups and coalitions calling for global and common core standards and college readiness as a means for preparing our youth to prosper and maybe to survive in an uncertain future.

Distilling what they all are espousing is to teach students those characteristics, moral principles and dispositions that will be needed to survive and to function effectively in the centuries beyond 21. This book provides the vision and leadership for teacher training institutions to incorporate these new curriculum needs into the preparation of future teachers. The role of teachers has been shifting and calls for a new pedagogy. Teachers need to be grounded in not only sound but also future-oriented curriculum and instructional practices.

This is vision reflects a curriculum of *process* that serves as leverage for learning any content. It is a curriculum that gives students practice engaging with complex problems, dilemmas and conflicts the resolutions of which are not immediately apparent. And, what is most significant about these processes is that they are as worthy for university teacher educators as well as for the teachers they educate. These processes are referred to as dispositions that reflect the necessary capacities that students will need to acquire, practice and continue to learn as they become more thoughtful in their education, in their family, their community and in their lives.

There are an increasing number of nations around the world that are experiencing an "Intellectual Spring" in which ministries of education are adopting dispositional teaching and learning. As an example, the Global Competencies (2011) set forth by the Council of Chief State School Officers address the knowledge, skills and dispositions to understand and act creatively and innovatively on issues of global significance. Those competencies competencies and the dispositions they require include: *Investigating the world beyond their immediate environment*: Curiosity, wonderment and questioning, problem posing. *Recognizing their own and others' perspectives*: Empathy for others, flexibility, collaboration, inhibiting impulse, listening, humility. *Communicating their ideas effectively with diverse audiences*: Thinking and communicating both orally and in writing with clarity and precision, striving for accuracy. *Translating their ideas and findings into appropriate actions to improve conditions*: Taking responsible risks, persisting.

It is apparent that outcomes such as these require educational mind shifts (Costa & Kallick, 2011) such as:

1. From knowing right answers to: knowing how to behave when answers are not readily apparent. In the past, schools tended to teach, assess and reward convergent thinking and the acquisition of content and with a limited range of acceptable answers. Life in the real world, however, demands multiple ways to do something well. A fundamental shift is required from valuing right answers as the purpose for learning, to knowing how to behave when we *don't* know answers--knowing what to do when confronted with those paradoxical, dichotomous, enigmatic, confusing, ambiguous, discrepant and sometimes overwhelming situations which plague our lives. An imperative mind-shift is essential--from valuing knowledge *acquisition* as an outcome to valuing knowledge *production* as an outcome. We want students to learn how to develop a critical stance with their work: inquiring, thinking flexibly, and learning from another person's perspective.

As our paradigm shifts, we will need to let go of our obsession with acquiring content knowledge as an end in itself, and make room for viewing content as a vehicle for developing broader, more pervasive and complex goals such as the Habits of Mind. The focus is on learning FROM the objectives instead of learning OF the objectives. And

2. From transmitting meaning to constructing meaning. Meaning making is not a spectator sport. Knowledge is a constructive process rather than a finding. It is not the content that gets stored in memory but the activity of constructing it that gets stored. Humans don't *get* ideas; they *make* ideas. As neuroscientists study the processes of learning they are realizing that a constructivist model of learning reflects their best understanding of the brain's natural way of making sense of the world. Constructivism holds that learning is essentially active. A person learning something new brings to that experience all of their previous knowledge and present mental patterns. Each new fact or experience is assimilated into a living web of understanding that already exists in that person's mind. Learning is neither passive nor simply objective.

Furthermore, meaning making is not just an individual operation. The individual interacts with others to construct shared knowledge. There is a cycle of internalization of what is socially constructed as shared meaning, which is then externalized to affect the learner's social participation.

Constructivist learning, therefore, is viewed as a reciprocal process in that the individual influences the group and the group influences the individual (Vygotsky, 1978).

Little or no learning will take place unless the learning environment is trustful and the others who are significant to the learner (parents, teachers, coaches, etc.) model the desired outcomes. One of the greatest distractions to trust is when there is incongruity with how a teacher acts and what the teacher professes. This suggests that teachers must learn how to "walk the talk" through modeling the dispositions of a continuous and inquiring learner.

This book sends a message to teacher education accreditation agencies to include in their ratings, criteria and rubrics that include teaching the dispositions. The challenge is to consider how to make certain that the teachers of teachers use the habits as the mission of their and their institution's curriculum design. This book provides strategies to accomplish and assess the development of the Habits of Mind as well as commentaries of how students in the program at Florida International University have responded to a program in which dispositions were made explicit, taught along with content and modeled by the professors and master teachers.

An overarching message is to show what happens when an entire teacher education faculty adopts a common vision, a shared vocabulary and a dedication to incorporating these dispositions (Habits of Mind) into the curriculum and instructional program. It provides an inspiration for educators who are desirous of making the world a more thoughtful place.

Arthur L. Costa, Ed.D
Granite Bay, California
Bena Kallick, Ph.D
Westport, Connecticut
Co-Directors and Founders of the Institute for Habits of Mind

References

Darling-Hammond, L. (2012, June 25). No: Teaching is too complex. *Wall Street Journal*. PR4.

Dweck, C. (2006). *Mindset: The new psychology of success*. New York, NY: Ballantine Books.

Friedman, T.L. (2005). *The world is flat: A brief history of the 21st-century*. New York, NY: Picador.

Hargreaves, A. and Fullan, M. (2012). *Professional capital: Transforming teaching in every school*. New York, NY: Teachers College Press.

Costa, A. and Kallick, B. (2011). It takes some getting used to. In Jacobs, H.H. (Ed.) *Curriculum 21: Essential education for a changing world*. Alexandria, VA: ASCD.

Mansilla, V.B. and Jackson, (2011). *Educating for global competence: Preparing our youth to engage the world*. New York, NY: Council of Chief State School Officers' EdSteps Initiative & Asia Society Partnership for Global Learning.

Pink, D. (2009). *Drive: The surprising truth about what motivates us*. New York, NY: Penguin.

Ravitch, D. (2010). *The death and life of the great American school system: How testing and choice are undermining education*. New York, NY: Basic Books.

Vygotsky, L. S. (1978). *Mind in society*. Cambridge, MA: Harvard University Press.

Wagner, T. (2012). *Creating innovators: The making of young people who will change the world*. New York, NY: Scribner.

Wagner, T. (2010). *The global achievement gap: Why even our best schools don't teach the new survival skills our children need-and what we can do about it*. New York, NY: Basic Books.

PREFACE

The germinal seeds for this work were planted between 1994 and 1996 when the co-editors worked closely to bring conceptual coherence to accreditation efforts in the College of Education at Florida International University. The focus on dispositions by the National Council for Accreditation of Teacher Education provided the flowering of this work. One of the co-editors received the College's Frost Professor Award in 2010 and used that platform to create a Faculty Learning Community to focus on dispositions as habits of mind for making professional conduct more intelligent. The community's goals are (1) to understand how dispositions as habits of mind may be used to promote good thinking in the COE faculty. (2) To appreciate how dispositions as habits of mind can enhance the COE faculty's teaching and learning. (3) To understand, document, and support individual and group learning. This work is a manifestation of the community's experiences and efforts to link conceptual understanding of dispositions as habits of mind to their pedagogical efforts with teacher education candidates at both the undergraduate and graduate levels.

ACKNOWLEDGEMENTS

The co-editors and chapter contributors to this work would like to acknowledge those who have provided particularly strong support in helping them to bring this book to fruition. First Dr. Delia Garcia, the Dean of the College of Education who assisted the growth of the learning community administratively and financially. Second Dr. Milton Cox, the national leader on faculty learning communities, who provided directional clarity for the group. Third Dr.. Arthur Costa and Dr. Bena Kallick national and international leaders on habits of mind who shared their intellectual acumen with the group graciously.

INTRODUCTION

The Moral Dimension

We are in an era of accountability in which the salient focus is on what one knows and what one can do. The accountability spotlight has not avoided teacher education, and, as such, "business" in teacher education is driven by performance outcomes - what teacher education candidates, teacher education graduates and their K-12 students know and can do. In fact, the report put out by The Center for American Progress entitled, *Measuring What Matters: A Strong Accountability Model for Teacher Education*, reinforces the foregoing (Crowe, 2010).

But, there is another dimension to teacher education as noted by Gary Fenstermacher, "We need to prepare and encourage our teachers to be as concerned with their moral manner as they are with their subject matter methods" (Fenstermacher, 1994, p. 15). Fenstermacher's exhortation makes sense if put in a context of teacher educator as professional as done by Lee Shulman (2005):

> Professional education is a synthesis of three apprenticeships-a cognitive apprenticeship wherein one learns to think like a professional, a practical apprenticeship where one learns to perform like a professional, and a moral apprenticeship where one learns to think and act in a responsible and ethical manner that integrates all three domains (para. 8).

What one may draw from Shulman is that while understanding (having knowledge) and acting are critical to teacher educators, they are necessary, but not sufficient, in light of the moral dimension for professional educators. In fact, Sullivan (n.d.) cautions that "professionals are inescapably moral agents whose work depends upon public trust for its success" (para. 5).

The literature is replete, therefore, with calls for teacher educators to encourage candidates to be as concerned about the moral dimension of pedagogy as they may be about content and methods (Ducharme & Ducharme, 1999; Goodlad, Soder & Sirotnik, 1990; Hansen, 2001; Osguthorpe, 2008; Richardson & Fenstermacher, 2001; Sockett, 19993; Sockett, 2006; Tom, 1984).

It is one thing to encourage the moral dimension of pedagogy, and it is another, however, for many teacher education programs to establish conceptual understanding of the moral dimension of pedagogy, to have faculty engage in substantial discourse, discovery and understanding of the moral dimension, and to engage candidates in meaningful learning experiences. The Task Force on

Teacher Education as Moral Community of the American Association of Colleges for Teacher Education concluded that "the injection by NCATE into its procedures of an explicit attention to moral agency in students and teachers has left many institutions in difficulty" (Sockett, 2006, p. 7).

This book will help to provide guidance to teacher education programs in this arena, in a manner similar to that provided by the Task Force in *Teacher Dispositions: Building a Teacher Education Framework of Moral Standards* (Sockett, 2006).

The Essential Moral Interest

Some scholars suggest that to make the moral manifest in teaching, it must be guided by an Aristotelian perspective on moral development (Osguthorpe, 2008; Sockett, 2006). This view holds that "the young acquire virtue by being around virtuous people" and "virtue is 'caught' or 'picked up' by interacting with those who seemingly possess it through habituation" (Osguthorpe, 2008, pp. 288-289). In contrast, this current work subscribes to the Deweyan idea of moral practice as "the disposition to respond intelligently to new circumstances" (Anderson, 2010, para. 1) or more specifically, as "the use of reflective intelligence to revise one's judgments in light of the consequences of acting on them" (Anderson, 2010, para. 2). According to Dottin (2006), the dispositions that render action intelligent must "enhance our growth through the application of our thinking to things already known for the purpose of improving social conditions" (p. 39). These dispositions for effective problem-solving and continuous learning include the habits of mind of persisting, managing impulsivity, listening with understanding and empathy, thinking flexibly, thinking about thinking, striving for accuracy, questioning and posing problems, applying past knowledge to new situations, thinking and communicating with clarity and precision, gathering data through all senses, creating, imagining, innovating, responding with wonderment and awe, taking responsible risks, finding humor, thinking interdependently, and remaining open to continuous learning (Costa & Kallick, 2000).

Further, Hansen (2002) interprets Dewey's view of reflective intelligence as being grounded in "learning from experience" where dispositions as habits may be seen as expressions of growth. To retain the ability to learn from experience obliges a person to cultivate among other things, what Dewey calls, "'personal attitudes' toward thinking and acting in the world. These attitudes include.... Straightforwardness, open-mindedness, breadth of outlook, integrity of purpose and responsibility. Such qualities characterize a person who is extending and deepening an interest in learning from all of his or her contacts in the world, whether the latter be weighty or light, momentary or enduring, pleasant or trying" (Hansen, 2002, p. 269). This deepening of interest in learning from experience may be captured as "the essential moral interest" (Hansen, 2002). It is:

Moral...because it pivots around ongoing, responsive engagement with other human beings and their projects, purposes, and hopes...[and] it is essential because it is vital, significant, and decisive for the direction human life can take...Such interest fuels the possibility of a flourishing life for individual and society alike (Hansen, 2002, p. 269).

If education is the force of forming dispositions–intellectual and emotional–toward nature and fellowmen then teachers should play a central role in helping students develop the essential moral interest –through educative environments (Hansen, 2002, p. 269). The teacher's moral responsibility must, therefore be, to help the student grow from uncultivated impulses, to nurtured desires, to reflective planning and purposing.

The qualities of thought and conduct that the College of Education (The Unit) at Florida International University expects to see when teacher education candidates are demonstrating pedagogical intelligence are 12 of the habits of mind articulated by Costa & Kallick (2000). These dispositions (that is, habits of mind) are deemed as necessary to guide the essential moral interest of candidates in their being mindful educators. A requisite in the unit, therefore, is for faculty to structure learning environments that will enhance the essential moral interest for candidates.

The Historical/Developmental Process that Led to the Habits of Mind

But, how did the College of Education (The Unit) get to its focus on structuring learning environments to elicit in candidates the habits of mind that will enhance their moral interest? In 1972, the conceptual orientation of teacher education at FIU was structured as four-year undergraduate (B.S.) and advanced level (M.S.) degree programs for credentialed and experienced professionals (Arends, Winitzky, & Burek, 1996; Feiman-Nemser, 1990).

Typically, students entered the upper division program after receiving an A.A. degree from Miami-Dade Community College. A smaller number of candidates transferred lower division credits from other universities or from the liberal studies program at FIU. Undergraduate and graduate courses offered by the School of Education, (the college was referred to as the School of Education in 1972), were consistent with a technological conceptual orientation (Feiman-Nemser, 1990). "An orientation refers to a set of ideas about the goals of teacher preparation and the means for achieving them. Ideally, a conceptual orientation includes a view of teaching and learning and a theory about learning to teach" (Feiman-Nemser, p. 220). The technological conceptual orientation is one of five conceptual orientations in teacher preparation (i.e., academic, practical, technological, personal, and critical social), and focuses on the knowledge and skills of teaching with a primary goal to prepare teachers who carry out teaching proficiently (Feiman-Nemser, 1990; Gage & Winne, 1975; Joyce, 1975). The technological conceptual orientation is associated with a movement which spanned the late 1950s to early 1980s when constructing teacher education as a training problem was in vogue (Cochran-Smith & Fries, 2008; Urban, 1990). At FIU courses were designed to be performance or competency based as well as field-based for professional service in education and training. Typically, all courses included a requirement to spend time in schools as well as class time on campus. In this era...process-product research on teaching became prominent; this program of research had the goal of developing "scientific basis for the art of teaching" (Gage, 1978) by specifying teacher behaviors correlated with student achievement and applying them as treatments to classroom situations. Research on teacher education also emerged as an identifiable program of empirical study (Cochran-Smith & Fries, p. 1073).

State of Florida policy mandates in the early 1990s required all colleges of education to become nationally accredited by the National Council for Accreditation of Teacher Education (NCATE) or to be closed. The Unit, at FIU, approached the mandate from its technological conceptual orientation, and a technical competence framework of teacher education (Zimpher & Howey, 1987; Howey & Zimpher, 1989), but was denied national accreditation (the unit was approaching national accreditation from a more technical orientation). At about this time, the national accrediting body was engaged in revising its standards, and pointed to the need for units to articulate a "conceptual framework." NCATE indicated that the framework establish a common vision for the unit, and be grounded in an intellectual philosophy that provides guided coherence for programs, courses, teaching, and assessments.

The Unit's quest to gain national accreditation between 1994 and 1996 opened the door for the college's attention to coherence in its operation (see Dottin (2001) *The Development of a Conceptual Framework: The Stimulation for Coherence and Continuous Improvement in Teacher Education)*. The college's focus on coherence was supported in the literature by the work of Koppich & Knapp (1998) which showed that a key variable in effective teacher education programs is the extent to which curriculum, instruction, the integration of technology, and assessment and evaluation are aligned to form a coherent whole. Attention to coherence thus brought about healthy discourse among faculty about how life ought to be lived in the unit thus generating moral agency with regard to the unit's purpose (why – vision, mission, philosophy, outcomes; knowledge, skills and dispositions), curriculum (what – content to be learned), methods (how – the content would be delivered), and assessments (when – the measures to determine when outcomes were met). The result was the college gaining national accreditation in 1996, and receiving a best practice award from the American Association for Colleges of Teacher Education (AACTE) for its embryonic attention to coherence through its development of a conceptual framework.

Continued attention to coherence abated somewhat between 1999 and 2006 but was revived in 2008 as the college prepared for its second continuing accreditation visit. By this time, NCATE had increased attention to the concept of "dispositions" by asking units to assess their candidates' dispositions. NCATE provided little conceptual clarity for the construct "dispositions"as units and educators across the country were grappling to address the construct in relation to education. This afforded the unit another chance to attend to coherence and conceptual clarity vis-à-vis "dispositions." The unit revised its conceptual framework and articulated its desired future (vision) as one "in which the emphasis on inquiry is the means-ends connection to enhancing reflective intelligence" (The Conceptual Framework of the College of Education, n.d., p. 4).

Working Toward Common Ends

However, "the connection between the conceptual framework and the salient moral question – that is, the framework's articulation of how life in the unit ought to be lived and how that life will enable students to acquire requisite habits of mind and moral sensibilities or dispositions" (Dottin, 2006, p. 28) is not a simple translation and operationalization. Moral agency requires that one:

> Must know what he is doing…must choose it, and choose it for itself …the act must (also) be the expression of a formed and stable character….It must be voluntary; that is, it must manifest a choice, and for full morality at least, the choice must be an expression of the general tenor and set of personality. It must involve awareness of what one is about; a fact which in the concrete signifies that there must be a purpose, an aim, an end in view, something for the sake of which the particular act is done (Dewey, 1960, p. 8).

So, the end in view to be pursued cannot be pursued by just following prescriptive mandates. Reflective morality implies that one asks by what purposes one should direct one's conduct and why should one do so; in other words, the salient question has to be what makes one's purposes good (Dewey, 1960, pp. 29-30). But, in human endeavor, "many acts are done not only without thought of their moral quality but with practically no thought of any kind" (Dewey, 1960, p. 10), a phenomenon not absent from teacher education units. For example, in many instances in teacher education, there is a disconnect between evaluating faculty performance in relation to unit purposes and aims.

One idea to better connect between purpose and actions in a teacher education program, or in other words to consider conduct in the unit, is to view the unit through the Dewey's conceptual lens of the family: "the family in its moral aspects has one end, the common good of all its members" (Dewey & Tufts, 1913, p. 571).

It is an enduring form of association in which the members of the group stand from the beginning in relations to one another, and in which each member gets direction for his conduct by thinking of the whole group and his place in it, rather than by an adjustment of egoism and altruism (Dewey, 1960, p. 164).

If the idea of community is substituted for the idea of family then it becomes clear that:

Men live in a community in virtue of the things which they have in common; and community is the way in which they come to possess things in common. What they must have in common in order to form a community or society are aims, beliefs, aspirations, knowledge – a common understanding – *like-mindedness* [italics added] as the sociologists say .... The communication which insures participation in a common understanding is one which secures similar emotional and intellectual dispositions – like ways of responding to expectations and requirements (Dewey, 1916/1944, p. 4).

In fact:

Individuals do not even compose a social group because they all work for a common end. The parts of a machine work with a maximum of cooperativeness for a common result, but they do not form a community. *If, however, they were all cognizant of the common end and all interested in it so that they regulated their specific activity in view of it, then they would form a community* [italics added]. But this would involve communication. Each would have to know what the other was about and would have to have some way of keeping the other informed as to his own purpose and progress (Dewey, 1916/1944, p. 5).

Working to Call Forth Dispositions as Habits of Mind

The focus of this book is, therefore, on the efforts of faculty in a learning community to live out the foregoing by (1) working toward common ends as articulated in their unit's conceptual framework (the conceptual framework provides the aim which facilitates their acting with meaning) (2) sharing of purpose through communication – using the language in the conceptual framework, and (3) fostering a sense of community based on the things community members have in common – their working to structure learning environments, consistent with a particular conceptual orientation, to call forth in themselves and their students, key dispositions, that is, habits of mind that are consistent with democratic education.

The work operates on the assumption that the social environment is the catalyst for the development of the mental and emotional dispositions of behavior in individuals. It, therefore, follows that environments must be structured to enhance the acquisition and/or demonstration of habits of mind. But, to structure such environments requires that the learning environments promote the use of subject matter and skills toward social ends.

Overview of Chapters

The chapters in this book will highlight Dewey's concept of "plasticity" – learning from experience and retaining from one experience something used in coping with difficulties in another situation (Dewey, 1916/1944). The chapters will show that to learn from experience, that is, to act on the world, undergo the consequences, and make connections between the act and its consequences (learn) requires the cultivation of certain habits of mind or as called by Dewey

(1916/1944) "moral traits." Such habits of mind "characterize a [teacher and learner] who is extending and deepening interest in learning from all of his [her] contacts in the world" (Hansen, 2002, p. 269).

The pedagogical examples in the chapters will reinforce the idea of the teacher's moral responsibility to help the student (in a teacher education program) grow from uncultivated impulses, to nurtured desires, to reflective planning and purposing (acquiring reflective intelligence) (Anderson, 2010). The concurrent developmental process in dispositions (that is, habits of mind) will be seen in students' levels of awareness of the habits of mind, their seeing value in expanding their capacity to become better in their habits of mind conduct, that is, their choosing to behave more intelligently, and in their building a commitment to habits of mind by reflecting on how to improve their conduct.

The authors of the chapters share their stories regarding how as teachers and/or program leaders, working toward a common end, they nurture, and assess candidates' dispositions (that is, habits of mind for making candidates' conduct more intelligent):

Erskine Dottin, Barbara Johnson and Mickey Weiner use case analysis problem solving as the means to enhance professional knowledge and habits of mind for candidates in an Introduction to the Teaching Profession Course.

Teresa Lucas cultivates habits of mind through modeling in an undergraduate TESOL course.

Aixa Perez-Prado helps students become more aware of habits of mind by helping them make connections in a TESOL course.

Patsy Self Trand, reframes subject-area Reading for secondary students using habits of mind

Gwyn W. Senokossoff, develops candidates' habits of mind by living her educational philosophy in her Reading Course.

Joyce Fine demystifies habits of mind in her Reading Master's Course.

Joyce Fine and Lynne Miller work with candidates in a Literacy Master's experience to develop dispositions.

Angela Salmon and Debra Mayes Pane nurture habits of mind and visible thinking in a graduate childhood curriculum course

Charmaine DeFrancesco calls out the habits of mind by bridging the theory/practice gap in a Physical Education Course.

Lynne Miller, Helen Robbins, Maria Tsalikis, and Lynn Yribarren help graduate students see the value of dispositions in a Supervised Clinical Practicum in Reading.

Maria L. Fernandez, Roxanne V. Molina, Esther F. Joseph and Leslie Nisbet approach the habits of mind through their courses in mathematics.

George E. O'Brien and Kathleen G. Sparrow use an historical lens and reflection in presenting a vision of teaching Pre-service Elementary Science Content and Methods.

References

Anderson, E. (2010, Fall). Dewey's moral philosophy. *The Stanford Encyclopedia of Philosophy (Fall 2010 Edition)*, Edward N. Zalta (ed.). Retrieved from http://plato.stanford.edu/archives/fall2010/entries/dewey-moral/.

Arends, R., Winitzky, N., & Burek, A. A. (1996). Program structures and learning to teach. In F. B. Murray (Ed.), *The Teacher Educator's Handbook: Building a Knowledge Base for the Preparation of Teachers*. pp. 526-556. San Francisco, CA: Jossey-Bass Publishers.

Cochran-Smith, M., & Fries, K. (2008). Research on teacher education: Changing times, changing paradigms. In M. Cochran-Smith, S. Feiman-Nemser, D. J. McIntyre, & K. E. Demers (Eds.), *Handbook of research on teacher education*, 3rd edition, (pp. 1050-1093), New York: Routledge, Taylor & Francis Group and the Association of Teacher Educators.

Costa, A. L., & Kallick, B. (2000).*Habits of mind: Activating and engaging* Alexandria, VA: Association of Supervision and Curriculum Development.

Crowe, E. (2010, July). *Measuring what matters: A stronger accountability model for teacher education*. Washington, DC: Center for American Progress.

Dewey, J. (1960). *The theory of the moral life*. New York: Holt, Rinehart & Winston.

Dewey, J., & Tufts, J. H. (1913). *Ethics*. New York: Henry Holt.

Dottin, E. (2006). A Deweyan approach to the development of moral dispositions in professional teacher education communities: Using a conceptual framework. In H. Sockett (Ed.). *Teacher Dispositions: Building a Teacher Education Framework of Moral Standards*. pp. 27-47. Washington, DC: American Association of Colleges for Teacher Education.

Dottin, E. (2001). *The development of a conceptual framework: The stimulation forcoherence and continuous improvement in teacher education*. Lanham, MD: University Press of America.

Ducharme, E. and Ducharme, M. (1999, November-December).Responding to Goodlad: The primacy of teacher education in SCDEs. *Journal of Teacher Education*, 50(5), 358-363.

Feinman-Nemser, S. (1990). Teacher preparation: Structural and conceptual alternatives. In W.R. Houston, M. Huberman, and J. Sikula (Eds.). *Handbook of research in teacher education* (pp. 212-233). New York: MacMillan.

Fenstermacher, G. D. (1994). The absence of democratic and educational ideals from contemporary educational reform initiatives. ERIC Document. ED377542.

Gage, N. L. (1978). *The scientific basis of the art of teaching*. New York, NY: Longman.

Gage, N. L., & Winne, P. H. (1975). Performance-Based teacher education. In K. Ryan (Ed.), *Teacher education* (74th yearbook of the National Society for the Study of Education, Part II., pp. 146-172). Chicago: University of Chicago Press.

Goodlad, J.I, Soder, R., & Sirotnik, K. A. (Eds.). (19990).*The moral dimensions of teaching*. San Francisco: Jossey-Bass.

Hansen, D. T. (2001). *Exploring the moral heart of teaching: Towards a teacher's creed*. New York: Teachers College Press.

Howey, K. R., & Zimpher, N. L. (1989). Profiles of preservice teacher education: Inquiry into the nature of programs. Albany, NY: State University of New York Press

Joyce, B. (1975). Conceptions of man and their implications for teacher education. In K. Ryan (Ed.), *Teacher education* (74th yearbook of the National Society for the Study of Education, Part II., pp. 111-145). Chicago: University of Chicago Press.

Koppich, J.E. & Knapp, M.S. (1998, April). Federal research investment and the improvement of teaching 1980-1997. Seattle, WA: Center for the Study of Teaching & Policy.

Osguthorpe, R. D. (2008). On the reasons we want teachers of good disposition and moral character. *Journal of Teacher Education,* 59(4), 288-299.

Richardson, V. & Fenstermacher, G. D. (2001). Manner in teaching: The study in four parts. *Journal of Curriculum Studies,* 33(6), 631-637.

Shulman, L. (2005). The signature pedagogies of the professions of law, medicine, engineering, and the clergy: Potential lessons for the education of teachers. A speech delivered at the Math Science Partnership (MSP) Workshop, hosted by the National Research Council's Center for Education, February 6-8, 2005, Irvine, California.

Sockett, H. (2006). Character, rules, and relations. In H. Sockett, Editor. *Teacher dispositions: Building a teacher education framework of moral standards.* Washington, DC: American Association of Colleges for Teacher Education.

Sockett, H. (1993). *The moral base of teacher professionalism.* New York: Teachers College Press.

Sullivan, W. (n.d.). Preparing professionals as moral agents. Retrieved September 22, 2011, from http://www.carnegiefoundation.org/perspectives/preparing-professionals -moral-agents.

The Conceptual Framework of the College of Education. (n.d.). Retrieved on October 11, 2011 from http://education.fiu.edu/docs/Conceptual%20Framework%2006-19-09.pdf

Tom, A. R. (1984). *Teaching as a moral craft.* New York: Longman.

Urban, W. J. (1990). Historical studies of teacher education. In W.R. Houston, M. Huberman, and J. Sikula (Eds.). *Handbook of research in teacher education* (pp. 59-71). New York: MacMillan.

Zimpher, N., & Howet, K. (1987). Adapting supervisory practice to different orientations of teaching competence. *Journal of Curriculum and Supervision,* 2(2), 101-127.

CHAPTER ONE

Examining How Pre-Service Teacher Education Students Conceptualize and Frame Problems of Professional Practice in Light of Professional Knowledge and Habits of Mind

By

Erskine S. Dottin
Barbara Johnson
Mickey Weiner

Pre-service teacher education students must be challenged to become skillful thinkers and problem solvers. Why? The call has been made clear for the development of students in P-12 schools who can think critically, problem solve, and work collaboratively (Partnership for 21st Century Skills, 2009). Bellanca and Brandt (2010) editors of the book *21st Century Skills: Rethinking How Students Learn* note that "with 21st century skills, students will be prepared to think, learn, work, solve problems, communicate, collaborate, and contribute effectively throughout their lives" (p. xx). So, it follows that the teachers of these students must have the knowledge, skills and dispositions to facilitate the aforementioned goal.

But how might teacher education programs where pre-service teachers are educated structure their learning environments to enhance candidates' learning in a manner that will contribute to the pre-service teachers, when they are in the world of practice, nurturing skillful thinking and problem solving in their P-12 students? Some words of wisdom come from the empirical work of the National Research Council (2000):

> [pre-service teachers] need to make the transition from a world dominated primarily by college courses,..., to a world in which they are the teachers; hence they face the challenge of transferring what they have learned.... Transfer does not happen immediately nor automatically....People often need help in order to use relevant knowledge that they have acquired, and they usually need feedback and reflection so that they can try out and adapt their previously acquired skills and knowledge in new environments. These environments–the [schools of education]–have an extremely important effect on the beliefs, knowledge, and skills that new teachers will draw on (p. 203).

The key aspects of the foregoing are "the transfer of knowledge," and "the learning environments in schools and colleges of education. More specifically, is the learning environment that will have an effect on the kind of knowledge, skills and dispositions on which pre-service teachers will draw.

Historically, three knowledge components have been associated with teacher preparation: content knowledge, pedagogical content knowledge, and general pedagogical knowledge. However, Konig, Blomeke, Paine, Schmidt & Hsieh (2011) suggest that while a great deal of research has been focused on content and pedagogical content knowledge, there has been less focus on learning about teachers' general pedagogical knowledge. If a major function of teacher education is to help pre-service teachers transfer their learning from courses, and programs to other contexts, and problems in the world of practice, then Harry Broudy's (1977) proposition that educating people broadly is better than training them to perform specific tasks gives relevance to enhancing pre-service teachers' problem solving ability. On the other hand, according to Broudy (as cited in Tozer, Anderson & Armbruster, 1990), the failure of teacher education to develop and employ an appropriate method of case study is one of the major obstacles to the integration of research knowledge into professional preparation.

This work examines (1) how pre-service teachers in a teacher education program at Florida International University in the spring semester of 2012, exposed to problem solving through case analysis, conceptualized and framed problems of professional practice in light of professional knowledge, and (2) whether their being made aware of 12 habits of mind through case study, problem solving class learning experiences, and online and school site engagement with elementary students on habits of mind contributed to changes in pre- and post-self-ratings on the 12 habits of mind.

Common End to which Pedagogical Efforts are Directed

The course in this study is a lower division state mandated prerequisite course entitled Introduction to the Teaching Profession. To be delivered through the College of Education, requires that the experience be framed by the college's conceptual framework that is grounded in a vision that seeks "a desired future in which the emphasis on inquiry is the means-ends connection to enhancing reflective intelligence" ("The Conceptual Framework of the College of Education," n.d., p. 4). This is the vision, the common end to which pedagogical effort in the college is directed. A critical assumption in the college's conceptual framework is that "...educational environments conducive to this philosophy [of inquiry] are thus structured to challenge candidates to engage in the habits of thinking that are consistent with reflective inquiry or as termed by Dewey, 'the essentials of reflection' (Dewey, 1916/1944, p. 163)" ("The Conceptual Framework of the College of Education," n.d., p. 6). The concept of "dispositions" that emerges from the college's way of thinking is that "dispositions needed by teachers and other school personnel [should] be the habits that would render their actions (conduct) intelligent in the world of practice, and as such, those dispositions would guide how life is lived in the unit" ("The Conceptual Framework of the College of Education," n.d., p. 4). The faculty in the unit, therefore, seeks to create the kind of teaching and learning environments that elicit the mental and moral sensibilities consistent with reflective intelligence by engaging learners in intelligent action so that they might demonstrate wisdom in practice ("The Conceptual Framework of the College of Education," n.d., p. 9). The characteristics expected of graduates from the college, therefore, are that they be (a) stewards of their discipline, (b) reflective inquirers, and (c) mindful educators.

Enhancing Pre-Service Teachers' Knowledge, Skills and Dispositions

Research has indicated that pre-service teachers' knowledge, skills and dispositions may be enhanced through the study of cases. According to Cochran-Smith & Zeichner (2005), "The available studies provide initial evidence that cases may help improve the reasoning skills of pre-service teachers, enabling them to identify issues and analyze an educational problem more effectively. It is also clear from the research, that the instruction around cases matters not only in the use of case materials per se, but, also in candidates' learning" (p. 18). More importantly, the use of cases to structure the learning experience for pre-service teacher education students can provide them with the opportunity to experience in a vicarious manner a situation they are likely to encounter later as in-service teachers (Trier, 2010; Pitton, 2010). Furthermore, "By engaging in discussions using cases that present real-life…dilemmas, future educators are able to develop problem-solving strategies" (Pitton, 2010).

While the research on the impact of introduction to education courses on teachers' knowledge is scant according to Cochran-Smith & Zeichner (2005), these co-editors of the American Educational Research Association's report on research and teacher education indicate that "studies offer evidence about the effects of a small set of instructional practices used in the context of foundations courses" (Cochran-Smith & Zeichner, 2005, p. 12).

The available studies provide initial evidence that cases may help improve the reasoning skills of pre-service teachers, enabling them to identify issues and analyze an educational problem more effectively. It is also clear from the research that the instruction around cases matters not only in the use of case materials per se but also in candidates' learning (Cochran-Smith & Zeichner, 2005, p. 18).

It has been noted in the literature that:

> Teachers often do not see the relationship between the events they experience in their own classrooms and the generalizations about teaching and learning they are taught in universities. Many teachers report that they learned little of value about teaching until they began to teach. This finding challenges teacher education programs to create more effective ways to help prospective and

experienced teachers connect general principles of teaching and student learning to specific problems and events in classrooms ("Teacher Education," n.d., para. 14).

Case studies are a great way to enhance teacher education candidates seeing better the relationship between the events they experience in the field, and the information they are taught in universities. More importantly, case studies provide learners with an opportunity to solve a problem by applying what they know. Research, on expertise from the new science on learning, reveal that the ability to think and solve problems depend strongly on a rich body of knowledge about subject matter (Chase & Simon, 1973; Chi et al., 1981; deGroot, 1965). Case study learning by pre-service teachers should, therefore, make visible the candidates' meaning-making and knowledge construction (Murrow, n.d., para. 6). But, can case studies enhance how pre-service candidates conceptualize and frame problems of professional practice using general pedagogical knowledge?

General Pedagogical Knowledge

According to Shulman (1987) general pedagogical knowledge means aspects about pedagogy in general regardless of the content knowledge in which teachers are specialised (p. 8). It empowers prospective teachers with awareness of the educational system as a whole (Banegas, 2012), and comes from philosophy, history of education, social aspects of education, politics of education, curriculum, pedagogy, psychology and research.

The research literature on enhancing candidates' pedagogical content knowledge highlights the importance of this knowledge base. For example, Gudmundsdottir (1991) noted that teachers with considerable experience demonstrated better pedagogical content knowledge than novice teachers. Gudmundsdottir concluded that beginning teachers' lack of pedagogical content knowledge may be attributed to the fact that many teacher education programs do not place an emphasis on "getting students to think about the subject matter they have to teach in terms of their pedagogical content" (p. 69).

On the other hand, the literature is scant with regard to how pre-service candidates' general pedagogical knowledge may be enhanced. In one of the few studies, Konig, Blomeke, Paine, Schmidt & Feng-Jui, (2011) developed a standardized test of general pedagogical knowledge and administered it to future middle school teachers in Germany, Taiwan and the United States. The authors found a relative strength in one of the cognitive sub-dimensions of the test, generating strategies to perform in the classroom, and concluded that the future teachers had acquired procedural general pedagogical knowledge during teacher education. On the other hand, Cheng (2005) (as cited in Benegas, 2012) studied students at Hong Kong Institute of Education by interviewing them to understand their construction of pedagogical knowledge during the field experience component of their program. The findings from this study show that the students' construction of pedagogical knowledge is enhanced by working in interaction with peers and supporting teachers.

Since research has indicated that pre-service teachers' knowledge, skills and dispositions may be enhanced through the study of cases, this project combines the use of case study in campus learning for pre-service students, by drawing on a case from a real school, and uses the candidates' learning to transfer to improving practice at the public school. More specifically, the project asks the question: can pre-service teachers' general pedagogical knowledge and habits of mind be enhanced through the case study process?

Population

The participants in this project were 40 students enrolled in a lower-division state mandated prerequisite course for teacher education students, EDF 1005 Introduction to the Teaching Profession. The course was delivered in the College of Education at Florida International University during the spring semester of 2012. Students, other than intended education majors, were also eligible to enroll in the course. 76% of the students indicated their intended major to be education. 60% of the course enrollees indicated at the start of the semester that they were in the course because they wanted to learn more about becoming a teacher. On the other hand, 40% indicated that were enrolled in the course because it was required. 93% (37) of the students were female and 7% (3) were male.

Procedure

Can pre-service teachers' general pedagogical knowledge and habits of mind be enhanced through the case study process? Answers to this question were pursued through a pre-/post- design to monitor the effect of case study learning in an introduction course upon pre-service teachers' a) use of general pedagogical knowledge and (b) habits of mind conduct.

The pre-service teachers, at the start of the semester, were asked to read and offer their interpretation of a case (see Case of Jose in Appendix 1.1). They then were engaged in semester long case study learning using a heuristic problem solving process from the literature on problem solving and adapted by the instructor (of troubleshooting, investigating, analyzing, researching databases and information in the textbook, *American Education*, 15th edition, by Joel Spring, and offering interpretation(s) and solution(s). Each of the aforementioned problem solving components became a learning module in the course during the semester in which the students acquired the knowledge, skills and habits of mind germane to each module. They applied their learning in each module to the case under study, and captured their reflections regarding their learning to their meeting institutional, state and professional standards (in a

Meeting Standards Template), and to their awareness and demonstration of the habits of mind related to each module (in a Habits of Mind Inventory).

The case under study during the semester was drawn from the realities of a Miami-Dade County Public School–Charles Wyche Elementary (see Appendix 1.2), and developed collaboratively by the instructor, Professor Erskine Dottin, Principal of the school, Dr. Barbara Johnson, and Resource Teacher, Dr. Mickey Weiner.

Toward the end of the semester, and prior to learning how to provide an interpretation of and offer solutions for the problem in the above case, the pre-service teachers were asked again to read and offer an interpretation of a case (see Case of Joey in Appendix 1.1). A propositional case knowledge framework adapted from Lee Shulman (1987) was used on the pre-service teachers' pre- and post- interpretations (of the cases of Jose and Joey) to understand: (1) How they examine a problem(s)-to what/which aspects of the problem do they attend? To what perspectives or dimensions do they explore? (2) How the problem is represented–do they describe interrelationships among the people and events in the case? (3) How they think through the problem–Do they generate options in resolving dilemmas in the case? On what types of knowledge do they draw in developing and evaluating their interpretation and solutions? Do they use any theoretical information to enhance their interpretation and solutions to the problem in the case? If so, were theories used: research theories, theories of practice, and/or values for teaching?

The pre-service teachers' responses to the cases of Jose (at the start of the semester) and Joey (toward the end of the semester) were read by a Graduate Assistant, a total of three times. The first reading was used to gain a sense of how the learners, in general, chose to approach the case and/or questions with which they were presented. On the second reading, the graduate assistant engaged in a simple, single-level coding process that primarily involved identifying key words such as bullying, special treatment, language barriers, rules, and attention. These key words were inferred as a result of the first reading, after gaining a basic knowledge of the general perspectives that were represented by the pre-service teachers. On the third and final reading, these key words were considered in the context of the response in which they were situated to help identify the common themes among all pre-service teachers' responses.

A pre-/post- design was also used to monitor changes in the pre-service teachers' self-ratings of their conduct in 12 habits of mind. The 12 habits of mind items were adapted from David Hansen (2001) *Exploring the moral heart of teaching* and Arthur Costa & Bena Kallick (2000) *Activating & engaging: Habits of mind,* and are questioning and posing problems, thinking flexibly, managing impulsivity, persisting, thinking about own thinking, striving for accuracy, thinking and communicating with clarity and precision, applying past knowledge to new situations, responding with wonderment and awe, taking responsible risks, thinking interdependently, and listening with understanding and empathy.

The pre-service teachers were asked, at the start of the semester, to rate their past conduct, as learners, along a continuum, for 12 habits of mind (from demonstrating the habit of mind very little to consistently). Their self-ratings were captured through a Habits of Mind Rating Scale (see Appendix 1.3) that was part of a Habits of Mind Inventory developed by the instructor. They entered reflective entries, throughout the semester, about their demonstrating or not demonstrating specific habits of mind associated with each learning module in the course. They rated themselves again, at the end of the semester, on the 12 habits of mind, using the same rating scale.

Analysis/Case Problem Solving

Examining the problem: To what aspects of the problem did they attend? What perspectives or dimensions did they explore?

Pre-assessment. In their interpretation of the case of Jose at the start of the semester, the pre-service teachers examined the problem presented by bringing up one or more of the following issues: (1) bullying, (2) "special treatment" of particular students, or (3) language barriers. Bullying was discussed primarily from the standpoint that the way other students chose to interact with Jose was inappropriate and inadequately addressed in the classroom. They indicated that Jose should not be given "special treatment," as this ultimately would lead to more issues with Jose's isolation from other students. They thought that Jose's difficulty with English might be related to both his academic performance and his interactions with others. The following are representative samples of the pre-service teachers' responses in the three thematic issues:

Bullying
As far as the bullying goes, if I have not personally witnessed any of the students teasing Jose then I cannot rightfully take any actions against it. What I can do is speak to Jose separately and ask him how he feels in respect to the other students. If for any reason he happens to mention being mistreated by someone or by a group of students then I will proceed to have a class discussion along with class work and homework oriented towards the concept of bullying and how it makes people feel when they are bullied. If the situation appears to be severe, then I will contact the parents of the children who have chosen to tease Jose and speak with them directly in regards to the actions that must be taken in order to rectify the situation. I would continue to have class discussions on the issue of bullying throughout the week in which I would address the end results of bullying on both the bully and the victim. I will reassess the situation in two weeks by once again taking Jose aside and speaking to him.
Special Treatment
The first thing that needs to stop is Robert's special treatment towards Jose. This will only agitate the other children more and give more cause for them to single him out.

Robert is giving him special treatment because he most probably has pity for him and since he is giving him more attention and letting him get away with certain things, the other students may feel like he is preferred over them or better and that may be a trigger to the way they are acting towards them. The students may feel left out just like Jose is feeling, but Robert isn't seeing it that way. He needs to find a balance and get Jose involved with the other students.

He can put them to do activities together and get them to communicate and bond so that they can see he's just human like everyone else.

Language Barriers

Any child that enters a new academic environment is prone to feel out place while his mind and emotions adjust. However, when the student comes from an entirely opposite background than that of the people he will be sharing his daily routines with and does not know the same language with which others communicate, adjusting becomes even more difficult.

As far as the language barrier goes, it is important to give him extra attention when possible until his understanding of the language develops into a more appropriate level for a child his age. I agree that he needs help with class work and homework.

It is not right for other students that know the language and are in the same classroom as him to get the consequences when they do something wrong and for Jose to just not get punished when he has done something wrong.

Post-assessment. In their interpretation of the case that was presented to them, after they had learned how to troubleshoot, investigate, analyze and research in problem solving, the pre-service teachers examined the problem primarily by concentrating on: (1) Joey's feelings and reactions to the situation, (2) the other students in Joey's class and (3) understanding of Joey's home life and how it might affect him at school. The dominant perspective was that Joey was being bullied, that it was wrong, and that the situation was more complex than the other kids simply being "mean." They considered other factors, such as socioeconomic status, in the examination of the problem. Some of the responses focused first on identifying the problem and facts in the case in very simple terms before moving on to interpretation and solutions.

There are 24 third graders in my class.
No one sits with Joey at lunch.
Joey has a poor home life.
He is hurt by the treatment of his classmates.
Joey demonstrates difficulty when socializing. Joey's classmates do not sit with him to eat lunch or play with him during recess time. Joey shows that the way his classmates treat him affects him. Joey's home does not present him with optimal conditions.
Joey demonstrates difficulty when socializing. None of the other students sit with him at lunch or play with him at recess. Joey has a poor life at home. Is being affected by the way the other kids treat him.
How does mistreatment affect his social skills?
How does his economical status affect his self-esteem?
Does being picked on distract Joey from learning in class?

Joey's economic status is different and his classmate's are aware of this.
Joey's classmates alienate him because of his differences.
Joey is hurt by his classmate's mistreatment of him.

Problem representation: Did they describe interrelationships among the people and events in the case?

Pre-assessment. In recognizing the interconnected nature of language barriers, bullying, and "special treatment," many of the learners were able to connect how what was happening with Jose might affect his learning, his relationships with the other students and with the teacher, and his overall experience of the classroom. Further, learner responses were indicative of the recognition that the ways the teacher chose to interact with his context (classroom) and his students were potentially a problem, though learners could not always easily articulate their reasoning adequately.

Post-assessment. As noted above, in general, learners recognized that the situation was more complex than other students simply "being mean" to Joey. Many of the learners noted that there might be more going on with Joey than just the bullying in class. Most wanted to have more information from the parents and to better understand his socioeconomic status and home life before making a judgment about his reactions to his treatment at school. Above all, most learners recognized that it would be necessary not only to talk to the other students in the class, but also to Joey himself and to Joey's parents, and that constant communication would be necessary to fix the problem presented in the case.

Thinking through the problem: Did they generate options in resolving dilemmas in the case? On what types of knowledge did they draw in developing and evaluating their interpretation and solutions? Did they use any theoretical information to enhance their interpretation and solutions to the problem in the case? If so, were the theories used: research theories: theories of practice, and/or values for teaching?

Pre-assessment. The pre-service teachers relied on personal experiences to develop and evaluate their interpretations. Some also indicated that they had certain values that they believed should be reflected in effective teachers, but no particular theoretical or conceptual frameworks of understanding were applied beyond their own experiences. This is perhaps best indicated in the types of suggestions that they were able to offer for the problems in the case. Still, they generated some tangible solutions to the problems they identified in the case:

> I would bring in books to read to the children about diversity and how it should be celebrated. Later we would discuss the importance of understanding, accepting, and loving each other's differences.
>
> Whoever is responsible for watching a group of kids needs to put any type of bullying to a stop. What I would do if any type of bullying was happening in my classroom is give a speech to the class on why everyone should just be friends and why bullying is not tolerated. If the bullying were to continue there would be consequences, such as setting up a meeting with the parents of certain students or maybe make the student

write an essay on why bullying is wrong and how to eliminate it from classrooms in schools. An activity that I would do with a class in a situation like this one is to divide the class into partners so they could get to know each other and a couple minutes before the class is over they both have to introduce their partner. I would do this activity like every month so different children get to know each other which I think will make more peace in a classroom setting.

A possible solution would be to speak to Jose and learn more about his culture so that his culture could be included in the classroom and bring awareness to other students about diversity. This could possibly make Jose feel more comfortable in his learning environment.

I think that in that class Jose can get the attention he needs. He can learn English and will be in a class with other students trying to make the same adjustment. If Jose stays in the class, who is going to help him with homework at home? Jose needs to be on a different curriculum until he can better understand English. As a last resort if there isn't any ESL classes then I would introduce Jose to the class and tell them that we are all going to be teachers. We are all going to try and help Jose and Jose can teach us. I would assign Jose a buddy, or do more group work where the kids are helping Jose. That way the kids can learn how to help someone that is different and Jose can feel included.

Post-assessment. Many of the pre-service teachers again relied on personal experiences to develop and evaluate their interpretations of the case. However, a few of the most poignant responses included information from third party data sources (primarily Internet resources) that informed their opinions and interpretations of the case. While none demonstrated a mastery of theory to guide their interpretation of the case, the best responses did consider that the problem may have multiple solutions depending on the true nature of the issue (i.e. reasons for Joey being bullied, parental involvement, etc.). One response offered a particularly excellent solution, clearly drawing on knowledge from literature and/or experience. This response was best understood in three ways: (1) causes of Joey's pain, (2) ostracism and other children, and (3) the potential need for counseling (see below):

Causes of Joey's Pain
The teacher must find and implement ways to lessen or eliminate Joey's pain. Having a poor home life doesn't mean that the student must have a poor school life. There must be something besides this causing Joey's trouble. It may be that he is a victim of prejudice, or it may be that he suffers a lack of social skills which prevents him from interacting well with other students and makes him unappealing to the other students. If the problem is that he needs help developing social skills then put him in an environment in which he can interact with children who have good social skills, so that he can learn from them.

Ostracism and Other Children

Children who have been ostracized often become sensitive to other people's emotional expressions and tend unconsciously to mimic the gestures and behaviors of more popular individuals in order to fit in. Children generally do not need to be taught social skills, however some have difficulty acquiring them on their own. If this is the case for Joey, he may benefit from another child's influence.

If the issue is prejudice, then I, the teacher, must monitor and correct my own behavior toward Joey so that I am not promoting his maltreatment by ignoring him in class. Studies show that students treat other students similarly to how their teacher treats the student. Studies also indicate that teachers as well as students tend to ostracize disabled students. If Joey has a disability, I have to take even greater precautions against treating him unfairly in class.

Potential Need for Counseling

Depending on the severity of Joey's lack of social interaction or experience and whether or not it is perpetuated by his own behaviors, he may need counseling. Ostracized individuals become either aggressive, withdrawn, or apathetic. The ones who become apathetic don't care that they are being ostracized. They may even value the experience as indicative of their specialness or superiority. They don't desire to belong to the group which ignores them, and their self-esteem is unaffected by the experience. Joey is not apathetic; he is "obviously hurt" by his classmates treatment. He may react with attention-seeking aggression, or he may withdraw from social situations in order to avoid the pain of being ostracized further, or already expecting that he will be ostracized. In this way he protects himself from the pain by eliminating positive expectations. Being aggressive and being withdrawn could both lead to one being ostracized. If Joey's situation isn't grave, it may suffice to help him with his social skills in class, but if he is overly aggressive or too withdrawn, he may need to be counseled by a professional.

Summary

While many of the pre-service teachers, in the case of Joey, still relied on personal experiences to think through the problem in the case, one clearly begins to see some pre-service teachers starting to conceptualize and frame the post-case problem in light of information from the professional literature or general pedagogical knowledge base. What became even more revelatory was that once the pre-service teachers were taught, at the end of the learning experiences in the course how to interpret a problem in a case, and were asked to apply that learning to the case they studied during the semester (the Case of Wydesee, aka Charles Wyche Elementary), then their reliance on general pedagogical knowledge was quite evident in their final case analysis documents. In fact, their use of general pedagogical knowledge about parental involvement in schools, and teacher effectiveness, and parent/teacher communication, was manifested poignantly when some of the pre-service teachers visited the school under study during the semester, at the end of the semester, and engaged in a focus discussion about the case with administrators and school faculty. The school's Resource Teacher, Dr. Mickey Weiner, the moderator of the discussion on the case, mentioned to all participants, that the FIU pre-service teachers were contributing to the discussion by drawing clearly on and sharing the research literature and knowledge base on key topics in the case.

Analysis/Habits of Mind

37 students completed the pre-assessment habits of mind rating scale and of those 37, 26 completed the post-assessment habits of mind rating scale. A paired, two-tailed, t-test was used on the pre- and post- results for those 26 students who placed an X in the learner's instead of the teachers' category on the Rating Scale. The results revealed statistically significant changes at the .05 level in students' perceptions for four of the 12 habits of mind:

Habit of Mind #1 Questioning and posing problems

Pre-assessment		Post-assessment	
Mean = 3.58		Mean = 4.27	
SD = 1.03		SD = 0.60	
SEM = 0.20		SEM = 0.12	

t =2.960; df = 25; statistically significant at the .05 level

Habit of Mind #3 Managing impulsivity

Pre-assessment		Post-assessment	
Mean = 3.85		Mean = 4.38	
SD = 0.92		SD = 0.70	
SEM = 0.18		SEM = 0.14	

t =2.6687; df = 25; statistically significant at the .05 level

Habit of Mind #4 Persisting

Pre-assessment		Post-assessment	
Mean = 3.77		Mean = 4.35	
SD = 0.86		SD = 0.69	
SEM = 0.17		SEM = 0.14	

t =2.7627; df = 25; statistically significant at the .05 level

Habit of Mind #10 Taking responsible risks

Pre-assessment		Post-assessment	
Mean = 3.46		Mean = 4.23	
SD = 0.95		SD = 0.91	
SEM = 0.19		SEM = 0.18	

t =3.8014; df = 25; statistically significant at the .05 level

End of semester reflective comments by the pre-service teachers offer some clues as to their perceived changes in habits of mind conduct. One can detect in the comments below growth in their asking questions to enable them to fill in the gap between what they knew and did not know, and their probing into the causes of things (Habits of Mind #1); in their being thoughtful in their actions (Habits of Mind #3); their working to stay on focus throughout the learning experience (Habits of Mind #4); and their working to go beyond established limits and accept failure as part of their growth:

Habits of Mind #1 Questioning and posing problems
I also learned that I need to continually ask questions in order to evaluate my own thinking, and the further I must always keep an open mind to new ideas.

I grew in all areas. I improved in some areas more than others, but overall I showed improvement in every objective. Some areas where I could have grown a bit more was. Questioning and problem solving. At the end of the journey I still felt that I can improve on my problem solving skills. Specifically, finding underlying causes and interpreting them.

Habits of Mind #3 Managing impulsivity
I learned that I have high standards for my work, but that I hinder myself in achieving these standards through impulsivity and procrastination
caused by frustration and boredom. I also learned that I have more patience than I give myself credit for and that I am capable of group work even though it's not my favorite way to work.

I think I grew in all areas, although some less than others. Managing impulsivity and persisting may still be issues for me. I can do them, but it is not as easy as I'd like it to be. I become frustrated and annoyed easily when I'm not in control.

I learned that I tend to jump into things too quickly, and sometimes it's better to analyze a situation and really research and investigate a problem before assuming a solution. In order to even reach to a concrete solution to a problem, a process is involved, and I learned that I need to be patient if I want to be a professional in the future in the field of education. I also learned that not everything is rainbow and butterflies, these cases and problems are real-life scenarios, and they need to be dealt with properly. I also learned that it is possible to have an effective group, my group all in all participated in all the assignments and put in outside class time to benefit our final product.

Habit of mind #3 managing impulsivity, and #8 applying past knowledge were very big growing areas for me throughout the journey. I typically just jump on my first thought or instinct and it doesn't always get me very far, which I learned throughout the beginning of the journey. This course has really helped me reexamine my thinking process and really take a step back and think, analyze, and research topics before jumping to any sort of conclusion. Also, because I used to jump straight to my first thought, I didn't even give myself an opportunity to apply past knowledge to my thinking process, these are two habits of mind that I really learned how to use together and gained a better understanding of throughout the journey.

Habits of mind helped me a lot in this course. I will definitely take it along with me in my career as well as in my personal life. As an educator I will always strive for accuracy for my students. Be the very best I can be so I can encourage my students. Work interdependently with people that come my way as I start my career. One of the most important ones is persisting and managing impulsivity. As an educator I will be persistent in doing what is right and fair. I will fight for social justice. By managing impulsivity, I will always remember to take my time and not to rush things to get the best results. And I will listen with understanding and empathy to my students and colleagues.

Yes, I did I became a better listener. I was able to understand people better and be put in people's shoes. I managed impulsivity well because sometimes I get very impatient. I improved in my impulsiveness because I took my time to do my work, I care a lot about producing excellent work. I did not like to be rushed.

The Habits of Mind I grew in most were Managing Impulsivity & Thinking Interdependently. I Managing Impulsivity, I acted after thinking, not before. I remained focused & analyzed & understood all problems, research, literature, situations, etc. presented to me. I stayed in control of distractions around me & considered all options or possibilities before taking those actions. I had to be very conscientious. For Thinking Interdependently, I learned how to work in a group setting. I grew in maturity by taking on tasks & responsibilities. I learned to be a lot more accountable as well as holding other people accountable. I was fair & non-judgmental. I listened to my group members opinions & shared my own thoughts. I worked hard & offered help in any which way I could.

I found that I had made improvements in Habits of Mind #3: Managing Impulsivity. For instance, when among my group members for our discussions, I was able to manage my impulsivity by not jumping to conclusions and letting other group members finish speaking before I voiced my own opinion. I learned to respect their views even if I had disagreements about them.

I believe I have grown in habit of mind 3, managing impulsivity. While working in a group there were many times when Vivian and Marcy wouldn't do the work and I would begin to get very frustrated and I really wanted to kick them off the bus, but instead of jumping the gun, I would think carefully what I was going to tell them and try my hardest to not disrespect them in any way.

Habits of Mind #4 Persisting

I think persisting was probably the hardest to overcome. I do at times give up easily but luckily I had a great group that taught me to really think about things before I give up on them, especially during the literature review.

I will try to want to know things for the sake of knowing, rather than to do well on a class. I will also try to always think of different new ways to look at things. I will remind myself to keep being persistent all the time, and most importantly, never stop listening to others with empathy.

Habits of Mind #10 Taking responsible risks

I definitely grew in the habits of mind especially in taking responsible risks. Through the habits of mind I was taught that in order to answer a question effectively you need to draw from past knowledge and take responsible risks in order to show people what you really do know/ what you have learned. Not only, but thinking and communicating with clarity and precision also plays a great role in group communication, which is something I have also mastered through the habits of mind inventory.

A look at the data for the remaining eight habits of mind reveal positive changes in the mean pre- and post- ratings for Habits of Mind #2 Thinking Flexibly (Pre- 4.38 and Post- 4.58); Habits of Mind #6 Striving for Accuracy (Pre- 4.12 and Post- 4.35); Habits of Mind #7 Thinking and Communicating with Clarity and Precision (Pre- 4.12 and Post- 4.38); Habits of Mind #8 Applying Past Knowledge to New Situations (Pre- 4.38 and Post- 4.42); Habits of Mind #11Thinking Interdependently (Pre- 4.08 and Post- 4.38); and Habits of Mind #12 Listening with Understanding and Empathy (Pre- 4.42 and Post- 4.65).

On the other hand, two habits of mind showed negative pre- and post-ratings: Habits of Mind #5 Thinking about own Thinking (Pre- 4.27 and Post- 4.19); and Habits of Mind #9 Responding with Wonderment and Awe (Pre- 4.54 and Post- 4.38). These data suggest that pre-service teachers may have realized from the educational experience that there pre-ratings were not consistent with their initial self-perceptions of their conduct in these areas.

Qualitative reflective comments by the pre-service teachers below, however, reinforce their awareness, valuing, and/or demonstrating the above habits of mind as a means to their growth in problem solving – moving from novice to expert problem solvers.

> I learned that I set lower expectations of myself prior to the journey. I actually effectively demonstrated the majority of the habits of mind and did well. I learned after analyzing events that lead me to be aware of habit of mind that I used them all them time to complete task. They are almost descriptions of the behavior of an excellent problem solver and inquirer... I can apply what I learned about myself to becoming a teacher by setting high expectations for myself and my students to use the habits of mind to be successful. I can now be more aware of the use of habits of mind when I am a teacher and focus more on each to ensure effectiveness of problem solving.
>
> To become a better critical thinker I learned to: identify the problem, investigate the problem, analyze the assumptions and arguments, research the topics around the problem, do more research about the problem through the textbook, and learn to interpret and find solutions for the problem..
>
> I will definitely take a different approach to solving problems. I will have to separate facts from opinions and determine what the possible problems in a case are. Then I would determine arguments and their assumptions. I will have to determine if whether the argument is valid. The research has to be done. Research is especially imperative in helping solving problems as a teacher. There is plenty of knowledge available that can help you be more effective when solving problems as a school professional. Once the final problem is found, causes of the problem need to be identified. Then I can determine the solutions.
>
> I will apply what I learned in this course in my teaching career by implementing all the habits of mind in my classroom and showing children at an early age to think interdependently, listen with understanding and empathy, managing impulsivity and etc. I believe that habits of minds makes you a well-rounded person who takes into consideration what others have to say and makes you apply past knowledge to new situations.
>
> Upon completion of the journey I learned how to be a professional and a great researcher! I was eager to explore many areas of education that I did not think existed before. In conjunction with the field experience and the feedback from the professor, I learned to strive for accuracy and leave behind many of my old

ways of thinking and embracing new techniques that will help me throughout my educational career. In addition, I learned to be a better group member and improved my listening skills...I will apply what I have learned on my journey in the classroom. I will teach my students to always go beyond the limits and question the world around them. In my classroom, I will create a learning environment that fosters creativity and encourages students to approach learning with wonderment and awe. In addition, I will instill a sense of professionalism in my students by making sure they turn in work that reflects their best effort...Some of the goals I will set for myself are to keep an open mind and consider all aspects of a problem before offering a solution. Also, I will continue to strive for professionalism and accuracy by producing work that reflects my best effort. This goal can be applied on a personal level and in my future classroom.

I learned that I tend to jump into things too quickly, and sometimes it's better to analyze a situation and really research and investigate a problem before assuming a solution. In order to even reach a concrete solution to a problem, a process is involved, and I learned that I need to be patient if I want to be a professional in the future in the field of education. I also learned that not everything is rainbow and butterflies, these cases and problems are real-life scenarios, and they need to be dealt with properly. I also learned that it is possible to have an effective group, my group all in all participated in all the assignments and put in outside class time to benefit our final product....As a pre-professional I obviously have quite a bit to learn, however this class has again, taught me that with every situation has a process in order to reach an adequate solution. I hope to one day have my own classroom and be about to effectively deal with a spectrum of different issues that come my way because this class has properly guided me through the proper process.

Habit of mind #3 managing impulsivity, and #8 applying past knowledge were very big growing areas for me throughout the journey. I typically just jump on my first thought or instinct and it doesn't always get me very far, which I learned throughout the beginning of the journey. This course has really helped me reexamine my thinking process and really take a step back and think, analyze, and research topics before jumping to any sort of conclusion. Also, because I used to jump straight to my first thought, I didn't even give myself an opportunity to apply past knowledge to my thinking process, these are two habits of mind that I really learned how to use together and gained a better understanding of throughout the journey.

Teaching is not always going to be easy and the answers aren't going to be right out in the open but the answers are always there if you look hard enough. If you give up it's pointless. A good teacher takes the time to solve the problem correctly. I hope to become a good teacher one day.

The habits of mind that I found the most growth was, thinking flexibly and working interdependently. Although I used many of the habits of mind while completing the objectives, the above two were extremely important in the completion of the course. Usually when I am in a group, we are given a task of creating something together, most of the time it's a PowerPoint presentation. I have never had to write a paper, (which I have always done alone), with a group. When writing a paper you know how well you do research, whether or not you know the format, how long it will take you to write it, and so forth. In a group setting everyone works differently. In my group some of the things that were written made no sense what so ever. When first completing the HOM inventory, I put that I was a 5 at thinking flexibly. I am very open-minded. I love hearing new ideas, and learning new things. This case however, showed me a new side to flexible thinking. At the start of the semester we had four people in our group. Only after a couple of weeks we were down to three. To complete our case I had to be very interdependent. I could not do the case on my own. We all needed to work together. I may not be a fan of group work, but with all of the problems and situations that arose during the completion of our case, I think that I did very well. Even though I did not agree with the methods used by some members, I know that everyone works differently. The point of working interpedently is to acknowledge the differences and still complete great work

Now that I am aware of the Habits of Mind, I can begin to use them. They are going to help me become a better educator, because if I am able to master all of them I think that I will be a great educator. They will help me grow as a person, and as a teacher. I am going to focus on those areas that I need help with. This new knowledge of the Habits of Mind will help me with future experiences. I am definitely going to incorporate the Habits of Mind in my lessons. It's a shame that unlike the students at Wydesee, I am learning about them toward the end of academic journey.

Conclusions

So, can pre-service teachers' general pedagogical knowledge and habits of mind be enhanced through the case study process? The data gathered during this project does affirm that teacher education programs, where pre-service candidates are educated, can structure their learning environments to enhance candidates' learning in a manner that will contribute to pre-service teachers, when they are in the world of practice, nurturing skillful thinking and problem solving in their P-12 students. Pre-service candidates in a teacher education program at Florida International University were able, though exposure to problem solving through case analysis, to conceptualize and frame problems of professional practice in light of professional knowledge and habits of mind.

Merseth (1996) notes that in teacher education, case purpose falls into three categories: (a) cases as exemplars; (b) cases as opportunities to practice analysis, the assimilation of differing perspectives, and contemplation of action; and (c) cases as stimulants to personal reflection. This project was more consistent with the use of a case to enable pre-service teachers to practice decision making and problem solving, in other words, to help them begin to "think like a teacher" (Shulman, 1992). In this situation, the case reinforced the idea of teaching as a complex, messy, context-specific activity (Merseth, 1996). More importantly, the use of a case in this project stimulated personal reflection on the part of pre-service candidates with respect to the development of personal professional knowledge, and habits and techniques of reflection (Kleinfeld, 1992, Richert, 1991), and served as a significant stimulus to questioning and posing problems, managing impulsivity, persisting and taking responsible risks.

Feedback collected from the school faculty at the elementary school about (1) their focus discussion with students in the FIU course on the case at the end of the spring 2012 semester, and (2) the FIU students online interaction with 3rd grade students about habits of mind revealed:

(a) The need for more campus and school learning connections:
We need more discussions like this! It was nice hearing others' points of view and sharing ideas.
We don't do this kind of thing often enough.
(b) Things learned by school faculty:
Persistence pays off
Watching how it all comes together
That we need to work more closely with parents
That regardless of what population of students you are working with or what kind of parental support you have, you should always have high expectations for your students.
(c) Things enjoyed by school faculty:
The FIU presentation
The interaction between my students and the FIU students
That our opinions were valued and respected
Hearing the FIU students and us as teachers speak about ways to involve our parents
(d) Things to learn more about by school faculty and administrators:
Using Habits of Mind as a school-wide project along with Conscious Discipline
Getting more information on how to increase parental support
How to implement Habits of Mind school-wide
Having parents involved with Habits of Mind

Appendix 1.1

Pre-test

THE CASE OF JOSE

Jose is an Hispanic American student who has just recently moved to your school and is having some difficulty adjusting. He is the only Hispanic student in the class and does not read or speak English very well. Your student teacher, Robert, is aware of Jose's difficulties and gives him individual attention and assistance whenever possible. You notice, however, that Robert allows Jose to get away with small classroom infractions that would carry consequences for other students. When you ask Robert about this, he says that Jose needs to be treated differently until he can get better adjusted to his new surroundings. Robert explains that he feels the other students pick up on Jose unjustly. You have not noticed students treating Jose any differently than they treat each other. What is your interpretation of the case? What solutions would you offer?

Post-test

THE CASE OF JOEY

You are the teacher of a class of 24 third graders. You notice that they all pick on one boy, Joey. No one will sit with him at lunch, talk with him at break, or play with him at recess. Joey has a poor home life, and you can see that he is obviously hurt by the class's treatment of him. What will you do? •What is your interpretation of the case? What solutions would you offer?

Appendix 1.2

THE CASE OF WYDESEE
Spring 2012

Gloria Bravo, a teacher at Wydesee Elementary, was surfing the internet looking for resources that might help her 5th grade students, when she noted an online review posted by a parent of a student at her school. "My daughter scored a 5 in math & a 5 in reading in the 3rd grade FCAT. They're doing something right here! Or is it just our parenting skills." Ms. Bravo had not seen such online reviews previously, and was brought to a state of cognitive dissonance by the implicit aspersion about her and her colleagues' pedagogical propensity in the parent's comments. FCAT School Improvement Data flashed in her mind's eye as she muttered to herself: "The FCAT is a standards-based test, which means it measures how well students are mastering specific skills defined for each grade by the state of Florida. The FCAT has 5 achievement levels, with level 1 being the lowest and level 5 the highest. Florida considers scores of level 3 and higher to be on or above grade level. The goal is for all students to score at or above level 3." But, she thought to herself, "the most recent State data showed Wydesee to be below grade level in reading and math (65% are meeting high standards in reading; 63% in math; 75% in writing; 40% in science; 53% of the lowest 25% are making reading gains and 65% in math); the school grade is a C, and yes, Wydesee has not met Annual Yearly Progress. Was the parent suggesting that her daughter performed well because of parental efforts, and not because of the instructional quality at Wydesee? "But, wait a moment!"she countered to herself, "the words on Wydesee's web site clearly state that 'We invite parents and the community to join our highly professional staff in pursuing high academic standards of achievement for all students': was the parental review intended to challenge the foregoing? If the student referred to in the parent's review achieved on the FCAT because of her parents and not her teachers at Wydesee, then does it follow that the other students below grade level are not succeeding because their parents lack the requisite parenting skills?

Ms. Bravo's thoughts race to her knowledge of the educational literature which shows that parental involvement in children's schooling does enhance their academic success. That literature, however, reinforces the relevance of teaching and the complementary nature of parenting. Suddenly, she found herself feeling trapped in a logical sense by the parent's comment; for if a student performing well on a standardized test is caused by teaching professionals? Would a teaching professional be expected in his or her pedagogical endeavors with students to just cover material and simply prepare them to pass a standardized test? Ms. Bravo begins to think of visits to Wydesee by school district and region administrative personnel and about the focus of these visits on whether each minute in teaching and learning is engaged, whether learning always begins promptly, whether student generated work samples demonstrate high standards. If she and her colleagues were true teaching professionals, should school district and region administrative personnel be interested as well about pedagogical purpose, in other words, about the moral agency of teaching? Would a true professional see teaching as simply "putting in time," or would the fiduciary relationship with clients, that is, his or her students require evidence of passion and enthusiasm in his or her work? Would a true professional admit openly and consistently that he or she has low expectations for his or her students?   At this point, Ms. Bravo coincidently clicks on a web page that offers teaching tips, and reads the following:

> Students respond to clearly set expectations. Rather than keeping those expectations low for students with poor classroom performance, raising them to high expectations brings everyone in the class to higher levels of performance. While students often enter the classroom at various learning levels, educators should always determine the level of the child when he or she enters the classroom and then work up from there. Helping all students reach high expectations doesn't happen overnight. Key to meeting high expectations is teacher planning. As a result, educators are on the same page, knowing what is expected of them and their students. Students depend on consistent expectations from teachers. No matter the distractions of the day, educators have the daily opportunity and obligation to impact all students.

Ms. Bravo's eyes move from the computer screen to Wydesee's School Improvement Plan (SIP). Her colleagues' teaching experience range from 19% having 1-5 years of experience; 38% having 6-14 years of experience; and 38% having more than 15 years of experience. But, she recalls hearing that some of her colleagues do openly hold low expectations for their students. Does that mean that those colleagues are creating a self-fulfilling prophecy of low outcomes with regard to FCAT outcomes? As Ms. Bravo continues to scan the SIP other data jump out at her: Teachers with advanced degrees (38%); highly qualified teachers (11%); reading endorsed teachers (4%); National Board Certified teachers (3%); ESOL endorsed (53%). "Is there any correlation between these data and student outcomes at Wydesee?" she ponders. Her mind drifts back to the parent review comments: "My daughter scored a 5 in math & a 5 in reading in the 3rd grade FCAT. They're doing something right here! Or is it just our parenting skills."   Now, the "doing something right here" takes the foreground in her mind's eye. She is aware that the Response to Intervention (RtI) Leadership team at Wydesee has set clear expectations for teaching, and that teachers are expected to meet weekly for grade level meetings and meet monthly for Professional Learning Communities to share best practices and resources. So, she thinks to herself, "doing something right at Wydesee would mean that if a student is merely copying definitions from a dictionary then that would not be the best way to teach and learn new vocabulary; it would also mean that one would see students in classrooms at Wydesee learning through conversation and working in groups because the current knowledge about how kids learn best reinforces such pedagogical strategies; more importantly, it would mean that the "teacher as person" would have to have his or her personal needs met (a la Maslow) before he or she could help his or her students meet their needs."

Appendix 1. 3

PRE-JOURNEY ASSESSMENT: Please complete a self-rating of your past and/or current performance vis-à-vis the following habits of mind.
HABITS OF MIND SELF RATING SCALE
Developed by Erskine S. Dottin, © May 2, 2005 Revised May 3, 2011
These twelve items were adapted from David Hansen (2001) *Exploring the moral heart of teaching* and Arthur Costa & Bena Kallick (2000) *Activating & engaging: Habits of mind.*

Look at each item below and rate your past conduct (overt behavior) in teaching and learning experiences along the continuum for each disposition/habit of mind (from low end on the right [1] to the high end on the left f [5]. Place an X in the respective box to represent your usual behavior/conduct as (a) ___ teacher or as (b) ___ learner.

adopt a questioning attitude	5-4-3-2-1	avoid asking questions to fill in unknown gaps
be open-minded	5-4-3-2-1	resist changing mind even in light of new data
withhold value judgment about an idea until understanding is achieved	5-4-3-2-1	blurt out the first answer that comes to mind
persevere on the task even though the resolution is not immediately apparent	5-4-3-2-1	write down and/or say things just to be done with the task at hand quickly
reflect on my experience(s)	5-4-3-2-1	not take time to reflect on my experience(s)
find reworking task acceptable because more of interest in excellent work than in expediency	5-4-3-2-1	more anxious to complete task than to take time to check for accuracy and precision

use clear language and thinking in both written and oral forms	5-4-3-2-1	use fuzzy language and thinking in both written and oral forms
begin new task by making connections to prior experience and knowledge	5-4-3-2-1	begin new task as if it were being approached for the first time and make no connection to prior experience
Have fun figuring things out	5-4-3-2-1	perceive thinking as hard work and recoil from situations that demand too much of it
be more interested in being challenged by the process of finding the answer than in just knowing the answer is correct	5-4-3-2-1	be more interested in knowing the answer is correct than being challenged by the process of finding the answer
contribute to group work by being able to work and learn from others in reciprocal situations	5-4-3-2-1	not contribute to group work either by being a "job hog" or by letting others do all the work
devote mental energy to understanding others' thoughts and feelings	5-4-3-2-1	not pay close attention to what is being said beneath the words

References

Banegas, D.(2012, April).General pedagogical knowledge in teacher education. Retrieved from http://www.teachingenglish.org.uk/blogs/dario-banegas/general-pedagogical-knowledge-teacher-education.

Bellanca, J. and Brandt, R. (2010). *21st- century skills: Rethinking how students learn.* Bloomington, IN: Solution Tree Press.

Broudy, H. (1977). Types of knowledge and purposes in education. In R.C. Anderson, R. J. Spiro, & W. E. Montague (Eds.), *Schooling and the acquisition of knowledge* (pp. 1-17). Hillsdale, N.J.: Erlbaum.

Partnership for 21st Century Skills. (2009). P 21 framework definitions. Retrieved from http://p21.org/storage/documents/P21_Framework_Definitions.pdf

Chase, W.G., & Simon, H. A. (1973). Perception in chess. *Cognitive Psychology,* 1, 33 - 81.

Chi, M.T.H., Feltovich, P.J., & Glaser, R. (1981). Categorization and representation of physics problems by experts and novices. *Cognitive Science,* 5, 121-152.

Cochran-Smith, M., & Zeichner, K. (2005). *Studying teacher education: The report of the AERA panel on research and teacher education.* Mahwah, NJ: Lawrence Erlbaum Associates.

Concept to Classroom. (n.d.). Retrieved on July 7, 2011 from http://www.thirteen.org/edonline/concept2class/inquiry/index.html

Costa, A., & Kallick, B. (2000). *Activating and engaging habits of mind.*Alexandria, VA: Association for Supervision and Curriculum Development.

deGroot, A.D. (1965). *Thought and choice in chess.* The Hague, Netherlands: Mouton. Gudmundsdottir, S. (1991). Pedagogical models of subject matter. In J. Brophy (Ed.), *Advances in research on teaching 2,* (pp. 265-304).

Hansen, D. (2002, Autumn).Dewey's conception of an environment for teaching and learning. *Curriculum Inquiry,* 32(3), 267-280.

Hansen, D. (2001). *Exploring the moral heart of teaching: Toward a teacher's creed. New* York: Teachers College Press.

Kleinfeld, J.(1992). Learning to think like a teacher: The study of cases. In J. H. Shulman (Ed.). *Case methods in teacher education* (pp. 33-49). New York, NY: Teachers College Press.

Konig, J., Blomeke, S., Paine, L., Schmidt, W. H., and Feng-Jui, H. (2011, March/April). General pedagogical knowledge of future middle school teachers: On the complex ecology of teacher education in the United States, Germany, and Taiwan. *Journal of Teacher Education,* 62, 188-201,

Lenz, B. (2011). What does successful project-based learning look like? Blog http://www.edutopia.org/blog/project-based-learning-definition-bob-lenz

Merseth, K. K. (1996). Cases and case methods in teacher education. In J.Sikula (Ed.), *Handbook of research on teacher education* (pp. 722-744). New York: MacMillan Publishing Company.

Murrow, S.E. (2005). Learning from recurring debates in education: Teacher education students explore historical case studies. *Educational Studies,* 37(2), 135-156.

National Research Council. (2000). *How people learn: Brain, mind, experience, and school.* Washington, DC: National Academy Press.

Pitton, D. E. (2010). *Developing preservice problem-solving skills through case studies.* Lanham, MD: Rowman & Littlefield.

Richert, A.E. (1991). Case methods and teacher education: Using cases to teach teacher reflection. In B.R. Tabachnik & K. Zeichner (Eds.), Issues and practices in inquiry-oriented teacher education (pp. 130-150). London: Falmer.

Schreyer Institute for Teaching Excellence. (2007). How to write a good case. Retrieved from www.schreyerinstitute.psu.edu/pdf/CaseWritingGuide.pdf -

Shulman, L. (1992). *Case methods in teacher education.* New York, NY: Teachers College Press.

Shulman, L. (1987). Knowledge and teaching, *Harvard Educational Review,* 57, 1-22. Teacher Education. (n.d.). Bluprints online. Retrieved from http://www.project2061.org/publications/bfr/online/Teacher/text.htm

The Conceptual Framework. (n.d.). Retrieved from http://education.fiu.edu/docs/Conceptual%20Framework%2006-19-09.pdf

Tozer, S., Anderson, D.H. & Armbruster, B. B. (1990). For the record: Psychological and social foundations in teacher education: A thematic introduction. *Teachers College Record,* 91(3), 293-299

Trier, J. (2010, summer). Designing a case study from the popular culture text Boston Public. *Multicultural Education*, 49-56.

Wiggins, G. and McTighe, J. (1998).*Understanding by design.* Alexandria, VA: ASCD Wilhelm, J. (n.d.) Inquiry-based learning. Retrieved from http://www.neiu.edu/~middle/Modules/science%20mods/amazon%20components/AmazonComponents2.html

CHAPTER TWO

Building Trust in Undergraduate ESOL Classes: Foundation of Democratic Habits of Mind

By

Teresa Lucas

It is the first day of my undergraduate course, TSL 4081, the second of a two-course sequence on preparing teacher candidates to work with English language learners (ELLs) in the elementary classroom. After a general introduction to the course, but before going into the syllabus and requirements, I ask the students to reflect back to a favorite teacher, and to consider why they remember that teacher and come up with a word to describe him/her. We then go to a "cocktail party," where everyone meets every other person, and shares his or her remembrances of special teachers. Invariably, students discover connections they have with classmates they had previously known only by sight, and come up with words such as "patient," "enthusiastic," "caring," "fair," "funny," "helpful," etc. to describe favorite teachers.

By putting personal connections before content, I am emphasizing the importance of relationships in education. By asking the pre-service teachers to reflect on teacher qualities, I am focusing on the development of dispositions important for educators. Participation in the Faculty Learning Community (FLC) in the College of Education at Florida International University has helped me to define what I had been doing more by instinct than with thoughtful purpose. This chapter describes how I am working to consciously encourage and document students' engagement in the social process of learning through my modeling dispositions.

Thoughtful educators and educational researchers are taking a step back from the frenzied focus on accountability systems, assessment instruments and unified curricula to ponder fundamental questions related to classroom effectiveness. As noted by Fitzsimons (2007): "Teachers and educational policy-makers are not encouraging young people to reflect on the meaning and purpose of their lives; nor are they doing it themselves. Instead, there is an unquestioning emphasis on personal diligence, employment opportunities and the virtue of technology" (p. 7). Tollefson and Osborn (2008) echo this sentiment when they note that educators today are encouraged to "devote their allegiance to the market values of efficiency and uniformity rather than the humanistic values described by the John Dewey Project on Progressive Education (2002)...respect for diversity...and critical, socially engaged intelligence" (p. 17).

The Faculty Learning Community at FIU shares a belief in a much broader mandate for education than preparing individuals for the workplace. The utilitarian view of education focuses on the development of knowledge and the perfection of skills, worthy aims, to be sure, but not sufficient for individuals to develop to their full potential as contributing members of society. As Martin Luther King (1947) noted: "We must remember that intelligence is not enough. Intelligence plus character--that is the goal of true education. The complete education gives one not only power of concentration, but worthy objectives upon which to concentrate" (para. 5).

Like King, Shields (2011) proposes character as the aim of education, suggesting four dimensions of character: intellectual, moral, civic, and performance, remarking that "developing beneficial and pro-social dispositions should be prioritized over acquiring more and more facts and formulas (p. 49). He suggests that these dimensions of character all share a focus on personal dispositions and patterns of interaction (p. 49). The dispositions may be equated with the Habits of Mind (HoM) articulated in the college's Conceptual Framework and enhanced by the FIU Faculty Learning Community.

The goal of education is to prepare students for life in the human community, not only for the workplace. The development of character is crucial, and this development occurs through both reflection and social interaction. For teachers to guide students to their own development, they must engage continually in their own development. Talking about dispositions has little effect if the instructor does not model them in the classroom. Indeed, we educate by means of an environment in which habits of life and intercourse are lived, not merely told, preached, lectured, written about (Dewey, 1916/1944, p. 38). Modeling the dispositions is of paramount importance, as is creating an environment "...of mutual respect and support in an ethical classroom climate" (Hulsart & McCarthy, 2009, p. 54), in which teacher candidates are disposed to develop the Habits of Mind that they will, in turn, model for their students. While pondering the issue of modeling the Habits of Mind discussed in this book, it seemed to me that for my students to perceive in me a model for their own development, they would have to see in me a person in whom they could have confidence. This brought me to the fundamental issue of trust.

Theoretical Framework

At a faculty meeting some years ago in the university in Venezuela where I worked, I was profoundly struck by the question posed by one of my colleagues: "how can we get anywhere when nobody trusts anybody else?" The question both peeked my curiosity, and saddened me. While I had been living in the country for many years by then, I often was puzzled by interactions that confused me. It might be a simple thing such as making a date to meet someone, only to be told by my Venezuelan husband that our interlocutor did not really mean it. Or it might be something more consequential as when a colleague would agree to collaborate, and then not do his/her part. There was a tendency towards "double-speak" embedded in the culture that I had not understood until my colleague posed the question that day. Serendipitously, a friend recommended I read *Riding the Waves of Culture* by Fons Trompenaars and Charles Hampden-Turner (1998), an exploration of the bases of cultural differences. Among the attitudes that vary across cultures is the perception of truthfulness. Intrigued, I investigated further to find that researchers were discovering the relationship between the ability of people in a society to trust one another and the creation of democratic institutions and economic development.

Fukuyama (1995) noted that "one of the most important lessons we can learn from an examination of economic life is that a nation's well-being...is conditioned by a single, pervasive cultural characteristic: the level of trust inherent in the society" (p. 7). He defined trust as

> ...the expectation that arises within a community of regular, honest, and cooperative behavior, based on commonly shared norms, on the part of other members of the community. Those norms can be about deep 'value' questions like the nature of God or justice, but they also encompass secular norms like professional standards and codes of behavior (26).

According to Fukuyama, "the prevalence of trust in a society or in certain parts of it" (p. 26) gives rise to the development of social capital, which signifies the human resources of a nation or an organization.

Uslaner argued: "Trust matters because it is part, perhaps the most essential part, of *social capital*" (Uslaner, 1999, p.122). He referred to social capital as the system of values and norms, especially social trust, that binds people to one another in communities where generalized reciprocity and cooperation flourish. "Trust is a rational gamble that cooperation with others will ultimately pay off" (p. 122). Uslaner defined two types of trust: a) particularized trust in those who are like oneself, family and close friends, which is typical of authoritarian and totalitarian societies; and b) generalized trust, which extends trust to persons in the community at large, and which operates in democracies.

Jamal and Nooruddin (2010) note that "studies of political culture have long emphasized the importance of generalized trust–the propensity to trust fellow citizens–for effective democratic governance" (p. 45). Like Fukuyama and Uslaner, Zmerli and Newton (2008) refer to the importance of trust in the development of social capital:

> Social capital theory argues that generalized social trust is an important and central element in a complex and virtuous circle of social attitudes, behavior, and institutions that act as the foundation for stable and effective democratic

government. Trust is said to sustain a cooperative social climate, to facilitate collective behavior, and to encourage a regard for the public interest (p. 706).

Tonkiss and Passey (1999) indicated that "recent debates within social and political theory reveal growing interest in issues of 'trust' as a basis for social organization, civic democracy and economic prosperity" (p. 257). According to Warren (1999), "without trust the most basic activities of everyday life would become impossible" (p. 2).   After years of working as a business consultant, Covey and Merrill (2006) suggest that:

> ...trust undergirds and affects the quality of every relationship, every communication, every work project, every business venture, every effort in which we are engaged. It changes the quality of every present moment and alters the trajectory and outcome of every future moment of our lives – both personally and professionally (pp. 1-2).

As trust is recognized as the foundation for both democratic societies and interpersonal relationships, it is logical that educators take a serious look at the development of trusting and trustworthiness.   Research on trust in education has centered on the levels of educational policy, educational institutions, and in the classroom.   Bottery (2004) wrote about educational trust after listening to a speech on "Professionalism and Trust" by the then Secretary of State for Education in England and Wales in 2001.   The Secretary was attempting to build better relationships with teachers in the face of increasingly low morale. Bottery was struck that:

> ...this speech seemed almost exclusively concerned with the problems of trust *by* government *of* teachers. This not only failed to recognize that trust is a two-way street; it also failed to recognize that *not being trusted* is perceived by the recipient as a moral judgment about them and their character (6). (italics in the original).

On the institutional level, researchers have found a direct relation between trust and positive outcomes in organizations (Covey & Merrill, 2006; Dirks, 2000; Nooteboom & Six, 2003; Putnam, 1993; Tzafrir, 2005).   Tschaannen-Moran (2004) described the role of trust as "a lubricant of organizational functioning, without it, the school is likely to experience an overheated friction of conflict as well as a lack of progress toward its admirable goals" (xi).

As affecting the classroom, "Trust is foundational to learning across all stages of the lifespan. Whether the focus is on student learning of new academic or social skills...learning is enhanced when the learner feels safe enough to take on the risks that learning entails" (Tschannen-Moran & Tschannen-Moran, 2011, p. 437).   Trust is fundamental for promoting academic integrity (Hulsart & McCarthy, 2011); in building an atmosphere that promotes engagement and learning (Robinson & Kokela, 2006); and in reaching unmotivated middle school students ((Walsh 2006).   The current chapter focuses on building trust in the classroom as the building block for trust across institutions and in policy. If trust does not exist at the center of the educational process–the classroom–then it is difficult that it can be achieved more broadly.

Trust in the classroom depends on the relationships that are built reflecting Rotter's definition quoted by Hosner that "…interpersonal trust [was] an expectancy held by an individual or a group that the word, promise, verbal or written statement of another individual or group [could] be relied upon" (Rotter as cited in Hosmer, 1995, p. 383). Hosmer elaborated on the trust that can be built between superiors and subordinates (teachers and students) by citing Butler and Cantrell (1984)'s notion of the five specific components of trust: integrity, consistency, loyalty, and openness, and competence (Hosmer, 1995, p. 384).

More recently, Tschannen-Moran (2004) defined trust in the educational setting as the "willingness to be vulnerable to another based on the confidence that the other is benevolent, honest, open, reliable, and competent" (p. 17). In establishing a relationship of trust, an individual assesses such characteristics as benevolence, mutual concern, goodwill, caring, integrity, authenticity, openness, and reliability (Tschannen-Moran & Tschannen-Moran, 2011).

Bottery (2004) proposes four stages in the development of a trust relationship. These are calculative, role, practice and identificatory. The trust becomes deeper as one moves from the first two that are basically cognitive in nature to "incorporate motivational, affective, and principled elements" (p. 6). The lowest level, calculative, is the measuring of a new acquaintance to form a preliminary judgment of trustworthiness. Role trust refers to the assertion by certain professionals (including teachers) that they can be trusted because of their education into a certain set of values. Practice trust ensues when the assertion of being trustworthy is borne out through interaction. Finally, identificatory trust, the highest level of trust, ensues when "individuals come to know each other so well that there is an almost intuitive knowledge of what the other will do, generating a mutual unconditional respect and trust" (p. 7).

In their work on academic integrity, Hulsart & McCarthy (2011) emphasize that "…trust reflects feelings of mutual respect and support in an ethical classroom climate" (p. 93). Trust is a reciprocal process, necessitating that the instructor both act in a trustworthy way and have confidence that the students will be trustworthy as well. To create this situation, "two necessary leadership roles are team building and modeling trust" (p. 93). Team building increases interdependence among members of the team, while modeling demonstrates that trusting relationships are possible. Modeling includes being consistent, engaging with the students, respecting their opinions, and believing that students are trustworthy. If an instructor indicates to students that s/he does not trust them, this may result, according to Bottery (2004), in a "…cycle of mutual distrust, …as being distrusted is perceived as a normative judgment, producing anger, lowered self-esteem, powerlessness and deep distrust of the those not trusting" (p. 7).

A dissenting voice as to the value of attempting to encourage and develop trust in the classroom is that of Schutz (2011). He considers utopian, Dewey's ideal of a collaborative democracy in which people participate as relative equals on common efforts to improve their society since Dewey's vision "require(s) extensive trust among participants" (p. 495). Schutz argues that encouraging collaboration and trust in schools ill-prepares students for the "contentious world outside the doors of protective progressive schools…(where) attempts to use intelligent action for social purposes are thwarted and balked by the competitive antisocial spirit and dominant selfishness in society as it is" (p. 496). However, the very notion of "progressive" is about seeing a society that can be transformed if the individuals within the society work on personal transformation, as evidenced by the work of individuals like Ghandi and Mandela, who trusted that change was, indeed, possible.

Key Ideas and Issues and Methodologies

Our experience in the Faculty Learning Community affirmed my belief that it is possible to create and develop an environment based on mutual trust among the individuals in a group. I was energized to work more consciously on the development of the Habits of Mind in myself and in my students within a climate of trusting and trustworthiness in the classroom. As seen above, building trust relies on the dispositions of integrity, consistency, loyalty, openness, competency, mutual concern, goodwill, caring, authenticity, and reliability, closely related to the Habits of Mind defined by the Learning Community. My focus is primarily on those Habits of Mind that promote the development of an accepting environment in the classroom, such as we experience with the Learning Community: questioning and posing problems, thinking flexibly (being open-minded), thinking and communicating with clarity and precision, taking responsible risks, thinking interdependently, and listening with understanding and empathy.

In preparing to work purposefully on the integration of the development of dispositions within a classroom climate of trust and trustworthiness, I developed the following plan: (1) Continual personal development of the characteristics that make one a trustworthy individual: integrity, consistency, loyalty, and openness, competence, benevolence, mutual concern, goodwill, caring, authenticity, and reliability. (2) Making sure I know my students and that the students know one another. (3) Respecting students' lives and opinions. (4) Creation of teams in which individuals are responsible to one another, creating a "dynamic for reciprocity" (Hulsart & McCarthy, 2011, p. 93), and (5) Believing in students.

My Own Development

In working to develop in future teachers the dispositions for them to become good teachers, we often focus on our students when we have to begin with ourselves. The foundation of trust cannot be laid if the instructor is not trustworthy. Hulsart & McCarthy (2011, p. 93) refer to questions for faculty to ask themselves to reflect on their own trustworthiness: Is my behavior predictable or erratic? Do I communicate clearly or carelessly? Do I treat promises seriously or lightly? Am I forthright or dishonest?

Once I went to a workshop for future teachers during which the presenter encouraged the attendees to be themselves with their students. I agree and am open about myself, my experience, my children and grandchildren, as part of forming a personal connection with my students. Having had the experience of emigrating to another country and living many years in another culture, and raising bilingual, bicultural children, has the additional advantage of offering a personal perspective on the challenges my students will have in dealing with English language learners. However, when the presenter elaborated that teachers had the right to let students see frustrations and anger caused by personal problems, I had to take issue. As a professional, an instructor needs to maintain a professional attitude so that his/her behavior is predictable and not erratic. As an ESOL instructor, the Habit of Mind of communicating with clarity and precision is at the foundation of our practice. Of course, this is more than enunciating clearly; it is making sure students understand the goals, objectives and expectations of the class. It means providing clear instructions, both orally and in writing for assignments. It means never losing patience with the inevitable requests for repetition of the instructions.

As much as I have learned to repeat instructions over and over again, I have also come to be very sparse with promises, learning to rely on the phrase that I hated as a child growing up when I asked my parents for something: "We'll see." Perhaps nothing erodes the development of a trusting relationship more than a broken promise, unless it is dishonesty. A student needs to know that the instructor is open and honest.

Knowing and Respecting the Students

I have made use of several different activities in the first class of the semester to begin to get to know my students, and for the students to get to know one another. For the "cocktail party" referenced at the beginning of the chapter, I give each student a paper with a table on it that has the number of rows corresponding to the number of students in the class. Columns indicate the information they should obtain from each of their fellow students: name, major, where they went to high school, and an adjective that describes the main characteristic of a teacher they have had and admired in the past. Student must fill in the table themselves; they cannot pass it around for others to fill out. This creates a situation in which students find out something about their classmates that they generally did not know before, discover connections among themselves, and share stories about their favorite teachers. I participate in the activity as well, sharing my information. In this way we begin to establish the personal connections that are essential for building a trusting environment. This activity lays the foundation for the development of the Habits of Mind of thinking interdependently and listening with understanding and empathy.

Another activity that is effective, as an introduction to Habits of Mind, especially when the class is relatively small (some 20 students or less) is described by a former student:

> We were instructed to write down five facts about ourselves that we would like to share with the class… crumple the papers up and throw them in the center of the circle (we) created with our desks. Each student chose one paper and read aloud the traits of another classmate. We guessed who we thought the descriptions belonged to. As a class, we laughed and became comfortable with each other as we shared personal narratives…At first, it was strange; no teacher had ever told me to move the desks in a class from the position they were in when we entered the room. And furthermore, no teacher had ever told me to crumple up a paper I had written on. However, while the activity made me uncomfortable at first, truth be told, I have continued to use this activity to lower affective filters on the first day of school in my classroom year after year.

Getting to know the students' names and encouraging them to share information about themselves in a relaxed atmosphere is the first step toward establishing mutual respect. I ask students to post a brief introduction of themselves in the Course Management System website so that we can all refresh our memories about each individual. As the semester continues, listening to students' questions and issues with respect and answering honestly encourages them to develop the Habit of Mind of questioning and posing problems, as well as thinking flexibly (being open-minded). I also encourage them to share their experiences and knowledge about the topics that we discuss. Many are second language learners themselves, so they have an important perspective to share as we talk about issues related to working with English language learners in the classroom. I encourage them to express their opinions and insights, and am happy when I can tell them that they have offered a perspective that I had not thought of before, thus engaging them in the Habits of Mind of listening with understanding and empathy and thinking interdependently.

Creating Teams

Listening with understanding and empathy and thinking interdependently are further developed by working together in teams that are formed for the entire semester. The aim is that through the development of Habits of Mind, the trust that contributes to holding individuals and societies together is generated.

Michaelson (2012) describes the power of team learning as the nurturing of the "development of high levels of group cohesiveness, which in turn, results in a wide variety of positive outcomes" (p. 1). In addition to promoting successful learning, "as the groups develop into teams, communication becomes more open…(with) trust and understanding building to the point that members are willing and able to engage in intense give-and- take interactions" (pp. 3-4). Individual and team success depend on the members of the team finding ways to work together harmoniously.

Basic to team-based learning are Readiness Assessment Tests. These are multiple choice quizzes that students first take individually. Immediately after they turn in their individual quiz, they work together in their teams to answer the same questions. Students learn to listen to their classmates and come to a consensus. Invariably the combined knowledge of the students results in a better grade for the team than for the individuals, resulting in the building of trust among the members of the team.

Several assignments throughout the semester are also team-based, including a research project and the preparation and execution of an authentic assessment. Research topics arise from the students' own interests in topics related to the course. Teams choose their topic and assign aspects to each team member, as well as roles in the elaboration of a website through which they present their research. As assessment of English language learners is a major focus of the course, teams prepare an authentic assessment in which they engage the entire class at the end of the semester. Again, team members are responsible for organizing and assigning tasks for each individual.

Believing in the Students

We often hear faculty conversations about students who plagiarize sources when writing a paper or cheat on exams. Hulsart & McCarthy (2011) cite numerous studies "demonstrating the pervasive nature of cheating among college students" (p. 92). Departments increasingly require students to submit their papers via "Turnitin". It is easy to fall into the current mode of suspicion when working with students. However, trusting my students is a way of modeling the Habit of Mind of taking responsible risks.

So, instead of taking as my starting point that students are not to be trusted, I assume a trusting attitude. Covey and Merrill (2006) developed the metaphor of the "Trust Account", described in the following way: "By behaving in ways that build trust, you make deposits. By behaving in ways that destroy trust, you make withdrawals. The 'balance' in the account reflects the amount of trust in a relationship at any given time" (p. 130). Walsh (2006) applies the metaphor to his experience working with disengaged middle school students. He builds trust by being kind, courteous and honest with his students, instead of falling into the trap of disrespecting difficult students. Over time, the small "deposits" in the students' "trust accounts" lead them to see him as "safe, trustworthy and approachable…what students continually see, hear, and feel from teachers has a cumulative effect on building trust" (p. 14).

The relationships built through the initial activities, and continued throughout the semester through respectful and open dialogue and team-based activities, all constitute "deposits" in the trust accounts. Creating assignments that minimize the possibilities of unethical behavior are another component to assuring that trust is maintained. Instead of asking students to write a paper to report the results of their research, teams build a website in which they develop a storyline to relate their research to their own personal practice. For their field experience project, students work in a school with a small group of English language learners. The assignment requires them to describe in detail the school setting, classroom dynamics, and the children. They must create a unit and lesson plan based on a pre-assessment of the children, and carry out several lessons, after which they conduct a post-assessment. They are required to include personal reflections on the lessons and on the experience as a whole. The entire assignment is contextual and based on the knowledge they have acquired related to the course.

Other assignments include creating and carrying out activities and authentic assessments in which the entire class is engaged. Students are encouraged to consult sources and incorporate ideas from these sources, but the nature of the performance assessment ensures that the work is their own.

I also incorporate traditional assessments in the form of online exams. These are meant to capture the students' grasp of the course concepts drawn from class lectures and readings. My goal is understanding, not rote memorization, so the students are allowed several days and open books to complete the exams. I even encourage them to consult with their team members. In this way, the possibility of "cheating" is eliminated!

Maybe there have been times when I have been "burned," with students taking advantage of my own trusting nature and my commitment to depositing trust in my students. But, like Neal A. Maxwell, as cited in Covey and Merrill (2006), I feel "It is better to trust and sometimes be disappointed than to be forever mistrusting and be right occasionally" (p. 319). As Covey and Merrill note:

> Trust brings out the best in people and literally changes the dynamics of interaction. While it is true that a few abuse this trust, the vast, vast majority of people do not abuse it, but respond amazingly well to it. And when they do, they don't need external supervision, control, or the "carrot and stick" approach to motivation. They are inspired. They run with the trust they were extended. They want to live up to it. They want to give back. (p. 319)

As Zuangzi (c 286 BC) noted long ago, "Reward and punishment are the lowest form of Education" (Lapham, 2008, p. 15). It is through "...creating a space for fun, interaction, and trust, (that) teachers and students together can build a learning environment that promotes engagement, deep learning and meaning" (Robinson & Kakela, 2006, p. 202). Education is about positive relationships, for which "trust is clearly a critical component...for being trusted nurtures a person's morale, self-esteem and feelings of self-worth" (Bottery, 2004, p.8). Bottery goes on to emphasize:

> ...whilst much teacher CPD seems concentrated upon the elevation of pedagogic skills, little is written on the integrity of educators in their relationships with students and yet...perceptions of trust are critical in the development of a rich and productive teacher-student relationship (p. 8).

Building relations on trust has wide implications that reach beyond the classroom. Democratic societies rely on a foundation of trust. But is trustworthiness inherent in the individual, or can it be developed as we have seen with dispositions, such as respect for others and diversity? According to Covey and Merrill (2006), who have worked advising business leaders for years, "we can increase trust – much faster than we might think – and doing so will have a huge impact, both in the quality of our lives and in the results we're able to achieve" (p. 3).

Student Reactions

What was the impact of placing trust-building at the center of my pre-service ESL education course by encouraging the development of Habits of Mind that lead to trusting and trustworthiness? The reactions of the students were recorded in a survey at the end of the semester. The first survey question referenced directly the students' perception of how effectively a climate of trust was created in the classroom. Since trust is built among people, the quality of interaction is key, so the second survey question related to the experience of working in teams, a strategy utilized to establish mutual respect and trust. At the end of the semester, the students responded to the following questions:

1. Do you feel a climate of trust was established in the classroom from the beginning of and throughout the semester? What factors aided or inhibited the sense of trust?
2. Were you able to experience learning through interaction during the team-based activities (research project and RATS)? Why or why not?

Climate of Trust

Referring to the perception of the climate of trust, students reported that they felt that trust was established, mentioning several main factors that contributed to the building of trust. These included: 1) getting to know one another; 2) positive interactions with the instructor and classmates, including constructive feedback; and, 3) being responsible for their own learning.

1) Getting to know one another: Research has shown that trust is built on quality relationships (Hulsart & McCarthy, 2011; Kensler, et al., 2009; Robinson & Kokela, 2006; Walsh, 2006). Building these relationships with and among students from the beginning of the semester was seen as pivotal to creating a trusting environment. The "cocktail party" in the first class set the stage, followed by respectful class discussions, the building of teams and interactive activities, all couched in my attempt to model trustworthy behavior through reflection on the questions noted above. One student noted:

> I feel that a climate of trust was established in the classroom from the beginning of and throughout the semester. The reason...is because our class had grown into this large yet close community of teachers.... the first day of

class, we walked around the classroom and introduced ourselves to one another. We were able to get to know one another and from then on, we always maintained that open and friendly connection with one another…

Another student specifically noted the importance of getting to know one another's names: "I knew everyone in the classroom and everyone knew each other by name which makes you feel like friends, that you can trust each other". As an English as a second language (ESL) instructor, I have always been sensitive to the importance of getting names right, since in dealing with people from other languages and cultures, it is often difficult to learn to pronounce names correctly. ESL students are grateful when their instructor makes the effort to pronounce their names. One of the students in the class made reference to this issue:

> I do feel that there was a sense of trust established in the classroom from the beginning of the semester to the end because as a professor you didn't butcher our names the first day of class; on the other hand, you asked if we wanted to be called something else. I think that by doing this you made us feel comfortable.

By getting to know one another by name, and by learning something about one another's live, students felt comfortable contributing in class. One commented that "I got to know several of my classmates. This class was the most I have spoken in the classroom at FIU. I felt like my opinions mattered". Knowing whom they were talking to helped students to feel comfortable contributing in class, as evidenced in the following reflection:

> Whenever my group and I would go up in front of the classroom to present an assignment, I would personally feel a sense of comfort and trust since I know each one of my classmates…Often time in my previous classes, I don't even get to know the name of my classmate that is sitting next to me and in those classrooms, every time I would go up to present, I would feel frightened and uncomfortable presenting since it felt as if they were all a group of complete strangers.

Making the effort to know the students' names and ensuring that they know one another clearly make a difference in the classroom environment, leading to fruitful interactions among all of the participants in the class, including students and teacher. When interactions are positive, both trust and learning are encouraged.

2) Positive interactions among students and teacher / constructive feedback:

According to Tschannen-Moran and Tschannen-Moran (2011), change results from focusing on strengths rather than on debilities, with positive energy generated through "the quality of the conversations and interactions people are having with one another. The social context is viewed as the crucible that creates the present moment and changes future moments" (p. 423). Feeling that one's opinions matter is important for the development of self-esteem. Students come to the classroom with a vast store of experiences and background knowledge. All of their contributions matter, and should be accepted with respect, even if they may need guidance in correcting mistaken impressions.

In their comments, students seemed to appreciate the respect given to their contributions.

> ...the class felt like a safe environment where the students were not afraid to answer questions or be silly participating in a game or activity,' noted one, while another remarked: I feel that I was able to go to the professor or my fellow peers with questions or concerns without feeling like I would be judged. In the same vein, another student noted: The lectures were open for discussion and everyone was welcome to comment and responses were never wrong.

Of course, it is not exactly accurate to say "responses were never wrong", but by framing the feedback in a respectful way, students are more likely to learn from their mistakes. As one student expressed:

> Every time we would turn in an assignment or a project, she would always have a positive thing to say about it and acknowledge all of our hard work. Whenever we would have mistakes in our assignments, she would suggest various ways to fix it. Never did she make you feel belittled so I always felt that I could trust her whenever I sent out any assignment of mine to her. I knew that if I did an error, she would provide me with positive feedback.

While both positive and negative feedback can impact learning, research has shown that students with teachers who give constructive feedback and encouragement are apt to learn more than students whose teachers emphasize criticism and punishment (Acheson, 1987; Ovando, 1994). Positive feedback also contributes to the general positive environment in the classroom. The comments that students were comfortable asking questions indicate they were developing the Habit of Mind of questioning and posing problems. At the same time, they felt comfortable participating in the trusting environment, showing that they were listening to one another with understanding and empathy.

3) *Personal responsibility for learning*

Several students made reference to the relation between personal responsibility and trust. One noted: "I feel a climate of trust was established in the classroom through the semester because our learning was in our hands". Another elaborated:

> The professor gave us the opportunity to be creative and trusted that what we chose to teach or create would be in the best interest of our students and most importantly ESOL students. The professor allowed us to create lessons and activities we thought were best for our students.

This was a new connection to me and in searching for antecedents, I found reference in the corporate world. According to Mostovicz, et al (2011), we only trust those who are committed and undertake full responsibility for their actions.

Depositing trust in the students encourages them to become actively involved in their learning and to assume ownership of the process. While students are often "frustrated with assignments and assessments that require memorization and regurgitation" they respond positively when they are able to "creatively demonstrate content knowledge" (Hulsart & McCarthy, 2011, p. 94). The nature of the assignments in the class was such that student input and creativity were essential to completing them adequately. Assuming ownership of their own learning process involves the development of the Habit of Mind of taking responsible risks, as students must make decisions in the elaboration of their class work.

Working in Teams to Create Trusting Relationships

A responsible risk was involved in adapting the team-based learning strategy developed by Michaelson (2012). We had experimented with it in a previous class with good results, so I decided to implement it in this teacher education class. Michaelson (2012) attributes the power of team learning to

> the high level of cohesiveness that can be developed within student learning groups. In other words, the effectiveness of team learning as an instructional strategy is based on the fact that it nurtures the development of high levels of group cohesiveness which, in turn, results in a wide variety of other positive outcomes (p. 1).

Among the positive outcomes mentioned by Michaelson are the development of higher level thinking skills, providing support for at-risk students, and promoting interpersonal and team work skills (p. 19). By creating teams that worked together throughout the semester, and whose members depended on one another to complete assignments and the Readiness Assessment Tests (RATS), my hope was that the interdependence would be a motivation for each individual to perform his or her responsibilities and thus lay the foundation for building trust among the members of the team. Of course, there was risk involved. As one student noted in the survey: "Working with groups has always scared me because of bad experiences..." Since the students worked together over the course of the 15-week semester, I hoped that they would arrive at Bottery's level of *practice trust*, "where relationships can be built which take trust beyond the merely logical into the affective and value areas (Bottery, 2004, p. 7), causing a deeper relationship. Trusting and being trustworthy were essential to their success.

The risk seems to have paid off, as students noted that working in teams resulted in: 1) gaining from different perspectives; 2) achieving better results by working in a team; and 3) building cohesiveness.

1. Gaining from different perspectives:

According to Bottery (2004), one of the foundations for trust is agreement over values and value priorities. However, value diversity may be an even better foundation for practice trust , "because it is by learning to respect others and their differing views that one may come to realize that respect of difference is as important for trust as is a unitary agreement on values" (p. 7), echoing the Habit of Mind of thinking flexibly (being open-minded) As one student noted:

> I learned a lot of creative ideas from the people I have been able to work with this semester. I have also been exposed to different ways to look at a subject or topic, and while working together on the RATS I have seen that a question can be interpreted in many different ways from other's perspectives. I have learned to keep an open mind.

As the semester progressed, the level of comfort grew, so that one student remarked: "we all became more and more comfortable with one another to share our ideas as well as present our information to each other. I think this was possible because everyone in the class was always open to everyone's ideas and always willing to listen to what each other had to say." The student seems to indicate that the students were developing the Habit of Mind of thinking flexibly, or being open-minded.

Competence is another foundation for trust (Bottery, 2004), and students were able to rely on the knowledge of their teammates when working on the RATS and in doing their research project. Sharing their ideas in their teams allowed the students to develop the Habit of Mind of thinking interdependently. They found that working together they were able get better results than each one individually. As one student saw it: "By going over the quizzes together, each person was able to talk about what they knew about topic." Another noted: "There were many times I was unsure of an answer or I just simply did not know it or understood it. While doing the RATs my team members were able to explain and define many things." Learning from others was a result of working on the RATS: "Hearing my classmates explain why they thought the answer they chose was correct taught me something about the specific topic."

The same held true when working on the research project. Each person in the team had something to offer. As one student noted: "When you work together you can end with a wonderful ending product. I... learned that everyone has a special quality that can be useful for group work." Another highlighted the benefit of sharing ideas: "As far as the research project in my group was concerned, the second my team members and I got together to create the website, we all offered different ideas that none of us would've thought of by ourselves." The students also relied on one another, for example, to solve technical difficulties in creating the website: "All of my group members would work together. If we did not know how to add the title in the website, we would text or call one another and figure it out." Again we can see that working in teams seems to have provided an opportunity for the students to exercise the Habit of Mind of thinking interdependently, as shown in the next section as well.

2. *Getting better results working in a team:*

Lev Vygotsky (1978) considered that "…all the higher functions originate as actual relations between human individuals. The internalization of socially rooted and historically developed activities is the distinguishing feature of human psychology" (p. 57). In other words, learning occurs in the interaction among people and with the environment, and is then internalized within the individual.

Based on their reflections, the students experienced this phenomenon in working together. The group input resulted in learning:

> I found working on the research project to be helpful because within our groups we gave our own ideas and feeling towards what was going on. Working in groups helps us develop our thought process on the topic.

In reference to the RATS, one student noted the efficacy of the group interaction:

> In a group we can understand more than to do by myself. When I try to understand some questions the other group members had an easier method to solve the questions…In a group we almost always ended with a higher score than the individual one.

And another, commenting on the RATS, was surprised at the benefit of working with the team:

> There was even an instance when we all individually got a question working but when we came together as a group to discuss it, we got it right!

3. *Building cohesiveness:*

Being open to differing perspectives or cultivating the Habit of Mind of thinking flexibly (being open-minded), often led to better results for everyone, further leading to the development of trust among the team members. Several students recognized that there are both challenges and benefits of working in a team. As one put it:

> Working in groups can be challenging when you have different personalities on the team, but when interaction takes place, it provides benefits to the group and as an individual.

Another reflected:

> It teaches you to cope with people and compromise and solve problems together. Working as a group, you learn to work with different personalities.

Learning to work with the diversity was beneficial for most of the students, and is a vital component for establishing trust on a broader scale. It is said that tolerance of difference may make for a stronger society, and one student commented:

> The different perspectives and reasoning we all had to offer led us to open our minds to various potential explanations that we might've not thought of ourselves.

Appreciating the diversity of opinions within her team was reflected in one student's comment:

> We were given the chance to listen to each other's ideas which benefited my group members and I since what I said might have never crossed my partner's mind and what she said could've never crossed MY mind. So the sharing of ideas made us grow in our learning. I got to learn from my teammates and they served as a great support in my education.

Developing tolerance and appreciation for diversity is closely connected to the third level of trust, practice trust, defined by Bottery (2004), that ensues when the assertion of being trustworthy is borne out through interaction., "...because it is by learning to respect others and their differing views that one may come to realize that respect of difference is as important for trust as is a unitary agreement on values" (Bottery, 2004, p. 7).

From their responses to the survey questions, students expressed that they had felt a climate of trust was established in the classroom, and that they had experienced learning through working in teams. The initial activities aimed at making sure everyone knew each other, followed by positive interactions among the instructor and the students, and by students assuming responsibility for their own learning, all impacted the development of a climate of trust. Through working in teams, students found they were able to gain from different perspectives and achieve better results, thus helping to create cohesiveness within the teams. Cultivating the Habits of Mind of questioning and posing problems, thinking flexibly (being open-minded), thinking and communicating with clarity and precision, taking responsible risks, thinking interdependently, and listening with understanding and empathy, modeled as much as possible by the instructor, contributed to the development of trust and trustworthiness.

Conclusion

Is Dewey's vision of a collaborative democracy based on trust a utopian ideal, as characterized by Schutz (2011), who considers that students should be prepared to join in what he views as the "antisocial spirit and dominant selfishness" (p. 496) in today's society? Or can educators believe in and direct their efforts to making a more positive vision reality? Kouzes and Posner (2007) note that "people who are trusting are more likely to be happy and psychologically adjusted than those who view the world with suspicion and disrespect" (p. 225). And their work centered on people within corporations, Trust is not utopian. It is the basis for functioning democratic societies, and for successful businesses, as well.

Educators, and particularly educators who prepare future educators, should be the first to assume and model the Habit of Mind of taking responsible risks by being willing to trust their own students, thus encouraging them to become trustworthy and trusting. In learning to question and pose problems, and think and communicate with clarity and precision, students develop confidence in their own ability to contribute to the creation of a positive environment. As they participate more confidently in class and engage in team-building activities, they learn to think interdependently and flexibly and listen with understanding and empathy,

By developing these Habits of Mind, future teachers can join the ranks of the thoughtful practitioners and researchers who look for a broader mandate for educational reform than the focus on preparing students for the workplace. Along with knowledge and skills, individuals need to develop the dispositions that will allow them to achieve personal fulfillment and at the same time be contributing members of society.

References

Acheson, K.A. & Gall, M.D. (1987). *Techniques in the clinical supervision of teachers*, White Plains, NY: Longman.

Bottery, M. (2004). Trust: Its importance of educators. *Management in Education,* 18, 5, 6-10.

Covey, S. M. R., & Merrill, R. R. (2006). *The speed of trust: The one thing that changes everything.* New York: Free Press.

Dewey, J. (1916/1944). *Democracy and education: An Introduction to the philosophy of education.* New York, NY: The Free Press.

Fitzsimons, P. (2007). Social capital and education. Conference Presentation 2007 Philosophy of Education Society of Australasia. Retrieved from http://www.pesa.org.au/papers/2007-papers/Fitzsimons,%20P.pdf

Dirks, K. T. (2000). Trust in leadership and team performance: Evidence from NCAA basketball. *Journal of Applied Psychology,* 85(6), 1004-1012.

Fukuyama, F. (2000). Social capital. In Harrison, L.E. & Huntington, S. P. (Eds.), *Culture matters: How values shape human progress.* New York: Basic Books, 98-111.

Fukuyama, F. (1995). *Trust: The social virtues and the creation of prosperity.* New York: The Free Press.

Hosmer, L.T. (1995). Trust: The connecting link between organizational theory and philosophical ethics. *Academy of Management Review,* 20, 2, 379-403.

Hulsart, R. & McCarthy, V. (2009). Educators' role in promoting academic integrity. *Academy of Educational Leadership Journal,* 13, 4: 49-60.

Jamal, A. & Noorodin, I. (2010). The democratic utility of trust: A cross-national analysis. *The Journal of Politics,* 72, 1, 45–59.

John Dewey Project on Progressive Education,. (2002). *A Brief Overview of Progressive Education.* Retrieved from http://www.uvm.edu/~dewey/articles/proged.html.

Kensler, L.A.W., et al. (2009). The Ecology of Democratic Learning Communities: Faculty Trust and Continuous Learning in Public Middle Schools. *Journal of School Leadership*, 19, 6: 697-735.

King, M.L.K. (1947). The purpose of education. *The Maroon Tiger.* Morehouse College, Retrieved from http://www.drmartinlutherkingjr.com/thepurposeof education.htm

Kouzes, J.M. & Posner, B. Z. (2007). *The leadership challenge.* San Francisco, CA Jossey Bass.

Lapham, L. H. (2008). Playing with fire. *Lapham's Quarterly,* 1, 4, 12-21.

Michaelson, L. K. (2012). Getting started with team learning. Retrieved from http://www.med.illinois.edu/facultydev/classroom/interactivemethods/Michaelson.p df

Mostovicz, E. I., Kakabadse, A. Kakabadse, N.K. (2011) The four pillars of corporate responsibility: ethics, leadership, personal responsibility and trust. *Corporate Governance*, 11, 4, 489 – 500.

Nooteboom, B., & Six, F. (Eds.). (2003). *The trust process in orqanizations: Empirical studies of the detevininants and the process of trust. develop7nent.* Northampton, MA: Elgar.

Ovando, M.N. (1994). Constructive feedback: A key to successful teaching and learning, *International Journal of Educational Management*, 8, 6, 19 – 22.

Putnam, R. D. (1993). *Making denocracy work: Civic traditions in modern. Italy.*Princeton, NJ: Princeton University Press.

Shields, D. L. (2011). Character as the aim of education. *Phi Delta Kappan*, 92(8), 48 - 53.

Tollefson, K. & Osborn, M. (2008). *Cultivating the learner-centered classroom: From theory to practice.* Thousand Oaks, CA: Corwin Press.

Tonkiss, F. & Passey, A. (1999). Trust, confidence and voluntary organizations: between values and institutions. *Sociology*, 33, 2, 257-271.

Trompenaars, F. & Hampden-Turner, C. (1998). *Riding the waves of culture.* New York: McGraw-Hill.

Tschannen-Moran, M. & Tschannen-Moran, B. (2011). Taking a strength-based focus improves school climate. *Journal of School Leadership*, 21: 422-448.

Tschannen-Moran, M. (2004). *Trust matters: Leadership for successful schools.* San Francisco: Jossey-Bass.

Tzafrir, S. S. (2005). The relationship between trust, HRM practices and firm performance. *International Journal of Human Resource Managemient, 16(9),*1600-1622.

Uslaner, E. M. ((1999). Democracy and social capital. *Democracy and trust,* Cambridge: Cambridge University Press, pp. 121-150.

Vygotsky, L.S. (1978). *Mind in society: The development of higher psychological processes.* M. Cole, V. John-Steiner, S. Scribner, E. Soubeman (Eds.). Cambridge, MA: Harvard University Press.

Walsh, F. (2006). A middle school dilemma: Dealing with "I don't care". *American Secondary Education*, 35, 1: 5-15.

Warren, M.E. (ed.) (1999). *Democracy and Trust.* Cambridge: Cambridge University Press.

Zmerli, S. & Newton, K. (2008). Social trust and attitudes towards democracy. *Public Opinion Quarterly*, Vol. 72, No. 4: 706–724.

CHAPTER THREE

Making Connections: Starting to Incorporate the Habits of Mind in TESOL Classes

By

Aixa Perez-Prado

Lately, I've been starting all of my classes with the same idea; the idea that language, culture, and thought are so entwined together that it is imprudent to seriously consider one without also considering the other two. I think that this concept is so fundamental to everything I teach that I need to lay it right out there at the beginning of the semester, and hope that my students play with the idea until it becomes as central to their understanding of themselves, and the world, as it is to me. I teach teachers how to teach linguistically and culturally diverse learners. I also teach a class on diversity in ways of knowing that focuses on language, gender and culture. My students come from diverse backgrounds, and many of them are multilingual and multicultural, and as a result, this background may give them an advantage in understanding the language- culture- thought connection. Nevertheless, most of them have not thought about it at all. They approach the ideas as if they were novices who need to be coaxed to look at their own experiences, and to value the knowledge that they bring to the classroom. They also frequently need to be convinced that their interpretation and perspective is not the only one worth mentioning, and not the only one with value.

In an effort to take the concept of connection from the abstract to the personal, I ask my students to participate in a variety of creative and reflective learning activities. They maintain blogs in which they articulate their thinking on these topics as they arise in the course of the semester; they participate in cooperative learning task-based activities that demand problem solving; and they create short videos to demonstrate these relationships.

The videos are meant, on the one hand, to provide a visual and auditory experience on the close connection between language, culture and thought as it relates to cross cultural interactions, and, on the other, to inspire viewers to critically consider this relationship and draw their own conclusions. Sometimes the videos are truly inspiring. They demonstrate that the students have used flexible thinking, set forth clear goals, looked at their own knowledge from a new perspective, strived for excellence and accuracy, and truly listened to the voices around them. Other times the videos are very one dimensional, demonstrating little thought or sensitivity, fraught with stereotypical encounters, and even highly prejudiced scenarios. In an attempt to promote more of the former and less of the latter videos, I have recently turned to the habits of mind for help in encouraging my students that more thoughtful and reflective thinking is both necessary and good, and that they are capable of doing it.

The College of Education (COE) at Florida International University (FIU) has a visionary theme about which I talk to my students at the start of each semester. The theme is, *"facilitating personal, intellectual, and social renewal within diverse populations and environments"* ("The Conceptual Framework of the College of Education," n.d., p. 4). The students, at this particular university, are well versed in diversity, it is one of the largest minority serving universities in the country. Many of them are from Hispanic backgrounds, yet they often grew up in areas where the ethnic minority was the majority and so they often do not have the same set of experiences that another less represented ethnic minority group might have. They also, sometimes, have difficulty with the idea of renewal. Many of them seem to feel that they are not in need of renewing themselves or their ways of thinking and tackling problems. It is a challenge to open them up to new ways of thinking, and new ways of processing information. One of these new ways involves utilizing the habits of mind in order to enhance their learning and teaching experiences.

The College of Education at FIU is committed to promoting student self-discovery and reflection as part of the experience of becoming teachers who are mindful practitioners ("The Conceptual Framework of the College of Education," n.d.). As a result, mindfulness in the college is translated as dispositions, that is, habits of mind that make professional conduct more intelligent by adopting a critical eye toward ideas and actions (Being Analytical); withholding judgment until understanding is achieved by being thoughtful in one's actions.(Managing Impulsivity); working to see things through by employing systematic methods of analyzing problems (Persisting); thinking about one's own thinking (Reflective Thoughtfulness); thinking and communicating with clarity and precision (Communicating Accurately); showing curiosity and passion about learning through inquiry (Being Inquisitive); showing a sense of being comfortable in situations where the outcomes are not immediately known by acting on the basis of one's initiative and not from needing a script (Taking Responsible Risks); recognizing the wholeness and distinctiveness of other people's ways of experiencing and making meaning by being open-minded (Being Open-minded); taking time to check over work because of one being more interested in excellent work than in expediency (Striving for Accuracy); abstracting meaning from one experience and carrying it forward and applying it to a new situation by calling on one's store of past knowledge as a source of data to solve new challenges (Applying Past Knowledge to New Situations); showing sensitivity to the needs of others and to being a cooperative team member (Thinking Interdependently), and, showing a sense of care for others and an interest in listening well to others (Empathic Understanding) ("The Conceptual Framework of the College of Education," n.d., p. 11).

To enhance and nurture the aforementioned habits of mind, the environment of continuous renewal and thoughtful reflection is promoted in the college's classrooms, and is sought through the sorts of active learning that takes place in the classroom and throughout the community during the students' field study experiences. Our pre-service teachers acquire new knowledge by constructing that knowledge for themselves in the field as well as within the classroom. The idea is to lead our students to internalize the dispositions that they will need in order to develop into thoughtful educators of diverse students. It is with these goals in mind that I structure the learning activities that take place in my classroom, launch the websites that the students construct throughout the semester, and assign the field experiences and video projects that they will complete.

The Teaching English to Speakers of Other Languages (TESOL) program in the College of Education at FIU focuses on meeting the needs of linguistically and culturally diverse learners. Since the students at this university are often second language speakers themselves, and even more often the children of English language learners, they have a particular and rich background knowledge that they bring to the TESOL classroom. They are often full of opinions and insights on how languages are learned and how cultures can mingle or collide. It becomes my job to give my students the tools that they need in order to critically examine their own ideas and analyze from where they came. Sometimes, theory and practice in second language acquisition directly contradicts their strongly held ideas, and it is important that they learn to examine the research and the evidence in relation to their personal experiences in order to develop new ways of thinking about the language and culture acquisition process.

Although there is not one specific methodology that the field recognizes as the best methodology for learning languages, there is a wealth of data that lead researchers to recognize some important best practices for English language learners. These best practices are put forward to the students during active learning activities using a variety contexts as well as different languages so that they are able to experience the process of being language learners themselves. Among the most important characteristic that these language learning activities share is that they are interactive. Students must work together, often cooperatively in order to complete tasks, and solve problems using authentic language as the medium for getting the job done (Ellis, 2003; Johnson, 1995). This emphasis on active learning, cooperation, problem solving, and creativity is in line with both the mission of the COE at FIU and the habits of mind that lead to the dispositions we wish to promote in our students.

Second language acquisition theory relies heavily on the idea that language must be comprehended in order to be acquired (Krashen, 1981, 1982). In order to comprehend language, it is necessary to be an active participant in the linguistic environment in which it is used. Learners must engage in decoding messages in the target language (Prabhu 1987, Long 1996). In order to ensure that participation occurs, learners must be interested, engaged, and as relaxed as possible. The ideal environment for second language acquisition promotes and supports learners who are not afraid to take risks, who are willing to make mistakes, who are creative and flexible in their thinking, who listen carefully to others, and who actively construct language over time. In other words, the ideal second language acquisition environment very closely resembles the ideal first language acquisition environment.

When language is learned in a natural environment, such as the environment where first languages are learned, the focus is primarily on meaning. Babies and their caretakers are striving to communicate with one another, get their messages across and attend to basic needs. Similarly, second language instruction needs to recognize this basic concept and create language learning activities that focus on the content of messages. Some second language theorists surmise that only when learners are engaged in decoding messages during communicative acts are they then ready to acquire language (Long, 1996). The use of task-based approaches in which students work cooperatively to solve problems and resolve tasks are pregnant with learning opportunities that lead students to employ higher order thinking skills and use language to express their thinking. The habits of mind come in to play naturally with the use of these approaches that demand creativity, persistence, listening, flexibility, managing impulsivity, and the rest. Learners are taking part in activities that are real, motivating, and challenging, and they are using language as the medium to do so thus helping to develop fluency in the process (DeKeyser, 1998).

Similar to first language acquisition, second language acquisition takes time. Learners need the time and the conditions to receive a great deal of input in the target language. If learners do not receive this input, they will not acquire the language (Krashen, 1982). Although Krashen (1982) has argued that input that is comprehensible along with motivation is all that is required for successful acquisition, others have argued that it is also necessary for students to produce language in order to acquire it.

Either way, students must be interactive, either as listeners who act upon the information heard or as interlocutors who engage in negotiating the messages going back and forth among the participants in linguistic encounters. With these ideas in mind, teachers of second language learners must create environments which promote extensive use of the target language in the classroom. These environments are logically interactive and participatory so that learners have the opportunities necessary to engage in the language for as much time as possible. The environments also need to be nurturing and accepting of errors, just as the first language acquisition environment is naturally.

When I talk to my students about the challenges facing second language learners as they navigate a new linguistic system and corresponding culture, I often take them back to the first language acquisition process. The habits of mind seem to be an almost perfect fit for explaining how babies learn to think and can in the matter of about five years acquire the vast amount of knowledge, skill, and ability which is the underlying foundation of becoming culturally and linguistically competent. In order to achieve the monumental task that babies take on at birth, persistence is certainly necessary. Babies and toddlers go through a huge amount of trial and error as they learn to become active participants in their own cultural groups. They begin by experimenting with sounds and discovering how these sounds are interpreted by their caretakers. They are soon able to refine the sounds they create in order to maximize the interactions they receive thereby ensuring that they become participants in the dialogue of their native languages. Babies are masters of persistence.

Listening is another skill that is essential during the language acquisition process. It is only after much listening that first language acquirers begin to produce, and they continue to listen mainly, for years. As their listening skills become more developed, so do their abilities to interpret how others feel, and how they will react, thus making them aware of cultural norms and expectations. All of this is going on as these learners are starting to think abstractly, a process which demands the use of increasingly complex language. As they continue to hypothesize about the world around them, and build their schema, they are encouraged to think flexibly and creatively through play. It has been said that play is the work of children, and this is certainly the case when it comes to the work of acquiring a language and becoming a member of a cultural group that has a whole unwritten code of behavior and values. These unwritten rules are learned through play which is laden with opportunities for problem solving, repetition leading to mastery of tasks, communicating intentions clearly to others, cooperating, data gathering through all of the senses, imagination, innovation and humor. The process of first language acquisition is a continuous learning journey full of wonderment and awe for these youngest of learners who seem to employ virtually all of the habits of mind as we know them naturally and consistently.

These habits which seem to come so effortlessly to children as they become active members of a cultural group do not seem to come as naturally to older learners who are second language acquirers. Somewhere along the way these habits are lost and need to be relearned.

I tell my students, many of whom will be teachers of second language learners, that it is their job to recreate an environment where these habits are practiced in the classroom because it is through these practices that language and culture are best acquired. Just as babies do, older children and adults need to have time to listen, freedom to question endlessly, the strength to be persistent over time, and the time to develop mastery in a problem solving environment that is playful, uses humor, and is laden with opportunities for interaction. Second language learners must be encouraged to gather data all around them about their new language and culture so that they can form their own hypotheses, create their own schema and acquire the flexibility of thought they need to change their hypotheses as more linguistic and cultural data is accumulated. They need to be inspired and their curiosity needs to be stimulated so that they too can capture the wonderment and awe of the learning process just as they did when they were first language acquirers.

I spent years talking about these ideas with my students. I didn't call them "habits of mind" because I didn't know that terminology. I called these ideas other things such as: English Language Learner (ELL) friendly strategies, culturally responsive teaching, multiple perspectives valuing, and just good teaching. However, I fear that many of my lectures, activities and readings did not have a lasting effect because I did not often see the results in final projects, teaches and videos. I have now come to the realization that I may have neglected to inspire my students to examine their own ways of thinking before trying to teach others using these ways and turning them into teaching strategies. Although most of my students could recite many of my suggestions by the end of the semester on how to create an optimum environment for teaching linguistically and culturally diverse learners, I noticed that when they actually taught demo lessons or created videos, they weren't exactly putting into practice what they could so easily recite. Their teaching and their videos often lacked creativity, flexibility, and imagination. They didn't gather enough information, build on prior knowledge, strive for accuracy or clarity, and they really didn't think through the process enough. They often demonstrated an almost alarming impulsivity, jumping to conclusions, and lack of empathetic listening when encountering diverse opinions and ways of knowing. Finally, I have realized that many of my students simply need more practice and focus in thinking about thinking and I am using the "habits of mind" to that effect. In fact, I need some more attention in that area myself.

Recently I started to give my students readings on the habits of mind, and to ask them to make connections about these habits and best practices in second language acquisition teaching and learning. Since I teach some of my classes partially and fully online, I was able to create links that led my students to different websites that discussed the habits of mind and how they have been utilized by teachers and students in a variety of disciplines. After giving students a few weeks to look over these websites, I created a blog for my students on the habits of mind. The task was for them to reflect on what they had researched online and draw connections between this information and what we were learning in class about language acquisition.

The habits of mind blog in our website included some of the following postings from students in one course that focuses on the knowledge and skills that content area teachers and counselors need when faced with English Language Learners in the classroom.

> The habits of mind of a student are important for a teacher to understand and try to identify in students as it is what makes the students connect to the content being taught to them. The Habits of Mind are essential to the integration of language, culture, and thought with diverse students in that each student assimilates what they are learning in different ways according to the habits they use most .for the typical ELL "diverse" student language, culture, and thought process go hand in hand. The ELL student has a particular thought process

based on their education they have received up to that point in their respective cultures and language. The ELL student usually uses both language of origin and English in their though process as they learn in an American environment.

...I think perseverance would be a very important habit for an ELL student to practice as they should strive to achieve their goals and ambitions using baby steps- first learning the English language and then go after their dreams. In terms of listening with understanding and empathy, I believe I am a very compassionate person, and I always try to live by the golden rule and be there for those who need me; whether it be my friends, family or students. As the reading passage states, listening is the beginning of understanding. In order for ELL students to fully comprehend the material being taught, they should listen attentively and if they understand, they should be empathetic and explain to other fellow ELL students.

I feel that Habits of the Mind translates to character. Our ability to think, communicate, listen, question, persevere, create, gather information, apply and respond to different situations make us who we are. Understanding how our minds work and knowing that we are all capable of creating these habits, allow us to better understand our students and try to reach them at an intellectual level...

The habits of mind are important in understanding the relationship between language, culture, and thought because humans are not learning in a set environment or in a box, the environment and factors affecting the learner during this process are unique to that individual. As the article states "employing habits of mind requires a composite of many skills, attitude cues, and past experiences." As a result of these experiences, we decide to engage in a specific behavior. Because each of our experiences are different, we each approach problems differently utilizing different skills. The same applies to learning a language, a student is building on previous experiences of what works for them or does not work for them in regards to learning,

One habit of mind that I feel I am strongest in, at times perhaps a bit too much so, is persisting. It was through persistence that I have been able to get to where I am. I was an ELL student throughout elementary, I had many family issues growing up and there were many indicators that suggested that I would not succeed, yet here I am working on two Master's. It is that sense of self and my oft times annoying trait of persistence that has kept me in line, and focused on attaining my goals. As a counselor, I would advocate for my students but also teach them to advocate for themselves and to keep fighting for their goals, even when it seems impossible...

The "habits of the mind" information is very interesting because it talks about how an intelligent person thinks. In regards to this class, it is very useful because as teachers we need to teach our students how to better think about their actions and the purpose of their actions. As a graduate student, I often find myself thinking a lot about what my purpose is and how I can do things better. ...When interacting with people of diverse backgrounds, we need to be self-aware of our own biases and knowledge about that culture. If we want to teach or counsel people, we, as educators, need to be multiculturally aware and be respectful of other people's backgrounds. It is especially essential in Miami, where we have such a cultural overload. I think I need to work on all the habits of the mind because there is always a moment when I say, "I wish I would have thought about that before I did this."

These blog postings indicate that the students in this particular class are beginning to think of their own experiences as teachers and learners in the context of the habits of mind. They are starting to analyze these experiences and reflect on them in a way that they didn't do previously. As a part of this course, as well as my other courses, I also have students prepare short videos in cooperative groups. The aim of the videos is to provide students with an opportunity to creatively express one of the fundamental ideas learned in the course.

They are encouraged to use their imaginations in creating the videos, and to use their personal content area knowledge and skills in the undertaking. Some students choose to perform skits, others conduct interviews, others make pseudo public service announcements, and others come up with a variety of alternate scenarios to get their points across. Recently I have asked my students to incorporate the habits of mind as one of the key concepts in our course, and to use them in their videos if they are inclined to do so. This past semester, summer 2012, we had a few examples of students groups who chose one of the habits and created a scenario around it that tied it to the teaching and learning of linguistic and cultural minority students. One group followed a learner around campus demonstrating the importance of persistence in getting things done and in negotiating meaning in a second language. The scenes were sometimes funny, and other times heart breaking as the learners struggled to comprehend the different uses of language, gestures and intonation used by native speakers as they attempted to navigate his way around the university in order to change is class schedule. Another video created by art and music pre-service teachers focused on integrating more creativity in the classroom by having students express their personal narratives through the use of rap and drawing to create story boards that were performed for varied audiences. The videos are often difficult to follow and technically primitive, but as the semesters pass, they are becoming more sophisticated and focused in the messages that they convey.

Finally, at the end of the summer 2012 semester, I added a question on the final regarding the habits of mind as they related to the students' field experiences. The students in most of the methods classes in the COE spend hours of service in the field working with actual learners. In my class, they are asked to work with one English Language Learner in order to complete an action-based research project. Students are paired with a learner who is usually chosen by the mentor teacher as someone who could use some extra help. They are asked to work ten hours with that learner after observing him or her for several class periods and interviewing the teacher and the learner regarding what areas of difficulty are being experienced. They then identify one particular area to work on, such as speaking, and focus the rest of their time with the learner on that particular area. In order to assist the student they must go back to the readings in our textbook, website, and outside articles to find what the research tells us about that particular area and what are the best practices to employ with the learners.

This is a very difficult assignment for my students. They tend to want to help their students with things that are necessary, but not based on developing language skills in a significant way. For example, students often tell me that their case study students need to do better on spelling tests so they will focus their energies on memorizing spelling words. I quickly ask them to rethink the situation since having great spelling is not exactly an important part of language acquisition and has little to do with the interactive methods that we have been studying in class. When they do go to the research and review our class activities they begin to create mini-lessons for their learners that are interactive, creative, cooperative and engaging, and that help them increase their ability to comprehend in the target language. They begin to employ the habits of mind in their own thinking about how to interact with their case study learners and encourage their learners to do the same in their language acquisition process.

The question I added to my course during summer 2012, in an effort to assess my students' understandings of the habits of mind is the following:

> Review the habits of mind reading in your course. Choose a few of the habits of mind that you feel that you need to work on as a teacher or counselor of English Language Learners. How did you implement these habits in your interactions with your case study learners and how did you teach them to do the same through learning activities that are good for language acquisition, while keeping cultural considerations in mind? For example, if you worked on 'managing impulsivity...' how did you do that? Was it in the form of a game, an activity, a reading, a project...?

My pre-service teachers and counselors provided a variety of responses to this question. A sampling of some responses is included below.

> As a teacher it is our responsibility to identify areas of concern and provide students with tools that will help strengthen their mind and be better able to globalize their learning to all aspects of life and give students the tools to improve their minds. A few habits of mind that I feel I need to continuously work on are, of course, empathy, managing impulsivity and thinking interdependently.

> As a counselor, having children participate in role playing games, teaching them to assert themselves in a respectful manner, discussions about needs and feelings, stories that discuss empathy and bullying, teaching them what careful or attentive listening is, discussing conflict resolution, use of a talking stick and many other creative methods can help children improve their empathy skills.

By doing so, we are not only setting the foundation for healthier interactions and relationships but also fostering bully-free behavior.

To assist with managing impulsivity, I would start with structure. The students who came to me with this problem would have a clear structure in counseling, along with predetermined schedules and activities. By providing consistency in counseling, we are enabling students to be prepared for appropriate behavior. Practicing appropriate behavior during times of transition will also help gear students away from disruptive behavior. This would apply in the classroom as well, and should be utilized by both counselors and teachers. Promoting self-reflection will also help impulsive students to think about their actions and how they negatively affect them. Through use of a daily journal, students are able to write about situations in their own words and self-identify behavior that is causing them unfavorable attention or repercussions. Discussing journal entries with the student will give me the opportunity to assess whether or not the child is able to accurately assess and recount their own behavior.

I believe that my students and I still have a long way to go in incorporating the habits of mind into our interactions with others. At the same time, I feel that we are off to a good start at least at the awareness level. In the future, I plan to have students create second language task-based interactive activities that focus on a habit of mind for use with language learners. I think that through this process they will get a chance to reflect more on the habits and as they encourage thinking and the language of thinking in their learners.

References

DeKeyser, R. (1998). Beyond focus on form: Cognitive perspectives on learning and practicing second language grammar. In C. Doughty & J. Williams (Eds.), *Focus on form in classroom language acquisition* (pp. 42-63). New York: Cambridge University Press.

Ellis, R. (2003). *Task-based language learning and teaching.* Oxford: Oxford University Press.

Johnson, K. (1995). *Understanding communication in second language classrooms.* Cambridge: Cambridge University Press.

Krashen, S. (1982). *Principles and practice in second language acquisition.* Oxford: Pergamon.

Krashen, S. (1981). *Second language acquisition and second language learning.* Oxford: Pergamon.

Long, M. (1996). The role of the linguistic environment in second language acquisition. In W. Ritchie & T. Bhatia (Eds.), *Handbook of second language acquisition* (pp. 413-468). San Diego: Academic Press.

Prabhu, N. S. (1987). *Second language pedagogy.* Oxford: Oxford University Press.

The Conceptual Framework. (n.d.). Retrieved from
http://education.fiu.edu/docs/Conceptual%20Framework%2006-19-09.pdf

CHAPTER FOUR

Reframing Subject-Area Reading for Secondary Students Using Habits of Mind

By

Patsy Self Trand

Teaching secondary subjects is as rewarding as it can be daunting, especially when it means teaching pre-service teachers to guide their students through options and choices of solving problems within and related to their subject area readings. Many teacher education candidates focus their attention on the subject, losing sight of the thought and interpretations that must accompany the subject and its quandaries. As infusing reading skills and strategies may be far from subject-area pre-service teachers' focus, so may be the need to nurture dispositions that their students may use to solve problems. But, it is subject-area reading that starts to guide students through that intellectual thinking process of the subject, so much, that many secondary teacher education programs require a course to help secondary pre-service teachers learn how to help their students learn to read content area material more effectively. With these thoughts in mind, each semester I begin my instruction in Subject-Area Reading, a required course for pre-service secondary education majors at Florida International University.

My experience and research affirms that in many secondary teacher education programs, teaching reading in subject-area reading courses serves to address candidates' undiluted focus on subject and guides them to thread into their instruction literacy skills and strategies. However, while these subject-area reading courses assist pre-service teachers in learning how to help students read subject-area material, they do little to help students learn to solve problems or think openly about issues in their field.

The missing relationship with most of these courses may be the relationship between reading-to-learn strategies and the fostering of problem solving and intellectual inquiry followed by oral and written discourse.

This chapter has a ternary approach. I will focus first on helping my pre-service teachers understand what it means to be literate in a subject-area. Next I discuss a routine that helps pre-service teachers integrate subject-area material and Habits of Mind (HoM) ("The Conceptual Framework of the College of Education," n.d.). Finally I will share several strategies that further integrate subject-area knowledge and skills with HoM.

Bridging Understanding Text and Literacy with College of Education Learning Outcomes

The Subject-Area Reading course I teach provides pre-service teachers with knowledge and essential learning strategies that may be applied to secondary content subjects to maximize students' comprehension and retention. The pre-service teachers in the course learn these strategies experientially, and I guide them to apply the strategies with secondary students during the required field experience component of the course.

At the beginning of the course, I help pre-service teachers learn the difference between understanding the text and literacy. For many of my pre-service teachers, these concepts mean the same thing. But, understanding the text and literacy stem from two different knowledge bases, although one depends on the other. From my experience, understanding the text is considered the ability to read, write, and comprehend the appropriate instructional materials in a given subject-area. Literacy is the ability to negotiate (e.g. read, view, listen, taste, smell, critique) and create (e.g. write, produce, sing, act, speak) texts in discipline-appropriate ways or in ways that other members of a discipline (e.g. mathematicians, historians, artists) would recognize as "correct" or "viable" (Draper, Broomhead, Jensen, Nokes, & Siebert, 2010, p.30). If I am to truly guide my pre-service teachers towards educating their students in subject areas, then I know I must teach my pre-service teachers to acquire and develop this concept of literacy, as well as learn to guide their students into literacy within any given discipline, or subject area.

To make the distinction between understanding the text and literacy, I begin with an oral discussion in which pre-service teachers are asked to give examples of each. They are encouraged to think about instructional practices they learned in previous courses in their respective subject areas. This is a very important task, because it helps the pre-service teachers process what they already know about these two constructs, as well as what they need to learn to fully understand them.

Through this initial discussion, I help the pre-service teachers make other very important connections to the course, their program and the college's learning outcomes. I weave into the discussion the idea that the knowledge they are learning about subject-area literacy in this course supports their development as Stewards of the Discipline ("The Conceptual Framework of the College of Education," n.d.). As stewards of the discipline, they must remain current about subject-area literacy and pedagogical content that further supports this knowledge. I extend the discussion to help pre-service teachers explore their role as Reflective Inquirers. This second College of Education (COE) learning outcome highlights the importance of educators' on-going reflection about educational practices, while they strive to make changes when needed, with a focus on the continuous improvement of their teaching as it reflects diversity, sensitivity and collaboration with others. Finally, our discussion turns to the third COE learning outcome, one of high importance, that of becoming a Mindful Educator. I introduce to pre-service teachers the importance of their developing essential professional dispositions. In our college we call these Habits of Mind (HoM). These HoM include being analytical, managing impulsivity, persisting, reflective thoughtfulness, communicating accurately, being inquisitive, taking responsible risks, being open-minded, and striving for accuracy, applying past knowledge to new situations, thinking interdependently, and empathic understanding ("The Conceptual Framework of the College of Education," n.d.).

In the paragraphs above, I share how a variety of important concepts are brought out through discussion. In actuality, these discussions take place over several class meetings as I help the pre-service teachers understand their roles as Stewards of the Discipline, Reflective Inquirers and Mindful Educators as a bridge for their development in teaching subject-area literacy. In my course, initial understanding of knowledge, skills and HoM are brought about through discussion, but they are developed as pre-service teachers learn to implement effective instructional routines and strategies.

Using an Overarching Subject Area Reading Routine, Inclusive of Habits of Mind

Subject-area reading equips students with literacy strategies that they use to more effectively understand and process subject-area content in texts. In a subject-area reading course, pre-service teachers learn to facilitate student learning strategically through well-chosen sets of strategies. From my experience, the strategies seem to be best learned by pre-service teachers and best used by students through the use of a coherent instructional routine. This routine incorporates HoM as an essential component. The routine should be so natural that their students use effortlessly both literacy strategies and HoM as they process content text.

There are six major steps that I developed for my pre-service teachers to use as part of a coherent instructional routine. This routine should not be used as a separate instructional activity, but as a natural seamless framework for subject-area reading and writing. Through this routine, I want my pre-service teachers to develop an instructional synergy in which the combination and regular implementation of instructional strategies are sequenced logically, in support of student learning. The steps of the routine are as follows:

1. *Formulate beliefs about your approach to instruction.* As participants in a teacher education program, pre-service teachers are developing their approaches to instruction. Their beliefs about objectives, expectations, and professional and personal theories of teaching the subject are developing so I

encourage pre-service teachers to include literacy within the context and fabric of this set of beliefs. If literacy is not an integral part of their mind set, then chances are it will not be an integral part of their practice. Further, I encourage pre-service teachers to include HoM as an integral part of their beliefs for similar reasons. In choosing literacy strategies and HoM, I ask students to consider the atmosphere, content of the text, appropriateness of the material, and their students' emotional and educational background and capabilities.

2. *Develop instructional foci including habits of mind.* I help my pre-service candidates recognize that school districts expect instruction based on local, state and national standards. I want them to understand that it is not enough to merely teach from the book. I help them become skillful in selecting the knowledge and skills they need to teach related to a subject-area based on both the texts and the standards. Through this process candidates develop instructional foci. However, this is not enough. I help pre-service teachers understand that HoM are nurtured in conjunction with knowledge and skills. HoM are necessary for thinking and inquiry. My goal is that pre-service teachers develop instructional experience for their students that integrate subject area knowledge and skills plus HoM seamlessly. When pre-service teachers have clear instructional foci, they are more likely to effectively support their student learning.

3. *Create seamless instructional blocks:* Typically my pre-service teachers enter the subject-area reading course with proficient subject-matter knowledge in their respective subject areas. They seem to be lacking in two areas: (1) they may not have developed sufficient pedagogical content knowledge to break down and organize the subject matter so that students may best learn it; and, (2) they have not yet developed an understanding of literacy strategies that facilitates students' processing of content area text. Without integrated understanding of subject area knowledge, pedagogical knowledge, literacy strategies, and HoM, pre-service teachers are likely to use less effective methodologies, such as, "listen to my lecture," "read the book," and "answer the question at the end of the chapter." The benefits of the seamless instructional blocks that I share with the pre-service teachers is that they bring together various aspects of instruction that otherwise would be delivered in a fragmented way. Main components of seamless instructional blocks include elements of direct instruction: explanation, demonstration, 6 components of comprehension, guide, practice, apply, student reflects, closure, and ESE and ESL support activities. The following diagram provides a graphic representation of seamless instructional blocks.

Explanation	Pre-service teachers briefly introduce the content material, literacy strategies and habits of mind that will be a part of the lesson for that day.
Demonstration	Pre-service teachers give an example of the lesson for that day.
6 Components of Comprehension	Pre-service teachers engage their students

	in a skill builder activity related to phonics, phonemic awareness, vocabulary, comprehension, oral language and fluency. Pre-service teachers guide students in previewing the reading material (textbook) by choosing words from the reading that are unfamiliar to students. Pre-service teachers and students discuss the meaning in context, phonetic rules, and pHoMenic tactics that help with the pronunciation of the words. Together students and pre-service teachers read a selected section together, and students orally discuss the meaning of the text. Students are asked to talk about the text making text-to-text, text-to-world or text-to-self reflections. These processes set the stage for students to think critically about what they will be reading.
Guide	Pre-service teachers teach the subject matter using the literacy strategy as a before, during, or after component of the lesson. Likewise, HoM are nurtured in the lesson where they best facilitate students' learning the knowledge or skills. Pre-service teachers use textbooks and materials on the students' instructional level.
Practice	Pre-service teachers continue to teach the subject matter, using the literacy strategy and the relevant HoM, but now enlist the participation of the students.
Apply	Pre-service teachers ask students to continue the activity. Pre-service teachers monitor students' progress.
Student Responses	Pre-service teachers ask students essential questions about the subject matter and literacy strategy. They also help students reflect about their use of related HoM. Questions may include known and unknown facts about the subject and how a situation or problem may be or was solved. Other questions may be asked about the usefulness of the literacy strategy and HoM.
Closure	Pre-service teachers and students close the lesson by reflecting about information learned about the subject matter. Pre-service teachers and students also

	discuss the literacy strategy and HoM, revealing how they felt they contributed to their learning of the subject. Discussions should also include if they enjoyed the process.
ESE/ESL	Pre-service teachers must describe how support for ESE students is embedded into the lesson. Pre-service teachers must describe how support for ESL students is embedded into the lesson.

4. Watch *for patterns of behavior across situations and time.* My pre-service teachers enter my subject area reading course as novices to the education field, while having had many courses in their subject area. Typically, they have had only one education course prior to taking my course. As a result, I take time to point out, from an education perspective, obvious and subtle patterns of student behavior when problem solving a particular topic. Behaviors may range from complete silence or indifference to strong, adamant voices. I want my pre-service teachers to be aware that student reactions to problems and situations vary according to topic and task. Patterns of behavior vary due to experiences, interest and knowledge of the topic. I ask my pre-service teachers to watch for signs of maturity in patterns of behavior across situations. I also have them watch for students' application of HoM. Additionally pre-service teachers must help their students find healthy and reasonable use of time in investigating problems. Rate of time should not be a factor, but use of time should be a point for observation

5. *Focus on patterns of involvement.* I inform my pre-service teachers that students bring different interest and experiences to the subject-area class. Therefore, students will be more interested in solving some problems and situations and less interested in others. There are times when students will need to be encouraged and times when the pre-service teachers must close the discussion. Pre-service teachers must monitor responses and note which topics generate excitement.

6. *Develop a plan to assess your instruction and students' progress.* I help pre-service teachers understand that planning for assessment is an integral part of quality instruction. I want them to know that they need to plan assessments in four areas. One assessment must focus on the subject-area knowledge or skill being developed. A second part of the assessment should focus on the literacy strategy. Are students comfortable enough with the literacy strategy to transfer to other contexts? A third part of the assessment should provide student feedback on their use of relevant HoM. Finally, the fourth part of the assessment pertains to the pre-service teachers' self-assessment of the effectiveness of their instruction.

Consistency employing this coherent instructional routine will help the pre-service teacher and students learn and develop a composite of behaviors when learning content and literacy strategies and when employing HoM. The pre-service teacher must begin changing paradigms to include literacy strategies and HoM when teaching content. A coherent instructional routine will become consciously and subconsciously a natural component of teaching and learning. As a result, student reading achievement and problem solving ability performance should improve over a period of time.

Literacy Strategies that Encompass Habits of Mind

Once pre-service teachers understand the benefits of teaching from a coherent instructional routine, I begin to teach them strategies that may be used flexibly within the routine and that vary by subject matter. To illustrate this point, I will provide an example of the use of two different literacy strategies, one that may be used with a technical discipline, mathematics, and one that may be used with a non-technical discipline, history. Given the content and the literacy strategies associated with both examples, I have identified relevant HoM that are integrated into the lessons as students learn content and skills. This first strategy is one that I often model for my secondary pre-service teachers so that they see how content, literacy strategies and HoM maybe integrated. A first question I often get from my subject-area students comes from the mathematics majors. Each semester they ponder how literacy strategies and HoM fit into the mathematics classroom. I call to their attention that math textbooks are written with mathematical operations/ equations and word problems to solve. However, this information must be processed, in part, by a reader. Students must be able to process complex mathematical ideas through reading, and teachers must be able to help students process information- presented to them in the form of text. I teach my pre-service teachers that it is imperative for them to introduce literacy strategies to their students that help them to process. Further, I show them how they may introduce HoM to enhance thinking related to the task at hand.

In approaching mathematics, students are often faced with these options: 1) how to solve an operation/equation without any scenario or case of why the equation exists or 2) how to solve a word problem, that is, a scenario or case study, building a numerical problem equation or formula around it and then finding a solution. It is the latter, reading a word problem and solving it, with which students struggle the most (Kintsch, 2004). Students are more challenged with a word problem as compared to the same problem if presented in a mathematical equation. A mathematical equation using numerals directly tells the student what must be solved. The student simply must know how to manipulate the numbers in the operation to find the correct answer. However, with word problems, a student must read the complex and sometimes abstract language of mathematics (Harmon, Hendrick & Wood, 2005).

One strategy that I introduce to my class that seems to be embraced by my mathematic majors is discussion webs (Alvermann, 1992). Discussion webs are a subject-area reading strategy that helps students evaluate, analyze and discover a probable solution to a multifaceted topic, in this case, solving word problems. Discussion webs force students to examine more than one side of a topic, such as, supporting a topic or rejecting a topic.

They may be used to gather relevant information through ways of knowing, thinking or solving, and separating this from irrelevant information that may be emotional or extraneous. I encourage my pre-service teachers to use discussion webs in group settings that give each student an opportunity for discussion. The graphic organizer for a discussion web typically looks like this:

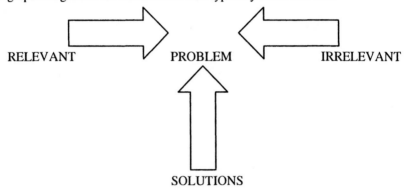

Discussion webs are enhanced when they are integrated with students' use of HoM. This combination enhances the learning and thinking experience in three succinct ways: (a) discussion webs call for students to use persist and to think analytically; (b) discussion webs offer students a platform for thinking flexible, thinking about thinking, and thinking interdependently while problem solving and (c) discussion webs build on student's ability to legitimize independent thought outside the prescribed text through questioning and posing problems. I help my pre-service teacher understand where these HoM support student thinking when using discussion webs. Then, I help them understand why they need to make transparent to their students the usefulness of HoM. Let's examine a discussion web using a typical word problem found in secondary education.

> Word problem: Harry is 55 years old and is very tall. He loves to eat 5 pieces of fruit a day to keep his blood pressure down. Then he runs five miles for exercise. Harry is 15 years older and twice the age of his son, Allen. Allen is much taller than his father and eats junk food. Allen can only run ½ mile when exercising. How old is Allen?

Discussion webs are enhanced when they are integrated with students' To solve this problem using discussion webs, I ask my pre-service teachers to pretend they are in a seventh grade math class. I then ask them to get into groups and read the word problem.

While they are in their groups with the discussion web and math problem attached, I walk them through the strategy and point out the HoM that can be integrated into the use of discussion web strategy when problem solving. As teachers, they can rely on these HoM to help students with their discussion webs. I inform my pre-service teachers that many of their students might find the word problem difficult, but as a group, the students should be encouraged to read the word problem many times. (HoM: Persisting). In their groups, the pre-service teachers reread and discuss the word problem. Then I instruct each group to write the math question in the oval (Problem) on the graphic organizer for the discussion web. I check the math question for accuracy. Groups are then asked to discuss all the information, relevant and irrelevant. Next, as a group, they fill out the discussion web's relevant and irrelevant boxes using the information from the problem.. Disagreements are common when deciding which information is relevant and irrelevant. In addressing disagreements, I use a think-aloud to help my pre-service teachers understand the literacy strategy and its integration with HoM. I explain, that students must discuss and defend their points. (HoM: Thinking about Thinking). Students should not be afraid to change their mind or go against the group's decision. (HoM: Thinking Flexibly) Everyone in the group needs to participate. (HoM: Thinking Interdependently) Working as a group allows students to listen to classmates' think aloud of their own personal problem solving techniques.

Once a group consensus is met on relevant and irrelevant information, the groups write relevant and irrelevant information in the appropriate box on the discussion web. Group members are asked to collectively review the word problem line by line and place the information in the correct box (HoM: Thinking about Thinking; Thinking Interpedently). A line by line review and reread ensures that nothing is missed.

Now, the problem solving equation must be created. Groups examine sample equations in the textbook (HOM: Applying Past Knowledge to New Situations). Each group discusses how the equation should be written. (HOM: Thinking Interpedently & Thinking about Thinking). Then the equation is written in the solution box.

In the solution box assign Allen's age the letter X. Use Harry age because it is needed to solve the equation. Allen is in the circle box that houses the question; he is what students are looking to solve. In the relevant box place Harry is 55 years old and that Harry is 15 years older than twice his son's (Allen) age.

So in the solution box the equation is:

$55 = 15 + 2X$. Now solve for X.
$55 - 15 = 2X$
$40 = 2X$
$20 = X$
$X = 20$. Harry A. Cook II is 20 years old.

Relevant	Problem	Irrelevant
	How old is Allen?	
1. Harry is 55 yrs old. 2. Harry is 15 yrs and twice the age of Allen.		1. Harry is tall. 2. Harry eats fruit. 3. Harry runs 5 miles and eats junk food. 4. Allen eats junk food and runs ½ miles per day.
	$55 = 15 + 2X$. Now solve for X. $55 - 15 = 2X$ $40 = 2X$ $20 = X$ $X = 20$. Allen is 20 years old.	
	Solutions	

Once pre-service teachers participate in this instructional experience they begin to understand, first-hand, the value of integrating mathematics, literacy strategies and HoM for enhancing students' learning in subject areas. To further process this experience, I lead a discussion to help my students reflect about each part of the lesson and the contributions of the literacy strategy and use of HoM to students' understanding. I find that my pre-service teachers become primed to learn more about subject area reading. After we complete the discussion webs using mathematics, we continue with another literacy strategy using a different subject. I want my pre-service teachers to understand that literacy strategies and HoM should be chosen strategically to best support students' engagement with subject area content. So, in the next instructional experiences, I model a different strategy in a non-technical content: History. This strategy focuses on student's processing of subject area text through writing.

To begin, my pre-service teachers and I discuss the nature of historical science texts. I explain that most history texts, for example, are packed densely with facts and are full of terminology that name people, events, and places (Harmon, Hedrick & Wood, 2005). I point out that the authors of history texts think about the prospective audiences for their text, as well as their purposes for writing. I ask my pre-service teachers to read history text through the eyes of the author. How has the author made connections among the topics (Shanahan & Shanahan, 2008), what biases has the author revealed through choice of topics and words, and how did the author organize the text to illicit or influence reader's understandings? I help pre-service teachers think about the author's intent in writing a text and about the extent to which the author is presenting fact and opinion. I want pre-service teachers to approach history texts thinking critically as they read, knowing that the author is presenting sets of beliefs and shaping those through purpose and awareness of the intended audience. I am able to help pre-service teachers internalize these concepts by having them write using a versatile literacy strategy, Role, Audience, Format and Task (RAFT2) (Santa, Havens, & Harrison, 1996), while integrating HoM. This literacy strategy works well when processing text in the historical sciences. The RAFT2 strategy provides a framework for writing. In this framework, the writer thinks about his/her role (R) as the writer. In this role, what is the purpose for writing? (e. g. to inform, to persuade, to compare/contrast). The writer also must think about the audience (A). The audience's background knowledge about the topic, interests or age, among other characteristics, will influence such things as the author's word choice, examples and register. As the author thinks about his/her role and the audience, the format (F) of the writing may be identified. Is the writing best presented in the form of a letter, essay, book chapter, etc? Finally, the author focuses the task (T), thinking about key aspects to be developed and how the information may be presented powerfully.

Students' use of RAFT may easily be enhanced through the integration of four HoM: being analytical; being open-minded; applying past knowledge to new situations; and, communicating accurately. I set the stage for using the RAFT, with the integration of HoM, with my pre-service teachers by reading to them a summary about the Navajo Native Americans who served in WWII as code talkers. I enlist the aid of my history majors to scaffold the class through a discussion of the summary so that all understand the content, subject area knowledge.

Then, I begin modeling the RAFT strategy, inviting the pre-service teachers to make decisions along the way. I use a SmartBoard or an LCD projector so that the pre-service teachers and I are writing together. We first discuss different roles that we might assume as authors of our writing. This requires pre-service teachers to think analytically (HoM) about what they understand about code talkers. At this point, I help students process how this HoM helps them to think about the task. To stretch their thinking, we often decide that we will write from the perspective of the feather pen that was at one of the code talkers' meetings. Then, together, we choose the audience who will be the recipient of the writing. This also calls for thinking analytically (HoM). We discuss who would benefit most from the information. In most cases, we choose deceased Navajo Native American code talkers. This choice gives a warm hush in the room with everyone in an engaged serious mood as we feel the distinctiveness of their experiences and respect their contributions (HoM: Being Open-minded). Next, we decide that we will write a note of appreciation, which becomes to our task, using a memorandum format. In our memorandum of appreciation, we emphasize what has changed based on their achievements. We talk about how applying past knowledge to a new situation (HoM) supports our task. We then draft our memorandum, while we work from a stance of communicating with accuracy and precision (HoM). Through careful instructional planning, teachable moments and targeted feedback, I am able to highlight for my pre-service teachers how content, literacy strategies and HoM work together to support student learning.

Conclusion

I close my subject area reading course by emphasizing to pre-service teachers that educators who integrate content, subject area literacy strategies, and HoM are fully preparing students to read to learn and to understand the wealth of information contained in the subject. I charge my pre-service teachers with the notion that as their students move through secondary classes, they must be guided by a teacher who has a solid plan for how to engage them in text and teach ways to problem solve in different subject areas. My pre-service teachers come to value that employing HoM that support and enhance problem solving, reading, writing and discussion should and can be a functional and necessary part of a subject area instruction. I believe that preparing teachers with this kind of perspective begins at the pre-service teacher preparation stage when instructional beliefs are developing. Then, as these educators leave their respective education programs, they carry with them a blueprint for effective subject area instruction in the classroom, inclusive of effective literacy strategies and HoM.

References

Alvermann, D. E. (1992). The discussion web: A graphic aid for learning across the curriculum. *The Reading Teacher,*45, 92-98.

Draper, R. J., Broomhead, P., Jensen,A.P., Nokes, J. D. & Siebert, D. (Eds). (2010). (Re) Imagining content area literacy instruction. New York: Teachers College Press

Harmon, J. M., Hedrick, W. B., & Wood, K.D. (2005). Research on vocabulary instruction in the content areas: Implications for struggling readers. *Reading and Writing Quarterly,* 21, 261-280.

Kintsch, W. (2004). The construction-integration model of text comprehendnsion and its implication for instruction. In R. Ruddell & N. Urau (Eds.). *Theoretical models and processes of reading,* (5th ed.), pp. 270- 1328). Newark, DE: International Reading Association.

Santa, C., Havens, L. & Harrison, S. (1996). Teaching secondary science through reading, writing, studying and problem-solving. In D. Lapp, J. Flood & N. Farnan (Eds.) *Content area reading and learning: Instructional strategies. (.*2nd ed. pp. 165 – 180). Boston: Allyn & Bacon.

Shanahan, T. & Shanahan C. (2008). Teaching disciplinary literature to adolescents: Rethinking content   area literacy. *Harvard Educational Review,* 78, 40 – 59.

The Conceptual Framework of the College of Education. (n.d.). Retrieved July 12, 2012 from http://www.education.fiu.edu/docs/Conceptual%20 Framework%2006-19-09.pdf.

Van de Walle, J. A. (2004). *Elementary and middle school mathematics: Teaching developmentally (5th ed.) Boston: Allyn & Bacon.*

CHAPTER FIVE

Living My Teaching Philosophy to Support Candidates' Development of Habits of Mind

By

Gwyn W. Senokossoff

Throughout my life, I have been immersed in teaching and learning. As a child, I would "play school" with my friends always wanting to be the teacher. As a student, I loved learning new things and later, as a "real" teacher, I enjoyed sharing what I had learned, and watching my students' growth. In my journey to continue my capacity for growth as an educator, I joined the faculty in the College of Education at Florida International University, and was soon invited to participate in a Faculty Learning Community that grew out of the members' shared beliefs and goals to develop habits of mind in themselves and their students based on the philosophy of John Dewey (1933) and the habits of mind praxis of Arthur Costa and Bena Kallick (2012). For the past two years, as my knowledge of the habits of mind has grown, I have looked for ways to use these habits or dispositions in my teaching. This chapter is the story of my journey, and that of some of my students.

A Philosophy to Guide Me

During my career, I have spent some time identifying my beliefs, and developing a philosophy of education. I believe that a teacher's philosophy is fundamental to the kind of teacher s/he will become. Whenever I work with teachers, I ask them to identify their philosophies as well. By definition, one's philosophy is "a set of precepts, beliefs, principles, or aims underlying [one's] practice or conduct" (Encarta Dictionary, 2012). Sometimes, one's philosophy is unconscious or includes assumptions that are taken for granted (Reber, 2011). When teachers identify their philosophies, they become aware of these assumptions and determine whether their beliefs make them an effective teacher or hinder their growth. A teacher's philosophy affects the way s/he responds to students. It also impacts the curriculum s/he chooses to implement and the methods used for instruction.

To become an effective teacher, it is important to evaluate one's beliefs and identify any inconsistencies between those beliefs and teaching practices. One researcher, Reber (2011) suggests that college faculty critically examine their own teaching philosophies, ask their students to describe what the faculty members believe about teaching and learning, and present their philosophies to students to develop a "shared philosophy of teaching" (p. 108). This process would allow faculty to improve the educational experience for themselves and their students.

Several years ago, the Faculty in the College of Education at FIU developed a Conceptual Framework that includes a philosophy. The College's philosophy highlights the concepts of self-renewal, social community, educative environments, and reflective intelligence ("The Conceptual Framework," n.d., p. 5). The Framework articulates that self-renewal implies growth through an interaction with the environment; that the faculty and students are immersed in an "educative environment" where content, professional, and pedagogical knowledge and dispositions are significant; that the faculty engages with each other as a "social community" and reflects upon this knowledge; and that through this engagement and reflection, the faculty continues to grow in its professional practice.

Habits of mind or dispositions emerged from the unit's philosophy. These habits or ways of thinking make professional conduct more obvious to students and provide a common language the faculty can emulate, model, and teach to others. The habits of mind adopted by the College of Education at FIU are: 1) Being Analytical, 2)Withholding judgment until understanding is achieved, 3) Persisting, 4) Thinking about thinking, 5) Communicating accurately, 6) Being Inquisitive, 7) Taking responsible risks, 8) Recognizing the distinctiveness of other people's experiences, 9)Striving for accuracy, 10) Applying past knowledge to new situations, 11) Showing sensitivity to the needs of others and working as a team, and 12) Caring for and listening to others. The faculty practices these habits as part of a supportive, educational environment where students reflect on and critique their own teaching, and then, share the wisdom and experiences they acquire with others.

Beginning the Journey

Since joining the Learning Community, I have examined my own teaching philosophy and the habits of mind, and tried to marry the two. I believed that if I could redefine my philosophy in terms of the habits of mind, I would develop a deeper understanding of the habits, and be able to model and encourage my students to develop habits of their own.

When I began this process, I wanted to utilize the habits of mind in my instruction so I reviewed the courses I was teaching and decided to begin with a graduate content area reading course. I chose this course for two reasons. First, the purpose of the course is to develop "understandings, skills, and dispositions that enable the literacy professional to support the reading and learning of all students as they interact with content area text" (Class Communication, RED6336 Syllabus, 2010, p. 1). Some of the students, who take this course, teach in a content area other than reading and through this course, they learn a variety of strategies and ways of thinking that they may use to support literacy in their respective disciplines. Other students taking this course are already teaching reading and plan to become reading specialists or literacy coaches. Whether they become reading specialists or remain content area teachers, they will all be responsible for mentoring other teachers and students and must find ways to develop a rapport and some common understandings with the other teachers and students. The habits of mind are the dispositions that will allow them to achieve these tasks. The second reason I chose to begin with the content area reading course is that I had just adopted two new textbooks for the course and was already redesigning it. Since many things were going to change in the course, it seemed like the perfect course to start with.

Once the course was selected, I spent time in the fall of 2011 working with my students. First, I explained the importance of understanding and developing a teaching philosophy based on the habits of mind. Then, I introduced the College's Conceptual Framework and the habits. I told the students we would define and discuss the habits of mind, and use them to identify and develop our teaching philosophies. We also began keeping a teaching journal where we would write about what we had learned from our teaching that day. I wrote about my experiences teaching them, and they wrote about their experiences with their K-12 students. At the end of our writing sessions, volunteers would share something they had learned about themselves, and, sometimes, I would share as well.

After a few weeks, I realized that we had drifted away from the original purpose of our sharing sessions to share insights from our teaching. Most of the discussions had turned into complaint sessions. Some students continued to discuss their learning, but many were just expressing their frustrations with parents, administrators, testing, and the public's perceptions of teachers. The students were reacting and not really reflecting on their teaching (Gun, 2011).

According to Gun (2011), effective, critical reflection should include "what" and "why" questions. These types of questions encourage a deeper understanding of one's teaching. When teachers contemplate their teaching earnestly and responsibly, they will act with foresight and planning rather than on authority or impulse (Dewey, 1933, cited in Moore & Whitfield, 2008). Dewey (1933) believed that learning improves according to the amount of effort that goes into the reflective process (as cited in Moore & Whitfield, 2008). Our reflections were not going well, so I reviewed some of the research on reflective teaching to find strategies to use with my students. Following is some of the research that I found.

Research on Reflection

According to Gun (2011), teachers are often asked to reflect on their teaching, but are unable to do so unless they are taught how to reflect. Reflection requires critical thought, self-awareness, and problem-solving. The ability to think reflectively may come naturally or must be cultivated through practice (Posner, 1989). Teachers must be willing to ask questions about their own assumptions and values (Zeichner & Liston, 1996). They must also understand the institutional and cultural context in which they teach (Zeichner & Liston, 1996). A teacher's beliefs and experiences shape his/her practice (Borg, 2001; Aguirre & Speer, 2000; Virta, 2002; Kupari, 2003).

Several researchers suggest there are levels or stages of reflection (Surbeck, Han, & Mover, 1991; van Manen, 1977). According to Surbeck, Han, and Mover (1991), the first level is reacting where "teachers react with a personal concern about an experience" (Moore & Whitfield, 2008, p. 586). The second stage, elaborating, is where teachers are able to compare one event to another event and refer to a general principle or theory. The third level, contemplating, is where teachers focus on educational issues, ethical matters, or moral concerns.

van Manen (1977) describes the stages differently. In his first stage, technical reflection, "teachers consider the best way to reach an unexamined goal" (van Manen as cited in Sparks-Langer, et al., 1987, p. 24). In the second stage, practical reflection, teachers examine the best way to reach a goal, and they examine the goal they are trying to reach. In the third level, critical reflection, teachers are able to look at the moral and ethical issues along with the means of reaching the goal and the goal itself.

As I read this research, particularly Surbeck, Han, and Mover's (1991), I realized my students were probably in the first stage of reflection. They were reacting with personal concerns and I wanted to move them beyond this level.

Reflective Teachers Employ Habits of Mind

Reading this research made me more determined than ever to "cultivate" reflective thinking in my students. Teachers who are reflective utilize several of the habits of mind during the reflection process. Reflective teachers willingly *question* (Being Inquisitive) and *take responsible risks* (Taking Responsible Risks) as they are learning (Halpern, 1996). Reflective teachers discuss with others and *analyze* (Being Analytical) the problems they face in their classrooms (Cunningham, 2001). They also use their *intuition and past experiences* (Applying past knowledge to new situations) to make *careful judgments* (Withholding judgment until understanding is achieved) about various teaching strategies (Markham, 1999).

The following week in class, I shared some of the research. I presented some of Martin Haberman's (1991) work on "Star Teachers" and brought in the article, "The Pedagogy of Poverty Versus Good Teaching." We had a rich discussion and continued to write in our teaching journals throughout the rest of the semester. Some evenings, we shared our journals as a whole class, and other nights, I asked students to share what they had written with a partner or small group. Next, I asked them to select three habits or dispositions that they felt most described the kind of teacher they were and invited them to explain. Near the end of the semester, the students were asked to write a short paper on their philosophy of teaching based on the three habits of mind they had identified. Of all the students that I have taught, I felt especially close to these students. During our final class meeting, several of them told me that this class was one of the best they had ever taken.

The Journey Continues

The following semester, I began another section of Content Area Reading with a new group of students and incorporated many of the same strategies. I introduced the habits of mind and the assignment they would complete on their teaching philosophies. Then, early in the semester, I attended a full-day workshop with Dr. Arthur Costa and Dr. Bena Kallick entitled, "Discovering and Exploring Habits of Mind." For one of the activities in the workshop, we were asked to work with a small group to create a poster about one of the habits of mind. The poster had to include a simile, a logo, and a slogan designed for the habit we had been assigned. I felt that this activity really helped me develop a better understanding of the habits of mind, so I used it with my students the following week in class.

Throughout the semester, the students in this class also kept a teaching journal and at the end of the semester, they, too, wrote a paper based upon the habits of mind. In the following section are samples of some of the students' comments from their philosophy papers from both classes.

Teaching with the Habits *in* Mind

Four students/teachers identified with the habit, caring for and listening to others or "empathetic understanding." Here is what one teacher wrote:

> The same school I volunteered in became the first school [where] I began teaching job. It was a dream come true and I was given that blessing because of my character. Ever since I started volunteering at the school, one trait that stood out for me was my ability to listen to others, especially with the children I worked with. Now, after five years, those same children are fourth graders and the number of children that know me for my ability to listen has grown from 18 to about 500 students. I make it a mission to know the names of all the students I meet. When I say, "Hi, Andy, I hope you have a good day," they know there is someone there who knows who they are and who is there to lend an ear.

Here are another teacher's words:

> As an educator, I understand the importance of caring and listening to others. It is my responsibility to create a positive learning environment. I initiate simple conversations [with my students], not only in academics but also in their lives outside of school. The students have become more comfortable with me and express their feelings, concerns and goals. I also engage my students in academic conversations related to goal setting. For example, I have meetings with my students individually to discuss their progress on high stakes testing and grades, as well as setting new goals for them to attain. I use this time to share my high expectations and motivate them to strive for academic success.

Three students/teachers felt that they often "apply past knowledge to new situations." Below are one teacher's words.

> I find myself drawing on past experiences to solve present problems in the classroom because I am familiar with behaviors certain children display. Having that base, or prior knowledge, on many things helps me organize my thoughts as to how I want to proceed each day in my classroom as a teacher. It helps me gain a head start to what the rest of the day with my students holds for me
> .

"Persisting" or sticking to a task until it is completed is another habit that several teachers identified with. Here is one example:

> According to the Oxford dictionary, persistence is the continuance of performing an act or task in spite of any difficulties or opposition. Persistent teachers do not give up. One of the key attributes of persistence is being able to analyze a problem and develop a systematic strategy to attack the problem. In the likely event that one strategy does not work, they know how to back track their actions and try again. When an individual decides to become a teacher, they not only assume the immense responsibility for young individuals, but they also take on the added position as a primary role model for them. It is therefore, imperative that our actions and dispositions as we interact with students and parents are positively reflected. Students often give up in despair when they are unable to answer a question or perform a task. Some have attention deficits and have difficulty staying on task for any length of time. Others are easily distracted or lack the ability to analyze and solve a problem. Whatever the case may be, as teachers, we must teach our students the necessary skills and model what it means to be a persistent learner.

Thinking about his or her own thinking or "reflective thoughtfulness" is another habit to which several teachers related. Here is an example.

> One of the most important habits in my teaching is thinking about my thinking. Teacher reflection is critical to being an effective educator. In order to develop and grow in my field, I need to think about planning a lesson, delivering instruction, and how to better meet the needs of my students. For instance, after

every lesson, I think about whether or not the students were able to successfully meet the goals of the objective. If I believe that a lesson was not as clear and concise as it should be, I can reconstruct a future lesson to reteach or enrich my [original] lesson. I also think about how to increase learning gains more effectively and efficiently for my students.

Two teachers identified with the habit, "taking responsible risks." Following are one teacher's words.

> The habit of mind, "taking responsible risks" means that one is willing to take a risk but is responsible enough to consider the outcome. One will weigh out both the positives and negatives of the risk and then will make the decision of whether or not the risk is worth taking. I do practice this habit of mind in both my personal life and my professional teaching career. I am a risk-taker and this attribute has assisted me with accomplishing many of the successes I have achieved. One risk I took professionally was answering a telephone call from the school [where] I currently teach. I received a phone call from the assistant principal for a phone interview. I completed the interview and at the end of the call, I was offered the job, and I was asked to start the following day. I took the risk and accepted the job. It has now been eight months and I couldn't be happier with my decision.

Some teachers felt that showing sensitivity to the needs of others and working as a team or "thinking interdependently" was a habit that they exhibited.

> Teacher 1:
> People need to remember that every person lives a different life than them; what may be easy to obtain for one person may be another's difficulty. We need to be more understanding and compassionate towards others, no matter what a person's gender, socio-economic status, or interest. There are many stories that people tell about someone who started with nothing and through diligence and grit made a name for himself. That is the concept I do my best to instill in my students and that is what other educators need to do as well. As long as you work as a team, you open the door to not just a few students, but for many others to join together and make something memorable with their lives.

> Teacher 2:
> I make sure to show sensitivity to the needs of others. Being an effective teacher means understanding that every student learns in a different way. I employ the use of differentiated instruction within my classroom to meet the needs of my diverse learners. For example, during the math instructional block, I begin with review followed by whole group instruction, independent work, and centers.

> Working in centers is extremely effective because the students are able to ask questions and get more of an opportunity to practice and have fun at the same time. The students that I work with do not ask many questions during whole group instruction, and sometimes fall behind.

Working in a small group, gives the students an important opportunity to ask questions that they are embarrassed to ask during class time. By making these necessary modifications students definitely benefit.

One student/teacher identified "being analytical" as a habit of mind that she uses often.

One way to address the learning styles of the students in the classroom is by having differentiated instruction. To have differentiated instruction, I need to be analytical in the way I teach. I must think of what I need to teach and how to teach it. I first find out my students' readiness level and then, I determine what the students need to learn and how I should teach them that information. I would differentiate my instruction by using tiered activities. By differentiating instruction, I will be giving my students the option of completing one assignment in different ways.

"Being Open-Minded" is one habit that many teachers embody. Here are the thoughts one teacher.

The ability to think flexibly and have an open-mind in working with students and parents is a disposition I practice in the classroom. Thinking flexibly involves the ability to change a point of view or trend of thought when presented with new ideas and/or additional information. In today's classrooms, where teachers are increasingly faced with socially diverse families, a successful teacher must recognize other people's points of view and thought processes. Jean Piaget discusses egocentrism (perceiving from one's own point of view) and allocentrism (perceiving through another person's orientation). Flexible thinkers operate in the latter perceptual position as they are able to empathize with other's feelings, predict how they are thinking, and anticipate potential misunderstandings. It is very important for students to recognize this disposition, as many young children perceive most situations from a very ego-centered point of view. They usually think their way to solve a problem is the only way.

My Teaching Philosophy Based On the Habits of Mind

As I said earlier, I believe one's philosophy is the force that drives everything one does in the classroom; the way s/he relates to students, the curriculum s/he selects, and the approaches s/he employs. Throughout my experiences thus far at FIU, I have been grappling with my own teaching philosophy, and like my students have chosen three habits of mind that represent the kind of teacher that I am. First and foremost, I am a good listener. I enjoy learning other people's "stories" and seek to understand what motivates them. When I am working with students of any age, I try to get to know them as people first, and then determine how I can support them in their learning. In my classroom, I try to create a sense of community where students can take risks and learn to encourage and listen to each other. I believe that each person has a unique perspective and that learning is enriched by multiple viewpoints.

Persistence is another habit of mind that is part of my belief system or philosophy. Whenever I am faced with a challenge, I immediately begin to seek a solution. With my own learning, I continue to study until I have a deep understanding of a topic. With my students, I maintain high expectations for them and will try numerous approaches, until they are successful. I am tenacious and do not give up easily.

A third habit of mind that I practice is being open-minded. By nature, I have a deep need to pose the question, "Why?" When I am asked to complete a task, I always want to know why it needs to be done. When I work with students or colleagues on tasks, I listen to their ideas and I enjoy learning new ways of thinking about or doing things. When someone has a very different viewpoint, I listen and try to understand their perspective and sometimes, will change my mind. Today as classrooms are becoming more and more diverse, we must be open to new ideas. We can discuss them intelligently and promote common understandings across viewpoints.

Moving Forward: Journey On

One of my colleagues, Dr. Erskine Dottin (2012), recently shared three levels or stages of development that one moves through as dispositions or habits of mind are acquired. The stages are awareness, seeing value, and internalization (Dottin, 2012). After reviewing the teaching journals and papers that my students submitted these past two semesters, I believe that they have developed an "awareness" of the dispositions and are beginning to "see value" in them. This fall as I prepare for another group of students, I am thinking about how I can move the next group farther along the continuum. One thing I plan to do is have them identify three habits they feel most represent them, earlier in the semester. Then, I would like for them to find opportunities in their own classrooms to apply these habits. I think this activity will bring the dispositions to life for the students, and move them beyond the awareness level of development. After all, for something to become a pattern or a habit it must be repeated often, reflected on, and tweaked to fit each new situation. To give my students the best opportunity to internalize these habits, I need to give them time to practice and reflect.

Prior to coming to FIU, I had some experiences with dispositions at another institution. I helped to place and supervise several groups of undergraduate elementary education interns and the interns were evaluated on several professional behaviors that one would expect to see in an effective teacher. I also worked with a group of reading faculty to develop dispositions for candidates in a graduate reading program. Yet, it wasn't until I came to FIU and saw dispositions defined in terms of habits of mind that I really began to value and internalize these dispositions. Because the habits of mind are based on patterns of thinking or ways of behaving, I believe that they make dispositions recognizable, concrete, and more easily understood. Faculty and students can identify some of these patterns in themselves and relate to each other as they would with a common language. "A 'Habit of Mind' means having a disposition toward behaving intelligently when confronted with problems" (Costa, 2012, p. 6). These intelligent behaviors provide a means for the faculty and students to create a "social community" where they can reflect on their professional practices to create an engaging, educative environment not only at FIU, but also in K-12 classrooms.

References

Aguirre, J., & Speer, N.A. (2000). Examining the relationship between beliefs and goals in teacher practice. *Journal of Mathematical Behavior, 18*(3), 327-356.

Borg, M. (2001). Key concepts in ELT Teachers' beliefs. *ELT Journal 55*(2), 186-188.

The Conceptual Framework (n.d.). Retrieved from http://education.fiu.edu/docs/ ConceptualFramework2006-19-09.pdf

Costa, A. L. & Kallick, B. (2012). Habits of mind. Learning guide from Discovering and Exploring Habits of Mind Workshop, 6-22, Miami, Florida.

Costa, A. & Kallick, B. (2000). Getting into the habit of reflection. *Educational Leadership, 57*(7), 60-62.

Cunningham, F.M.A. (2001). Reflective teaching practice in adult ESL Settings. Retrieved from http://www.marshalladulteducation.org/pdf/briefs2/Reflective_ Teaching_Practice_in_Adult_ESL_Settings.pdf

Dewey, J. (1933). *How we think: A restatement of the relation of reflective thinking to the educative process.* Boston, MA: Heath.

Dottin, E. S. (2012, March). Dispositions [Habits of Mind] Development. Handout given in Faculty Learning Community meeting at FIU.

Gun, B. (2011). Quality self-reflection through reflection training. *ELT Journal, 65* (2), 126-135.

Haberman, M. (1991). The pedagogy of poverty versus good teaching. *Phi Delta Kappa,* 290-294.

Halpern, D.F. (1996). Thought and knowledge: An introduction to critical thinking. Retrieved from http://www.kcmetro.cc.mo.us/longview/ctac/definitions.htm

Kupari, P. (2003). Instructional practices and teacher's beliefs in Finnish mathematics Education. *Studies in Educational Evaluation,* 29, 243-257.

Markham, M. (1999). Through the looking glass: Reflective teaching through a Lacanian Lens. *Curriculum Inquiry, 29*(1), 55-76.

Moore, J. & Whitfield, V. (2008). Musing: A way to inform and inspire pedagogy through self-reflection. *The Reading Teacher, 6,* (17), 586-588.

"Philosophy" (2012). In Microsoft Encarta (version 2.1) [software]. Redmond, WA: Microsoft Corporation.

Posner, G.J. (1989). *Field experience methods of reflective teaching.* New York: Longman.

Reber, J. (2011). The under-examined life: A proposal for critically evaluating teachers' and students' philosophies of teaching. *College Teaching, 59,* (3), 102-110.

Sparks-Langer, G., Simmons, J., Pasch, M., Colton, A., Starko, A. (1987). Reflective pedagogical thinking: How can we promote it and measure it? *Journal of Teacher Education, 41,* (4), 21-32.

Surbeck, E., Han, E. P., & Moyer, J. (1991). Assessing reflective responses in journals. *Educational Leadership, 48,* 25-27.

van Manen, M. (1977). Linking ways of knowing with ways of being practical. *Curriculum Inquiry, 6,* 205-228.

Virta, A. (2002). Becoming a history teacher: Observation on the beliefs and growth of the student teacher. *Teacher and Teacher Education 18,* 687-698.

Zeichner, K. M., & Liston, D. P. (Eds). (1996). *Reflective teaching- An introduction.* Mahwah: New Jersey.

CHAPTER SIX

DeMYSTifying Dispositions: Enhancing Teaching and Learning in the Organization and Supervision of a Course in a Reading Program

By

Joyce C. Fine

Teaching how to teach reading is just one aspect of the job of a literacy professor. Another aspect is shaping candidates in the Masters of Reading Education program to be literacy professionals. A literacy professional's job, besides knowing the content or knowledge-base and skill to teach reading, includes being able to deliver professional development, being a literacy coach to teachers so they can improve the reading performance of their students, being a curriculum designer, being an interpreter of data, being a spokesperson for the school when it comes to literacy issues, and displaying the high quality professional behaviors required by the latest P-12 standards. As such, literacy professionals must employ skillful thinking to meet all the cognitive tasks challenging literacy professionals today. Because practices in teacher preparation are a mirror image of practice for quality teaching in P-12 settings (Hollins, 2011), professors must create courses to include ways to develop these roles, a pursuit which has led to the infusion of professional dispositions or Habits of Mind (HOM) (Costa & Kallick, 2004) along with knowledge and skills. These dispositions emphasize fostering reflective intelligence so that their candidates know not only what should be done under different circumstances, but that they act in ways that demonstrate these dispositions. More specifically, the aim is to prepare reading specialists who know the field of reading education well enough to be able to apply knowledge and skills to problem solve when they are teaching all students, from proficient to those with severe disabilities, and adjust their instruction to accommodate the students, demonstrating these dispositions with reflective intelligence.

To develop the dispositions that the College of Education (COE) at Florida International University has identified, candidates are first introduced to the dispositions so that they develop an awareness of what they are. Then, the dispositions are integrated into the courses to move candidates to the stage where they value the dispositions. Towards the completion of the program, the goal is for candidates to demonstrate the internalization of these dispositions within course assignments. (See chapter   by Fine & Miller in this volume).

When the start of a Faculty Learning Community (FLC) was announced, I had been working as program director with our Reading Strand members to incorporate the dispositions throughout the program. In the courses I regularly teach, which are in the latter part of the program, I had started by infusing the dispositions and bringing candidates to a level where they valued them. Eventually, there was evidence that the disposition labels were attached to the activities that the candidates were asked to complete to meet the state and national standards.

Upon accepting the invitation to join the FLC, I had no idea how much the time spent talking and interactively learning with my colleagues would impact me and, consequently, my students. In this chapter I describe how the FLC impacted my thinking which, in turn, impacted how I developed ways to nurture the candidates' thinking as I redesigned one of our courses, Organization and Supervision of Reading Programs. I share examples of candidates' in-class and out-of-class thinking from their reflections about the COE dispositions in completing an assignment to move candidates to a deeper level of understanding of dispositions during the spring 2012 semester. Lastly, I provide evidence from candidate's reflections on their performance in a supervised practicum during the summer term of 2012 when they were able to demonstrate the extent to which they had internalized the dispositions.

Honestly, I joined the FLC because I liked the people involved, especially Dr. Erskine Dottin, a colleague who had been a leader in facilitating the faculty's development of the COE's conceptual framework. His work with dispositions is well-recognized and is elucidated in his book, *Dispositions as Habits of Mind: Making Professional Conduct More Intelligent*, (2010). It helped me view dispositions as moral habits of mind grounded in the work of Dewey (1916/1944) that can and ought to be developed in teacher education programs. Our college had collectively agreed upon using 12 of these Habits of Mind from Costa and Kallick (2004) as dispositions in our undergraduate and graduate programs. The focus of the FLC was developing dispositions, which my reading program associates and I had been working to develop for about six years for the Masters of Science in Reading Education program. I figured I might be able to contribute to the discussion what we had been doing. I had been using them in courses in discussion, in the assignments and rubrics for each assignment, and in reflections written after assignments. I did have some strategies for stepping the candidates through the process of becoming reflective practitioners. For instance, one objective in the Organization and Supervision course is for the candidates to plan professional development and to coach teachers to teach reading better. One strategy was using Cognitive Coaching simulations (Costa & Garmston, 2002). In-class Cognitive Coaching sessions helped the candidates learn to be sensitive to their colleagues' feelings when delivering constructive criticism. The simulation of Cognitive Coaching in the class helped with their preparation to coach at their school site, but there was still a need to bring the thinking process into more of the course meetings. Little did I know when I joined the FLC that through experiencing the use of certain strategies with my colleagues, that I would gain a means for bringing thinking into my in-class sessions. The Faculty Learning Community proved to be much more than I had anticipated.

The FLC members met and were introduced to some protocols developed by Harvard's Project Zero. These were thinking routines, patterns of learning called MYST and the Ladder of Feedback. These thinking routines enabled us to accomplish the goals of each meeting through their added structure to guide learning. During the gatherings, faculty had a chance to present their work with everyone listening attentively. We focused our attention with the intention of responding thoughtfully afterwards, making our thinking visible. I felt fortunate to have had the opportunity to learn about and appreciate the fine work of my colleagues, something that we rarely take the time to do considering our busy schedules. I left the meetings marveling at the time spent so well. We focused not only on our thinking but on enabling the thinking of others. After experiencing these protocols in the FLC, I thought these routines were wonderful models to facilitate thinking and that the protocols would be excellent routines for my candidates to use as they developed their dispositions to become reading coaches.

Because one of the goals of the Organization and Supervision course is for the candidates to develop skills needed to be caring and capable reading coaches, these routines, slightly modified for my classroom purpose, seemed appropriate tools to enhance the quality of an assignment to support the internalization of the dispositions while the candidates gained knowledge of the field and proficiency in creating professional development. The MYST protocol, which stands for **M**y thinking, **Y**our thinking, **S**pace and **T**ime, helps presenters think about how they are making their thinking visible, how they are helping candidates to make their thinking visible, how they are utilizing the classroom space and time to the maximum potential (see Appendix A). The Ladder of Feedback consists of a framework for giving feedback to a colleague after a presentation. It establishes "a culture of trust and constructive support by sequencing feedback" that is constructive (see Appendix B). Instead of candidates just saying what they liked about a presentation, they have the opportunity to seek clarification on an aspect that may have been confusing, tell what was valued in the presentation, raise questions about anything that may have raised a concern, make suggestions for refining the presentation and thank the presenters for enhancing their understanding of the topic.

The assignment that I had developed and had been using simulated an activity that Reading Coaches do in schools, conducting Teacher Study Groups. A Teacher Study Group is a group of teachers who have chosen to come together to discuss a critical article from a professional journal that the reading coach has distributed. To simulate this activity in the course, I asked the candidates to form communities of four and to lead class discussions on each of a list of assigned articles for literacy professionals. The whole class was to read all the articles in order to be prepared to participate with the group leading the discussion. Each member of the group presenting read the article critically, (noting the credentials of the authors to determine if they were credible sources and the context in which it was written to determine if the article had current information and application) and carefully outlined the information in the article. Then they created a presentation for the group.

There were several reasons why I chose this assignment as the one to modify with the use of the thinking routines. One was that the presentations were not challenging the other members of the class to think about the concepts in the articles. Another was my concern with the in-class behaviors of candidates. From my observation during other terms, when one group was presenting information from an article everyone was supposed to have read, it seemed not everyone had actually read the material. While the presenters knew the materials on the surface level, they often were more interested in just making a PowerPoint with key ideas and reading the information from each slide rather than leading a meaningful discussion about the issues in the article. They did not seem to be motivated to stimulate the thinking of their colleagues. It lacked the kind of cognitive behaviors needed to support learning. There needed to be a change to bring more thinking, mental stimulation, excitement and engagement with ideas. The FLC had introduced me to the means to achieve this end.

During the spring 2012 course, I adapted the MYST protocol in a few ways to improve the in-class learning and interactions from the Teacher Study Group assignment. The candidates had to think of ideas independently to present the article's information in an interactive way. This interactive requirement was a modification involving the use of the MYST protocol. When all the group members had read critically, thought of their own ideas for presenting using the modified MYST protocol, they met to share their ideas and to select one to use for their 15-minute class presentation. They also had to use the space to move their classmates about the classroom to do something related to the topic and to do this in only a total of 15 minutes time. The time limit was emphasized because candidates needed to appreciate that professional development often takes place before or after school when teachers have limited time to participate in a study group. By keeping to a time limit, they respected a tenet of andragogy, the study of teaching adults, an important dimension of coaching adults. The candidates need to respect that adults do not have unlimited time before or after work because of all their other responsibilities. (I will attend if you remember to respect that I must leave at the scheduled time.)

The use of the Ladder of Feedback was an interactive activity that the candidates participated in after the in-class presentations. The Ladder of Feedback allowed more serious comments and encouraged more analysis of the quality of the professional development presentation. The candidates moved beyond the idea of trying not to hurt anyone's feelings if they gave constructive feedback. By following the Ladder of Feedback guidelines, they quickly got to the point where they were giving constructive criticism using considerate language. The groups got better and better at pointing out attributes of good professional development and each subsequent group, as we progressed through the different weeks of class, incorporated lessons learned from the last groups' experiences. These presentations were spread from week 7 through week 12 and were interspersed with the other major assignments in the course (see the abbreviated course outline in Appendix C). As one student commented, "I like the Ladder of Feedback because it is specific and really does allow you to see what the audience members felt went well and in which specific areas one would need to improve." This reflection supported the notion that the thinking routine was helping to achieve the needed change in the design of the assignment.

The candidates presenting the professional development reflected on the assignment after their Teacher Study Group presentation by answering questions related to dispositions. It is important to note that, as in other semesters, from the very beginning of the course, we talked about their individual identities. We discussed James Gee's Identity Theory (2004), that we each have four aspects of our identity: a force in nature, a position in an institution, our primary Discourse identity or interactions with people, and our affinity groups, those with whom we choose to associate. They discussed who they were in terms of each of these categories. We each shared our self-descriptions and saw that each of us was quite unique. We may share some of the same attributes, but our identities are formed from the sum total of our natural self and experiences.   The purpose of this activity was to sensitize them into realizing that as a reading coach they will not be trying to wave a magic wand and make each teacher with whom they work into a cloned version of themselves.   As future reading coaches, they will be supporting teachers' professional growth so that each teacher may develop his or her own professional literacy educator identity.   In the same way, I encouraged them to express their thinking openly when they reflected on their assignments for even though we are each different, we are in a community of practice.

Their community of practice in this spring 2012 section was built upon social interactions.   They gained knowledge about literacy, how to interact with other candidates, and how to facilitate their ability to support the teachers and students in their school. Most of all, they learned to appreciate the value of reflective intelligence.

Analyzing the Responses to Questions about Dispositions

There were 16 candidates in the course who each answered a set of questions for their study group presentation both prior to their presentation and following their presentation. The set of papers including their outline of the article was turned in the week after their presentation.   By analysis of a representative sample of the candidates' written reflections, we discover the extent to which the candidates in this course were able to bring meaning to, or demystify, dispositions in response to questions about their work on the Teacher

Study Group assignment as related to the use of the College of Education's dispositions developed within the Masters of Science program in Reading Education. The questions have the shortened labels for the dispositions bolded within them. The candidate's reflections are represented in the bulleted comments, while the author's analysis/commentary is italicized. The author provided feedback to each candidate in passing back the reviewed papers, which included my italicized analysis/commentary below, at the end of the course.

1. To what extent did you strive for **accuracy** in making your outline?

> When making my outline I ensured accuracy though the usage of bulleted points which paraphrased the text for the most part. I attempted to avoid summarizing the article in an effort to remain accurate to the author's tone and ideas.

> *Here a student shows that she was paying close attention to the details in the article in order to not miss any points the author was making.*

2. Since this was a simulation of professional development, what **responsible risks** did you take?

> I don't think I took risks, because a lot of things that I planned on implementing came from watching and learning from the mistakes of the groups that presented prior to our group.

> *This student made decisions about how to present based on what she learned in class from participating in the class discussions using the Ladder of Feedback after prior groups presented She sees the ideas she incorporated not as a risk, but as being safe, since she learned these ideas in the context of the professional community established with this assignment. Other students describe taking responsible risks and were able to reflect on them related to dispositions.*

> I took responsible risk in the form of incorporating music and interactive activities that my audience might have interpreted as being quirky or corny.

> *This student felt that she was free to incorporate something from her social practices, using musical lyrics, to get the audience's attention and to make her point.*

> The responsible risk that I took was coming up with a different activity that didn't involve dividing the class up and answering a question on chart paper, like the rest of the groups. At first I thought maybe we should do something similar to ensure we are doing the activity part of the presentation correctly. Instead, we decided to change it up and come up with an idea of having the participants create authentic literacy by writing a letter to someone who has influenced them, instead of answering something about the topic.

This student recognized that there was a pattern in the way groups were beginning their presentations. She and her group thought flexibly and wanted to deliver the information in a unique way. She knew it was important to start the presentation on authentic literacy, literacy activities which mirror the out of school practices, by incorporating an actual authentic literacy activity to begin the presentation so the audience would be able to experience and appreciate the value of such activities before the abstract ideas were presented.

I took the risk of presenting information in a fun, creative way to my colleagues. When I learned that I would be presenting the portion of the chapter on the credibility of the authors, I came up with a fun and creative way to do so. I was hoping my colleagues would appreciate this, but I was unsure if my presentation was going to be successful or go well so this was definitely a risk I took. The following is an excerpt:

The authors of this chapter, there were a total of four, so listen up close, I'm about to tell you more. Nell K. Duke, is the first name that you see. She currently teaches at Michigan State University. Her areas of teaching and research specialization, is what I'll go over next. Her areas include reading comprehension instruction and informational text. So now I'll go into, some of the rest. She's also co-director of the Literacy Research Center, we're sure she does this best.

This student says he likes to write poetry and felt that the disposition of taking risks made him feel secure enough to allow the audience to see him in this role as a poet. He thought creatively and applied his talents so the class could all enjoy his part of the presentation.

I believe that in doing this assignment, I took many responsible risks. I am extremely goal-oriented as well as organized. Another member in the group stepped up and wanted to be in charge of doing the PowerPoint. I had to let go of my fear of not doing everything myself and simply put it aside. I was extremely pleased with the way the PowerPoint turned out as well as my handling my anxiety over letting others take control.

In taking a responsible risk, this student managed her impulsivity to take control and was able to listen to her colleagues. She built a connection of trust with her colleagues to the point where she was able to let go of a fear concerning her grades. This was therefore, an example of being able to think interdependently, also.

3. How did you contribute to being a cooperative team member (thinking interdependently)?

We were all responsible for reading the chapter, but we created our individual slides on our own and then combined them to form the presentation. I wanted my part of the presentation to be more personal so I reviewed my notecards before presenting and never looked at them during the presentation. I made eye contact with my audience and allowed my thoughts to be more fluid rather than rehearsed or robotic.

This candidate describes the roles that she saw her different classmates take in their presentation and decided that her role was to be the personal connector to the audience. She reflected and made a metacognitive plan about what it would take to be able to present more spontaneously to her audience and executed her plan well.

I contributed as a cooperative team member to my group presentation through organizing and delegating specific tasks within the group. I was able to manage the organization of the resources, snacks, and presentation order within the group. I determined what tasks and assignments we needed to address and the other group members were able to decide which responsibilities each would assume.

This candidate was able to think and communicate with clarify and precision. Her "take charge" attitude was somewhat tempered by the idea that she should work interdependently. She has said that to be a good coach, one needs to be confident above all else. Her confidence comes through even in her reflection on dispositions. We have been working on the importance of having the knowledge base to support others as being very critical to the role of reading coach and the importance of respecting other's abilities to perform well.

4. Were you an empathetic listener to the ideas of your group? How did you show a sense of care for the time of colleagues and location for meetings?

It was important that we listened to each other and shared the same vision for the outcome and what we wanted our colleagues to take with them after the presentation.

We have worked diligently on why having a shared vision is very critical to being able to move forward as a community so this use of the word "vision" resonates with our work on dispositions.

Because all of my group members are working professionals, it was very important to all of us to have flexibility in meeting times and contribution of resources. I was sure to recommend a time and location for meeting that was convenient for all the group members that did not impose on others.

As mentioned above, we have talked extensively about the difference in teaching students and in teaching teachers. As adults, teachers have workloads that leave very little time for extras such as professional development. This carried over to their planning for the assignment.

I was a very empathetic listener to the ideas of my teammates. Being a team player is very important to making things succeed in a group and that is something I always go by when   working in a group with others. I felt that if changes needed to be made to our presentation, we should make sure all members agree.

We have also emphasized being open-minded to other's ideas as a disposition to internalize.

The above comment shows that being an empathetic listener has been integrated with being   open-minded.

5. In what ways did you demonstrate persistence to see the project through?

In order to see the project through, I insured that we had contact information for all group members. One member was assigned the task of creating an email group. I also ensured that I responded to emails, text messages, and any other forms of communication in a timely and professional manner.

Group work is always problematic considering teachers' busy schedules. It took persistence to get everyone together. They worked systematically to use technology to solve their problem of finding time to work together.

6. How did you or your group communicate accurately to clarify the information?

Because each group member had a specific section of the chapter to present, I assumed the responsibility of being a clarifier of information at the end of the sections. I attempted to make connections of the chapter to real life simplified experiences and other text and research that the audience may have experienced or read.

When an article has been divided by a group whose job it is to present the information, it can be a problem. To have someone self-appoint themselves to check for cohesiveness and accuracy is a sign of the development of professionalism.

The above samples from students' reflections following the assignment to simulate professional development with Teacher Study Groups show that there was a deeper understanding and application of dispositions.   These candidates were near the end of their masters degrees in reading and had been exposed to the ideas of these dispositions first just to make them aware of them and then to get them to value what they mean. At this advanced point in their program, they had demonstrated the dispositions at a depth of understanding within the classroom.   The next step is to investigate if there is transfer of these dispositions to the level where they employ the knowledge, skills, and dispositions needed to be reading coaches in the real world. This transfer is the goal of our College of Education's vision. Through this assignment and others in the Organization and Supervision of Reading Programs course, they worked to develop their professional identities to bridge from the classroom to their own classrooms and the school leadership roles they seek.

Demonstrating Dispositions in a Supervised, Clinical Practicum

During the summer, 2012 term, many of the same candidates participated in a supervised clinical practicum, the Community Literacy Club (CLC), in which the Diagnosis of Reading Problems and the Programs of Remediation of Reading Difficulties courses were integrated. Each candidate assessed and intervened to develop the reading ability of an elementary student in a one-on-one tutoring program, on-site in a predominantly Spanish-speaking community. Candidates were again placed within a community of learners with their students in different classrooms. They collaboratively shared the findings of their assessments to create a Community Profile. Using the Profile, each candidate created lessons for her/his individual student and then hypothetically differentiated the lesson created for the child for the entire group of students in the Community. Each candidate was observed and her/his demonstration of knowledge, skills, and dispositions was noted. After the tutoring, each candidate wrote a summary analysis and reflection on their teaching experiences. The following representative sample of comments showed that the candidates had, indeed, internalized many of the dispositions. They were specifically asked to select three they felt they had accomplished and how they had changed as a result of their experience in the CLC and program. The following reflections, grouped under bolded headings for different dispositions, came from the Community Profile Summary Analysis and Reflection assignment from the same pool of candidates who had participated in both spring and summer 2012 courses as part of the Masters of Reading Education program:

Reflective Thoughtfulness
These courses made me reflect like no other courses. Every single action I took with my student happened because I thoroughly planned out what should be best for her. I looked at every angle to the situation. Every night I came home and thought about my day and considered what I was planning to do to make the following day an even better / productive day for her.

I have learned to think about the way I teach, what I teach, and how it worked out in terms of benefiting the student. Being able to reflect on my thinking will help me in the future because I will be able to correct my mistakes and figure out what works and what does not. I will be able to help myself improve because I can make the necessary changes in order to bring out the best in myself.
I will be persistent because I have learned that we can't give up on a child. We must use whatever resources necessary until we are able to help the student be successful. I must be honest with myself and be willing to make the necessary changes. I have learned that I should draw knowledge from my past professional experiences and apply this to new situations in order to improve my performance and for the benefit of all my students.

If the lesson was not effective, I can evaluate it to reteach using different teaching techniques. I am becoming more of a steward of the discipline, a reflective inquirer and most importantly a more mindful educator.

Thinking and Communicating with Accuracy

Throughout this experience, I was able to clearly communicate with my colleagues and student. I worked cooperatively in the CLC with other teachers who shared strategies and ideas. When working with the student, I provided clear and defined goals. Every day before starting the tutoring session I told my student what was on the agenda and what the objectives of each lesson/activity were.

While teaching my student, I constantly reiterated and rephrased certain statements and information in order for my student to comprehend the subject matter or skill that was being taught. When speaking to parents, I must maintain a respectful and clear way. I must say the most important information to get the maximum effect.

Empathetic Understanding, Showing Sensitivity to the Needs of Others

I have learned to be sensitive to my student's feelings and not jump to conclusions before giving her a chance to explain.

I have had the opportunity to work incredibly close with one single student and got to know her in a relatively short period of time. I was there for her when she cried about not wanting to attend therapy, when she got upset with her dad for not letting her play with her friends and was even there for her mother when she expressed her concerns for her daughter. Although I was not there to give answers, I was always there to listen.

The above statements by the candidates who were in both the spring, 2012 Organization and Supervision class and the summer practicum were descriptions of professional dispositions which met a goal of the program. They were able to act with reflective intelligence under an intense schedule to support students. The next question to investigate is: Will they continue to act this way in their own classrooms? The study should continue with the purpose of following these candidates into their teaching environments to determine if they teach with reflective intelligence, using the desired dispositions.

Appendix 6.1

MYST PROTOCAL

Me, YOU, SPACE, TIME: "MYST"
A routine to help teachers prepare and reflect on making thinking visible.

Me: How do I make my own thinking visible? **You**: How do I make my classmates' thinking visible? **Space**: How is space in the classroom organized to help facilitate thinking? **Time**: How do I give thinking time? How Does thinking develop during the presentation?

Use this framework to critically analyze your group's professional presentation.

Ask yourself the following questions. Think about what you do now in your classroom.

Try to capture ideas to use in the future, too.

• How am I (*Me*) making my own thinking visible for candidates in the program?

How and when do I display the habits of mind and thinking dispositions candidates need to develop?

• How is my thinking made visible to me and the rest of the class?

When and where do candidates share their thinking? Do I have a sense that I know what candidates' thinking is on our current topic of study? Am I able to see their thinking develop? How can I get more access to this thinking? As a class, do we examine and discuss the thinking of others?

• How is thinking displayed in the physical setting of the classroom (*Space*)? Could a visitor to the classroom see candidates' thinking? What artifacts of thinking do I put up on the wall?

How can I use the space to make my thinking and that of candidates visible for examination, discussion, and reflection?

• What are the opportunities for thinking in the classroom (*Time*)?

How much time do candidates really spend in meaningful thought around the issues and topics we are exploring? How can I increase their thoughtfulness?

Taken from: Project Zero, Harvard Graduate School of Education, Visible Thinking Protocol. Retrieved from http://pzweb.harvard.edu/vt/ VisibleThinking_html_files/05_SchoolWideCultureOfThinking/05c_Study GroupMaterials/01_MYSTRoutine.html and modified by Joyce Fine for Teacher Study Group Presentations in Organization and Supervision of Reading Programs, a Masters of Science in Reading Education Course.

Appendix 6.2

Ladder of Feedback Guide for Presentations

The "Ladder of Feedback" is a protocol or structure that establishes a culture of trust and constructive support by sequencing feedback in an order that is constructive.

1. Clarify- Are there aspects of the presentation that you don't believe you understand?	2. Value- What did you see in the presentation that you find to be particularly impressive, innovative, strong, or noteworthy?
3. Raise Questions- What questions, issues, tensions or concerns were raised for you within the presentation?	4. Suggest- Do you have suggestions for refining the presentation, moving forward, or on how to address the concerns identified?

Think- How has observing and giving feedback enhanced your own understanding of teaching and learning?

Adapted by Joyce Fine from Ron Ritchhart's adaptation from Daniel Wilson's "Ladder of Feedback", Project Zero, Harvard Graduate School of Education

Appendix 6.3

Abbreviated Course Outline for Organization and Supervision of Reading Programs, spring, 2012.*

Week 1	Overview of course; Teacher Dispositions; Creating a personal professional vision; Form Teacher Study Groups
Week 2	History of Reading Instruction beginning in 1607
Week 3	Reading Instruction from 1967 to the present
Week 4	Pedagogy vs. Andragogy
Week 5	Changing Role of the Reading Specialist
Week 6	Literacy Teams; vision statements for schools
Week 7	Determining a school's literacy needs; Culturally Responsive Teaching; Needs Assessment Assignment for the teacher's school; Teacher Study Group presentation#1
Week 8	Developing a School-Wide Reading Plan; Tier 1, 2, and 3 instruction; Response to Intervention; **Teacher Study Group presentation #2**
Week 9	Closing the Literacy Gap; Differentiating Instruction; Teacher Study Group presentation #3 ;
Week 10	Cognitive Coaching; Lesson Planning;
Week 11	Cognitive Coaching with in-class simulation
Week 12	Conducting Professional Development Workshops for Paraprofessionals, parents, teachers, and administrators; Teacher Study Group presentation #4
Week 13	Evaluation of curriculum materials, print and non-print;
Week 14	High Stakes Testing; Reading Plan Due
modified Week 15	Meet to discuss Reading Plan before uploading to TaskStream

*A spring break was between weeks but was not numbered. Bold type represents the Teacher Study Group assignment in which the two modified protocols, MYST and Ladder of Feedback were used.

References

Costa, A. L., & Garmston, R. J. (2002). Cognitive coaching: a foundation for renaissance schools. Norwood, MA: Christopher-Gordon.

Costa, A., & Kallick, B. (2004). Describing 16 habits of mind. Retrieved from http:www.habits of mind.net/whatare.htm.

Dewey, J. (1916/1944). Democracy and education: An introduction to the philosophy of education. New York: The Free Press.

Dottin, E. (2010). Dispositions as habits of mind: Making professional conduct more intelligent. Lanham, Md.: University Press of America.

Gee, J. P. (2004). Discourse analysis: What makes it critical? In R. R. (Ed.). An introduction to Critical Discourse Analysis in Education (2nd ed.). New York: Routledge.

Hollins, E. R. (2011). Teacher preparation for quality teaching. *Journal of TeacherEducation* 64.4, p.395-407. doi: http://dx.doi.org.ezproxy.fiu.edu/10.1177/002248711409415.

Project Zero, Harvard University. Retrieved from http:pzweb.harvard.edu/vt/VisibleThinking_html_files/03_ThinkingRoutines/03_CoreRoutines.html

Rogers, R. (2004). An introduction to Critical Discourse Analysis in Education (2nd ed.). New York: Routledge.

CHAPTER SEVEN

Nurturing Dispositions Programmatically: Awareness, Valuing, and Internalization

By

Joyce C. Fine
Lynne D. Miller

Our Masters of Science in Reading Education program at Florida International University strives to prepare literacy professionals who expertly address the literacy needs of the diverse students they teach and who effectively coach fellow teachers in support of their professional development in literacy teaching and learning. Towards this aim, we engage in processes of continuous program improvement, using the most current iterations of Florida's Department of Education Subject-Area Competencies, Section 35, Reading K-12, Professional Education Competencies, Florida Educator Accomplished Practices, and Florida Reading Endorsement Competencies. Additionally, we update our program regularly to remain current with the International Reading Association's (IRA) *Standards for Reading Professionals* (2010). This program qualifies graduates for state certification in Reading K-12. Further, graduates meet the IRA standards for Literacy Specialists/ Literacy Coaches. To maintain a cohesive, focused program given the many embedded standards and competencies, we rely on the central role of our College of Education's Conceptual Framework (n. d.) for lending coherence to the work of our program.

Working Towards a Common End in the MS in Reading Education Program

The College of Education faculty established a vision in which the emphasis on "…inquiry is the means-end connection to enhancing reflective intelligence" ("The Conceptual Framework of the College of Education," n.d., p. 4). We then operationalized this vision through our colleges' learning outcomes for its graduates to be Stewards of the Disciplines, Reflective Inquirers, and Mindful Educators. Extending these learning outcomes to our program means that we want our MS in Reading Education candidates to be Stewards of the Discipline of literacy knowledge so that they may effectively use it to teach reading to students, and to support teachers so they may teach reading better in conjunction with their own literacy skills they develop and apply as Reflective Inquirers. Additionally, we want our candidates to develop and refine professional Habits of Mind (HOM) (Costa & Kallick, 2004) that is, dispositions, so that as Mindful Educators, their use of the literacy teaching and learning knowledge and skills develop concurrently throughout our program. In this way, they may best be used for "facilitating personal, intellectual, and social renewal within diverse populations and environments" ("The Conceptual Framework of the College of Education," n.d., p.4).

The college-wide Comprehensive Assessment System, a critical part of the Colleges' Conceptual Framework, currently helps us to evaluate how successful we are in nurturing candidates' knowledge and skills ("The Conceptual Framework of the College of Education," n.d., p. 21). Many of the literacy competencies and standards mentioned above, along with the college's learning outcomes are assessed, using rubrics, through critical tasks that are uploaded to this system. We then use aggregated data derived from these assessments to monitor candidates' learning related to knowledge and skills and continuously improve our MS in Reading Education program toward common ends.

As we have made significant progress in assessing candidate's knowledge and skills, we continue in our quest to find meaningful ways to nurture and assess candidates' dispositions. We believe that dispositions develop concurrently with knowledge and skills, so we include the assessment of dispositions on our rubrics as they relate to relevant knowledge and skills. For instance, if a candidate is assessing a student, the related disposition would be to withhold judgment, manage impulsivity, and not to rush to label a student before a thorough assessment is made. We also believe that candidates must be active agents in the development of their dispositions. In other words, nurturing dispositions is a collaborative effort between faculty and candidates, and candidates should be aware of dispositions and understand their value as literacy professionals.

Our objectives for this chapter are to describe 1) how we begin programmatically to develop candidates' disposition, or habits of mind, as they enter our program, 2) how we structure our learning environments in our courses to nurture dispositions, and 3) how we have piloted the assessment of candidates' dispositions with a survey. We also discuss how we try to enhance the possibility that candidates transfer these dispositions to the learning environments they create for students in the K-12 environment.

As Candidates Enter the Program

When prospective candidates explore our College of Education's website and written program information, they begin to develop an awareness of terms and concepts related to dispositions, or Habits of Mind (HoM) as defined in our college, based on the work of Costa & Kallick (2004). They see that our college has identified twelve dispositions that we nurture throughout our program: (1)

Adopting a critical eye toward ideas and actions (Being Analytical); (2) Withholding judgment until understanding is achieved by being thoughtful in his/her actions (Managing Impulsivity); (3) Working to see things through by employing systematic methods of analyzing problems (Persisting); (4) Thinking about his/her own thinking (Reflective Thoughtfulness); (5) Thinking and communicating with clarity and precision (Communicating Accurately); (6) Showing curiosity and passion about learning through inquiry (Being Inquisitive); (7) Showing a sense of being comfortable in situations where the outcomes are not immediately known by acting on the basis of his/her initiative and not from needing a script (Taking Responsible Risks); (8) Recognizing the wholeness and distinctiveness of other people's ways of experiencing and making meaning by being open-minded (Being Open-minded); (9) Taking time to check over work because of his/her being more interested in excellent work than in expediency (Striving for Accuracy); (10) Abstracting meaning from one experience and carrying it forward and applying it to a new situation by calling on his/her store of past knowledge as a source of data to solve new challenges (Applying Past Knowledge to New Situations); (11) Showing sensitivity to the needs of others and to being a cooperative team member (Thinking Interdependently); and, (12) Showing a sense of care for others and an interest in listening well to others (Empathic Understanding).

Further, as advisors speaking with prospective candidates, we are able to introduce them to the concept of dispositions and the role they have for literacy professionals. We want the candidates to be aware from the start that just as they will be deepening their knowledge and skills related to the teaching and learning of literacy, they will also be focusing on their professional dispositions.

As Candidates Proceed through Coursework

Candidates take courses in the MS in Reading program, completing a total of 36 hours if they are already ESOL endorsed, in a general sequence. The following courses are suggested to be taken first:

RED 6314- Theory and Instruction in Literacy (3)–This is a prerequisite for all the courses.

LAE 6319-Integrated Language Arts (3)

LAE 5415-Children's Literature (3)

EDF 6211-Psychological Foundations of Education (3)

RED 6336-Content Area Reading (3)

EDF 5481-Foundations of Educational Research (3)-This is a prerequisite for RED 6747 and RED 6540.

Then, the following courses should be taken depending on the term that they are available:

RED 6546-Diagnosis of Reading Difficulties (3)-This course is integrated with RED 6515 Programs of Remediation. Both courses are only offered in the summer for they are taught as a clinical practicum on site, which we call the Community Literacy Club.

RED 6515-Programs of Remediation in Reading (3)-This course is offered in summer only.

RED 6747-Research in Reading (3)-This course is offered in fall and spring.

RED 6540-Reading Assessment (3)-This course is offered in fall and spring.

RED 6805-Practicum in Reading (3)-This course is offered in fall and spring. It is best taken following the summer integrated clinical program.

RED 6247-Organization and Supervision in Reading (3)-This is offered in fall and spring.

If students are not ESOL endorsed, they also take TSL 5361C, TEOL for Secondary Teachers.

This general sequence allows us to pace candidates through the program as we introduce them to specific knowledge, skills and dispositions early on in the program and then support further development in subsequent courses. We believe that for candidates to develop knowledge, skills and dispositions, they must continually be engaged in multiple, meaningful experiences.

Course syllabi set the stage for such experiences. Within course syllabi we have another opportunity to help candidates be aware of dispositions as associated with experiences in the respective courses. Our college-wide set of dispositions is stated explicitly near the beginning of each syllabus. Then, relevant dispositions are aligned with specific experiences in each course. We take the opportunity to highlight dispositions on assignment sheets. We assess assignments through the use of rubrics, and, once again, the rubrics provide still another opportunity for us to solidify candidates' awareness of dispositions associated with each course.

Nurturing candidates' development of dispositions, as they proceed through coursework, takes on various means, depending on such things as the instructor style of teaching and actual course assignments. Described below are several ways we have found to be effective for nurturing dispositions in courses.

One of the first courses candidates take in our program is RED 6314, Theory and Instruction in Literacy. The dual focus of this course facilitates candidates' understanding of major literacy models and theories, along with their understanding of major components of the reading process (e.g. comprehension, vocabulary, fluency, phonics, phonological awareness and oral language development). In one of the major assignments, Theoretical Models Paper and Presentation, candidates first develop in-depth knowledge about several theoretical models related to literacy. They write a paper in which they compare and contrast elements of the models. In order to complete this part of the assignment, candidates must integrate their knowledge about theoretical models with a disposition to be analytical in thinking critically about how the models are similar and different. The candidates' disposition, being analytical, is developed and nurtured throughout the assignment as they concurrently construct their knowledge about theoretical models.

Children's Literature, LAE 5415, is a course that candidates typically take early in their program. While this course provides candidates the opportunity to engage in a comprehensive exploration of children's literature and related issues, it also focuses on a variety of topics related to diversity. A major assignment in this courses calls for candidates to examine their classroom library through the development of a diversity chart. They look for books in their classroom library that treat such topics as ethnicity, religion, nationality, social class, gender, exceptionality and age. They then look at the match between the current collection of books and the population of children in the classroom. Candidates use this information to identify gaps in their collection of books related to diversity in general, as well to examine connects and disconnects between their library collection and the children under their care. Through the entire process of this assignment, we nurture candidates' HoM towards being open minded. This HoM focuses on recognizing the wholeness and distinctiveness of others. It honors other people's experiences and ways of experiencing the world around them. This diversity chart assignment could be completed without the added focus on the disposition of being open minded; however, nurturing the disposition along with content helps candidates be purposeful in the use of their reflective intelligence.

Towards the end of the program, in the clinical practicum at the elementary level in which two courses are integrated, RED 6546 Diagnosis of Reading Difficulties and RED 6515 Programs of Remediation in Reading, the Community Literacy Club, we have an assignment which we call the Community Profile. While candidates tutor one-on-one with an elementary struggling reader, they work in a classroom of a community of four to five teachers in a classroom on-site with their students. These teachers collaborate by producing a Community Profile of the areas for literacy growth of the students as determined by seven different assessments. The professor presents an example of a lesson and includes the candidates in a discussion of how they might differentiate the lesson for different students in a particular community. After the discussion, the professor emphasizes that each community will be working collaboratively to create the Community Profile. Each candidate creates a lesson for his or her one student, but also creates a chart describing how they would hypothetically modify the lesson for each student in the community. With the Community Profile assignment, they have an opportunity to develop the disposition of thinking interdependently, showing a sensitivity to the needs of others (both the students and the other candidates) to discuss ways of differentiating lessons to be able to teach the same concepts to all the children in the community using different materials or with different approaches. This disposition supports the expansion of knowledge to deliver the most appropriate lessons to all the students. While planning their individual lessons, the candidates support each other in creating the best accommodations for each student. As part of the Community Profile assignment, the candidates reflect on dispositions that they believe they developed with this assignment. One student in our summer 2012 delivery of these courses selected the disposition of thinking interdependently and wrote, "By working together with this aspect of the lesson, it was critical to communicate with our community of teachers and work for the best opportunities for our students."

Regardless of the course, candidates need to be given background information about the dispositions to help them deepen their understanding of what they are. It is not sufficient, for example, to merely tell candidates that a particular assignment will help them "develop their disposition of taking responsible risks." Candidates must be provided with opportunities to develop the conceptualization of what each means by engaging with ideas associated with the disposition. Candidates may begin by writing what they think a disposition is and then discussing their thoughts with other class members in a think-pair-share format and then with the rest of the class and the instructor, giving examples of how one might demonstrate a particular disposition. This activity in class raises their awareness of the important, relevant concepts, planting the seeds for further development. Additionally, discussion should help candidates understand and value the disposition within the context of the learning experience and how the disposition works to enhance the construction of knowledge and development of skills.

In class, the instructor should take advantage of opportunities to make candidates aware of how s/he is modeling a disposition. For example, in RED 6805, Practicum in Reading which is conducted at a predominantly Haitian High School, prior to the first tutoring session, the professor demonstrates how the candidates should interact with the high school students. She reminds the candidates that the students may be tired because they have been at school from early in the morning, may be a bit discouraged, having had a difficult times in their classes and may be quite hungry at 5:00 when tutoring begins. She explains that is why we offer pizza and a drink for their hunger, and a sympathetic ear about their day. As teachers, they have the opportunity to emotionally connect by asking the student how his or her day went and to offer empathetic understanding concerning what the student shares. The disposition, empathetic understanding, builds connections to the students, establishes a component that will nurture the student's emotional resilience. After each of the sessions, the professor invites candidates to share some of their exchanges. She reveals to the students by reflecting aloud how this is one way of developing the disposition, showing a sense of caring for others and an interest in listening well to others (Empathic Understanding).

By reflecting aloud, the candidates also provide personal examples of how they engaged a disposition related to particular knowledge or skills. Besides oral reflections, candidates' assignments provide opportunities for written reflection and feedback on their developing dispositions in relation to the knowledge and/or skills being implemented.

As described above, field experiences associated with courses and supervised clinical experiences provide yet another within-course opportunity to nurture the development of candidates' dispositions. Besides written reflections and feedback, the instructor may take the opportunity to discuss with candidates what the instructor has observed relevant to evidence of candidates' behaviors associated with different dispositions. Field and supervised clinical experiences give candidates thinking time for the concepts to germinate and opportunities to apply these concepts themselves in the course of acting professionally as they begin to internalize the dispositions.

Within courses, the assessment of most assignments involves the use of rubrics. Because we believe that dispositions develop in conjunction with knowledge and skills, we design our rubrics accordingly. We do not assess dispositions in isolation. For example, one learning outcome for an assignment described above in the Research in Reading course is: Candidate demonstrates the ability to extract important information from research articles and use it as a base to inform his/her thinking about an action research topic. One of our dispositions that may be developed in conjunction with this learning outcome is: Adopting a critical eye toward ideas and actions (Being Analytical). These two items, the learning objective and the disposition, would share a row on the rubric and both would be evaluated in terms of level of performance. In addition to the evaluation through the rubric, candidates regularly provide a written reflection highlighting how the disposition supported the achievement of the specific learning outcome. The instructor may then provide feedback about this reflection.

One can see that as candidates enter our program and proceed through coursework, they are introduced to dispositions strategically and systematically. Not only are they introduced to them, but candidates and instructors work collaboratively throughout the program in support of the dispositions being valued and internalized. It is hoped that as the candidates build an awareness of the dispositions and come to value and internalize them, they will nurture the development of similar dispositions, or HoM, by the students with whom they work.

Piloting a Programmatic Self-Assessment Survey

In further thinking about our program from a programmatic perspective, we wanted to examine the impact of the MS in Reading Education program on the development of candidates' professional dispositions. We recognize that candidates enter our program with vast amounts and types of knowledge, skills and dispositions, among other things. However, we wondered to what extent candidates had developed any of the twelve dispositions as a result of their participation in our program. Further, we wanted to know if candidates valued these dispositions as supportive of their professional work as literacy professionals.

We developed and piloted a self-report survey, MS in Reading Education: Survey of Professional Dispositions (SPD-R) (Miller & Fine, 2010), that we administered to candidates who had taken 12 credits or less in our program and to candidates who had taken at least 27 of the 36 credits in our program. The survey asked two questions related to each of the 12 dispositions: (1) How important is each professional disposition for literacy specialist/reading coaches? and, (2) To what degree have you developed each professional disposition as a habit of mind? For each disposition, candidates answered these questions using a Likert scale from 1-5 with 1 being not very important and 5 being very important for the first question and1 being not developed to 5 being very well developed for the second question. The results from the assessment of candidates who were finishing the program were that they highly valued each professional disposition, rating them all as very important for literacy specialists/reading coaches. They also indicated that, in general, they had further developed each of the dispositions through experiences in the program, but they did not rate themselves as possessing each disposition to the highest degree. This was interpreted to indicate that they were most likely being quite honest and felt that they still had room to improve.

In analyzing the data, we realized that in future research we would need to look at subgroups of students who had graduated from different FIU undergraduate programs as compared to those who were new to the university. Those who had been at FIU had undergone the effect of being exposed to working with these same dispositions. They, most likely, had developed these dispositions as undergraduates to some degree and so had started their master's degree program at a more advanced stage than others. By asking the students to indicate more information about their undergraduate careers and previous course work at FIU, we should be able to refine our data collection.

Overall, other changes to improve our programmatic work have been identified for the assessment of the dispositions. For instance, one of the areas that the candidates indicated they still needed to develop was taking responsible risks. As a result of this, we have worked to encourage the candidates to take risks such as being more creative in completing assignments. (See Chapter 6 by Fine for a description of this.) We also wish to refine ways of encouraging candidates to take ownership of the process of internalizing the dispositions.

In Conclusion

Because we believe that the process of developing dispositions is a cognitive development, we want to explore ways in which the candidates make the personal decision to act professionally as described in the dispositions. We believe that by nurturing dispositions programmatically, we are having an impact, but we have more to learn about effectively assessing the impact of the program on the development of candidates' dispositions. Besides these insights, we continue to modify the program as we work with the latest versions of national and state standards and the new Common Core Standards.

The challenge is on-going as we seek to continuously improve the quality of our program.

References

Costa and Kallick (2004) Describing 16 habits of mind. Retrieved from http://www.habits of mind.net/whatare.htm.

Fine, J. C. (2012). DeMYSTIFYING dispositons: Enhancing teaching and learning in a Reading master's course. In E. Dottin, L. D. Miller, and G. E. O'Brien (Eds.). *Structuring learning environments in teacher education to elicit dispositions as habits of mind: Strategies and approaches used and lessons learned* (pp. 100-108). Lanham, MD: University Press of America.

Florida's Department of Education Standards. Retrieved from http://www.fldoe.org/edcert.

International Reading Association. (2010). *Standards for Reading Professionals-Revised 2010)*. Newark, DE: Author.

Miller, L. D., & Fine, J. C., (2010) MS in reading education: Survey of professional dispositions (SPD-R). Unpublished document.

The College of Education Conceptual Framework. (n.d.). Retrieved from http://education.fiu.edu/docs/Conceptual%20Framework%2006-19-09.pdf

CHAPTER EIGHT

Shifting Teachers' Discourse in the Classroom: Implications of Cultivating Habits of Mind, Visible Thinking, and Teaching for Understanding in a Graduate Childhood Curriculum Course

By

Angela Salmon
Debra Mayes Pane

It is common for teachers to teach in the same way that they were taught. In their teacher discourse, teachers often communicate and reflect their philosophies of teaching and learning, teaching approaches, and habits of mind. This chapter presents our approach of embedding and consolidating the Habits of Mind (HoM) and using the Visible Thinking (VT) approach to develop thinking dispositions within a Teaching for Understanding (TfU) framework (Blyte & Associates, 1998) in a graduate course (Childhood Curriculum, EDE 6205) in the College of Education (COE) at Florida International University (FIU) which is designed for candidates to study curriculum theory, research, construction, and evaluation. The combination of approaches have been designed and applied to enhance thinking and understanding of teachers/master's degree candidates' enrolled in the MS Curriculum and Instruction–Jamaica program. Additionally, we designed a qualitative case study of course participants to explore the three important interrelated frameworks [HoM-VT-TfU] for developing dialogical and dialectical thinking through teachers' discourse (Flyvbjerg, 2011). The study took place in in several regions of Jamaica during the summer term, 2012. The study included the candidates' field notes and audio/videotaping of their lessons taught at early childhood, elementary, middle, and high school levels in very diverse learning settings in grades PK-12 schools. We triangulated the data from different candidates' artifacts that revealed how the three frameworks of EDE 6205 were a call to action in their current practices to reflect on their classroom discourse, and that the new ideas/approaches would have favorable implications in their students' learning outcomes.

Childhood Curriculum Course EDE 6205

Thinking is a critical component in the learning process. Learning is a consequence of thinking (Perkins, 1992); thus, we believe that it is important for teachers to interpret the concept of thinking and how it is reflected in their discourse in the classroom. EDE 6205 was designed with this end-goal in mind.

Our Philosophy: Setting the Stage for Dialogical and Dialectical Thinking

Paul (2001) distinguishes between two theories that reveal the teacher's discourse in the classroom: (a) the didactic teaching theory and (b) the dialogical and dialectical thinking theory. We differentiate between these two theories to illustrate how the performances of understanding for this course were planned with the end-goal in mind of helping teachers reflect on their initial didactic teaching and their shift to a dialogical and dialectical thinking and teaching practices. The didactic teaching theory is a teacher-centered approach that encourages the teacher's mono-logic thinking from beginning to end. Didactic instruction is teaching by telling (The Critical Thinking Community, 2012). Teachers provide students with explicit knowledge to memorize, and the teachers expect students to regurgitate the same knowledge back to them. In the didactic teaching approach, students' knowledge is separate from understanding and justification. In other words, didactic teaching assumes that teachers can give students knowledge directly without their having to think their way through it (See Appendix 8.1EDE 6205 Stories from the Authors' Personal Experiences Concerning Didactic Teaching Theory and Approaches).

On the other hand, the dialogical and dialectical thinking theory involves dialogue or extended exchange between different points of view or frames of reference. Teachers purposefully create a classroom culture of thinking, talking, and collaborative learning. Within this perspective, teachers show students how to use their own thinking to figure out the thinking of another as they listen carefully to the thoughts of another and try to make sense of those thoughts. For Dottin (2010), the effort of teacher education programs is to help candidates move, like children, past impulse to the more intelligent level of pedagogical conduct, that is, to grow in professional judgment (p 8). When students arrange their thoughts, orally or in writing, they are reasoning dialogically (Paul, 2001). In the next sections, we explore how to engage teachers/master's degree candidates in dialogical and dialectical thinking through the a process that ultimately aims for internalization of the Habits of Mind (HoM), the Visible Thinking (VT), and Teaching for Understanding (TfU) frameworks. The following passages represent the foundational aspects of the three frameworks.

Habits of Mind: Dispositions toward Behaving Intellectually

The Habits of Mind (HoM) are performed in response to people's questions and problematic situations (Costa & Kallick, 2009). HoM are defined as dispositions toward behaving intelligently when confronted with problems-the answers to which are not immediately known. Costa and Kallick (2009) propose sixteen HoM, such as persisting, managing impulsivity, listening with understanding and empathy, and thinking flexibly, among others. The HoM can enrich different curriculum models. We use Costa and Kallick's (2008) four levels of educational outcomes framework (see Figure 8.1) as a foundation to justify our interpretation of the HoM within the particular learning community in this study.

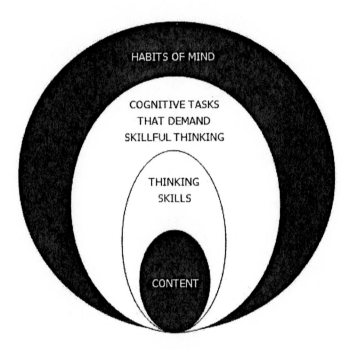

Figure 8.1: Four levels of educational outcomes. Reprinted with permission of ASCD

The HoM require a composite of many skills, attitude cues, past experiences, and proclivities. Internalizing the HoM means that we do not value one pattern of thinking over another, which implies we make choices about which pattern should be employed at the time.

Visible Thinking (VT): Cognitive Tasks That Demand Skillful Thinking

Our interpretation of the cognitive tasks that demand skillful thinking draws from our experience with the VT approach and the TfU framework. Both approaches are compatible with Costa and Kallick's (2008) idea of providing students with sufficiently authentic, engaging, and challenging curricula, instead of merely reproducing knowledge. The VT approach, developed by Project Zero researchers (Ritchhart & Perkins, 2008), is a broad and flexible framework for enriching classroom learning in the content areas while fostering students' intellectual development. The key goals of VT are to (a) deepen learners' understanding of content, (b) increase motivation for learning, (c) develop learners' thinking and learning abilities, (d) develop learners' attitudes toward thinking and learning, (e) develop learners' alertness to opportunities for thinking and learning—the dispositional side of thinking, and (f) shift the classroom culture toward a community of enthusiastically engaged thinkers and learners. Within this framework, an understanding of the eight cultural forces that Ritchhart (2002) proposes leads us to appreciate how teachers can create cultures of thinking in their classrooms.

Cultural Forces. Tishman, Perkins & Jay (1995) claim that schools are places of culture not only in the sense of intellectual achievements, but also the sense of community and spirit of common enterprise. A culture of thinking exists in a classroom when the cultural forces of that classroom are directed toward, and aligned with, the support of good thinking (Ritchhart, 2002). The use of Thinking Routines (TRs) uncovers children's thinking and provokes collective thinking, or dialogical and dialectical thinking.   Dialogical and dialectical thinking involve dialogue or extended exchange between different points of view or frames of reference (Paul, 2001).   The interplay between nature and nurture plays a critical role in promoting children's cognitive development. We do not teach children to talk, but we provide them with opportunities to engage them in talking. As Vygotsky (1978) pointed out-children grow into the intellectual life of those around them. Children are born with genetic codes that influence their cognitive development, however, we need to nurture their thinking. We can see these opportunities reflected in Ritchhart's (2002) eight cultural forces:

* Time for thinking, allocating time for exploring topics in depth.
* Expectations for thinking and learning, setting the agenda of understanding and value for thinking.
* Opportunities for engaging in thinking, providing purposeful activities that require students' cognitive engagement and understanding.
* Routines which are structures that scaffold thinking and learning.
* Language and conversations centered on thinking products and stances.
* Modeling who we are as thinkers.
* Interactions and relationships that show respect for students' contributions.
* Physical environments where we make thinking visible by displaying the students' process of thinking.

As we reviewed the literature, we noticed strong connections between the eight cultural forces and the HoM. We see the HoM as precursors for designing curriculum that cognitively engage students and help them understand concepts.

We also considered that the internalizations of these frameworks were critical to shift teachers' discourse in the classroom. Furthermore, the social environment plays a critical role in shaping dispositions of intelligent conduct (Dottin, 2010). Project Zero researchers designed a variety of thinking routines (Ritchhart, Church, & Morrison, 2011). The next passage addresses the origins of the thinking routines and connections with the HoM.

Thinking Routines (TRs)

The research-based TRs were developed by Project Zero researchers at Harvard Graduate School of Education (Ritchhart, Church, & Morrison 2011). Routines exist in all classrooms. A routine can be thought of as any procedure, process, or pattern of action that is used repeatedly to manage and facilitate the accomplishment of specific goals or tasks. Classrooms have routines that serve to manage student behavior and interactions, to organize the work of learning, and to establish rules for communication and discourse. Classrooms also have routines that structure the way students go about the process of learning. VT makes extensive use of learning routines that are thinking rich. These routines are simple structures-for example, a set of questions or a short sequence of steps that can be used across various grade levels and content. What makes them routines, versus mere strategies, is that they get used over and over again in the classroom so that they become part of the fabric of classroom culture. The routines become the ways in which students go about the process of learning (Visible Thinking, 2012). In other words, teaching thinking is an enculturation process. According to Tishman, Perkins & Jay (1995) enculturation involves a model, explanation, interaction and feedback. By using thinking routines the student becomes aware of the language of thinking or mental process. Words of thinking describe and evoke thinking. This is important because the process helps students organize and communicate their own thinking more precisely and intelligently, while it reinforces standards for thinking (Tishman, Perkis & Jay,1995). The teachers/master's degree candidates and authors selected the most popular TRs to analyze in connection with the HOM. In Appendix 8.2, we share our interpretation of the close relationship between TRs and the HoM.

Teaching for Understanding: Thinking Skills and Content

An important quality in children is the ability to use what they know in new and unfamiliar contexts by demonstrating their understanding flexibly as they respond to the moving target of tomorrow. For Perkins (2001), understanding something is a matter of being able to think and act flexibly with what you know, and are coming to know (p 446). Traditional education has been about educating for the known. Here, educators' attention is being called to the fact that we are educating for the unknown. In other words, "good learning is learning from a richly experienced today with tomorrow in view" (p. 218). It is worth mentioning that we do not know what is going to happen in 5, 10, or 20 years from now.

Content. Curriculum designers work under the influences of different forces that are mandated by the administration, state requirements, and so forth. However, practitioners should always keep in mind a critical question: *What is worth learning?* During the early nineties, Project Zero researchers developed the Teaching for Understanding (TfU) approach (Perkins, 2001), which encompasses four cornerstones of pedagogy with four elements of planning and instruction. The TfU is an educational pedagogy that uses the following four questions as a foundation for its framework (Blyte and Associates, 1998):

1. What topics are worth understanding? (Generative Topic).
2. What about these topics needs to be understood? (Understanding Goals).
3. How can we foster understanding? (Performances of Understanding).
4. How can we tell what students understand? (Ongoing Assessment).

Thinking Skills. It is important for educators to help students become aware of the thinking skills that they are using to perform an activity, solve problems, and so on (Salmon & Lucas, 2011). Learning is a consequence of thinking (Perkins, 1992). Thus, educators can foster learning when they use a language of thinking that directs students' attention to a particular thinking skill to solve a problem. For example, instead of saying, "Let's look at these two pictures," a mindful language would be, "Let's compare these two pictures" (Costa and Kallick, 2008). The intentional use of terminology creates students' thinking dispositions. Good thinking is not only a matter of skills, but also a matter of dispositions (Ritchhart & Perkins, 2008).

The 21st century calls students to become nimble learners who are trained to flex and stretch their thinking skills (Perkins, 2009). When children are aware of the thinking skills that help them understand concepts, they become independent learners. When talking about thinking skills, many people refer to Bloom's Taxonomy. Bloom's Taxonomy is a theory and is not based on research about learning (Ritchhart, Church, & Morrison, 2011). However, the taxonomy has become codified into how many teachers are taught to think about thinking. Ritchhart and colleagues (2011) disagree with the fact that Bloom's Taxonomy has a sequential or hierarchical way of seeing thinking that takes place at different levels. In contrast, they suggest that rather than concerning ourselves with levels among different types of thinking, it is better to focus our attention on the levels or quality *within* a single type of thinking.

Case Study Approach: Problem Statement and Research Questions

When we observe a teacher in her classroom, in many contexts, the stories she is telling to students, reflect the teacher's philosophy of teaching and learning. Teachers set the culture of their classrooms based on their values and beliefs about teaching and learning. The patterns of discourse reflect both the teacher's expectations about her students and determine the culture that the teacher is creating. Cultures of thinking are places in which a group's collective, as well as an individual's thinking is valued, visible, and actively promoted as part of the regular, day-to-day experience of all group members (Ritchhart, 2002). As with language, adults are responsible for nurturing children's thinking. There is a consensus among some scholars (Costa, 2001; Fogarty, 2001; Perkins, 2001) that thinking is teachable and learnable, and teachers play a critical role in making this happen. Ritchhart, Turner, and Hadar (2009) suggest that when teachers engage children in cognitive activities to uncover their thinking, they capture those critical moments when thinking is taking place. This allows teachers to get a hold of it and engage children cognitively in deep thinking and understanding.

The profile of the 21st century citizen requires thoughtful people who are curious, creative, collaborative, communicators and critical thinkers National Council for Teachers of English, 2012). Twenty-first century skills prepare citizens not only to be successful problem solvers, but also to be problem finders, and such skills are developed through the dialogical and dialectical thinking experiences. Thus, today's teachers need opportunities to learn how to implement the dialogical and dialectical thinking theory and associated approaches into their teaching, learning, and discourse practices. One of the purposes of EDE 6205 was to help teachers/ master's degree candidates' (graduate practitioners) gain ownership about building cultures of thinking in their own classroom. Our study explored whether or not there were any changes in the participants' discourse in their classrooms as a result of their self-reflection and discourse awareness, and if there were any implications for grades PK-12 children's thinking and learning. The research questions for this study were:

What are the implications of teachers' interpretation and value of thinking reflected in their philosophy and discourse in the classroom?

How do teachers reflect about changes that happen as a result of being exposed to the HoM, VT and TfU frameworks for thinking and learning?

Method

The qualitative case study explored the EDE 6205 candidate's implementation of three important interrelated frameworks—Habits of Mind, Visible Thinking, and Teaching for Understanding thinking frameworks—for developing dialogical and dialectical thinking through teachers' discourse in PK-12 classrooms in Jamaica (Flyvbjerg, 2011). The case study sought to understand and exemplify a case study of individuals, who were participating in the same graduate level course and program during summer, 2012. The case study was constructed through narrative inquiry, "a subtype of qualitative inquiry that centers around an interest in life experiences as narrated by those who live them" (Chase, 2011, p. 421), using storytelling, narrative practices, and content/discourse analysis (Rex, 2006; Rex & Schiller, 2009). This interpretive case study is framed within the social constructivist paradigm (Denzin &

Lincoln, 2011) in which "everyday realities are actively constructed in and through forms of social action" (Holstein & Gubrium, 2011, p. 341).

Participants

Participants were "selected on the basis of expectations about their information content" (Flyvbjerg, 2011, p. 307) and with informed consent. A cohort of Jamaican graduate student-practitioners serving PK-12 grade levels, who participated in the Master's in Curriculum & Instruction program at FIU in Jamaica, were selected to analyze their respective journeys toward becoming more thoughtful "thinking" practitioners. The cohort of degree candidates was a convenient sample, who worked in diverse educational settings, including early childhood, elementary, middle school, high school, vocational, counseling, and so forth (see Table 8.1).

Table 8.1 EDE 6205 Participant Demographic Data: Teaching Level, Education Level, Gender, & Age

Participants

Teaching Level	Education Level	Gender	Age
Primary-5	Bachelor-16	Female-16	20 to 29-3
Middle-2			30 to 39-10
High School-9			40 to 59-3

All 16 participants were female and had bachelors' degrees. Seven taught at primary or middle school levels, while nine taught at the high school level. Three participants' ages were in their 20s, ten were in their 30s, and three were in their 40s or 50s.

Curriculum and Instruction

The EDE 6205 curriculum and instruction course was designed to engage candidates (who are practitioners at the same time) in self-reflection about their current teaching philosophy and practice. Also, the course was designed to engage the participants in awareness, valuing, and self-reflection of shifts in their teachers' discourse. Shifts teachers' discourse included teacher practices that engaged their students cognitively after experiencing the power of HoM, VT, and TfU ideas in their own learning. Decisions for the course design with these end goals in mind included: planning for teachers/master's degree candidates' learning outcomes, understanding goals, and performances of understanding.

Learning Outcomes. Candidates' learning outcomes followed the FIU COE Conceptual Framework (CF) as follows:

Stewards of the Discipline (knowledge)—having the necessary concepts, knowledge and understandings in their respective field of study.

*R*eflective Inquirers (skills)—knowing how to use the requisite generic skills needed to apply the content and pedagogical.

*M*indful Educators (Dispositions)—being able to apply the dispositions, that is, habits of mind (intellectual and social) that render professional actions and conduct more intelligent.

Based on the CF, EDE 6205 included the following understanding goals and performances of understanding.

Understanding Goals

Specific understanding goals for this course include the following:

Knowledge. Understand and appreciate various approaches and philosophies used in curriculum development and decision making. Understand theories of child development and principles of learning. Understand how to create, design, and improve a course outline, unit and lesson plans to promote thinking and learning.

Skills. Develop the skills required to create, design, and improve a course outline, unit and lesson plans to promote thinking and learning. Develop effective teaching methods to design appropriate creative learning experiences for children including ESOL, ESE and LEP, and culturally diverse backgrounds.

Dispositions. Disposed to understand, broaden, expand, and improve their knowledge of curriculum development and theory both locally and within the international/global context to create thinking dispositions for teaching and learning.

Performances of Understanding

Specific performances of understanding or projects included the following:

Reading Log. Candidates were required to reflect on the course readings by addressing the HoM that they used to understand the topic. They also had to analyze how and why they used that particular HoM. They also were required to post one question for discussion about each chapter, following Arthur Costa's levels of questioning. During each session, the candidates and professor analyzed the students' questions according to Costa's levels of questioning, which led the discussion in the EDE 6205 class.

Self-Reflections. Each participant was required to document her practice in journals and audio/video documentary tools every week and analyze her documentation of practices and reflections in the Habits of Mind framework. Participants were given the option to have someone visit their class and videotape them, audiotape them, or write down their interactions with their students as documentation. Each candidate also was required to elaborate concerning her individual reflections and make conclusions about her understandings, skill development, and dispositions in a final paper using guiding questions provided them. This process encouraged the candidates to revisit their learning journeys and reflect on the growth and changes in their discourse in their classrooms and work setting. Some of the guiding questions for this assignment were as follows:

In a few words, describe your teacher discourse in your classroom.

How have the Habits of Mind and Visible Thinking influenced your teaching and learning philosophy?

What changes have you observed in your teaching discourse in the classroom as a result of internalizing HOM and the VT ideas?

How can you and/or your students describe your discourse in the classroom?

Wikis. This was a cooperative effort. The candidates were required to revisit their practice and analyze the implications of using the HoM, VT, and TfU in their classroom discourse using Wikis. Wikis is an online platform where each of the class members can add, modify, or delete its content via a web browser using a simplified markup language or a rich-text editor. The candidates were expected to contribute with questions, theory, connections between theory and practice, reflections, and discussion.

Collaborative Curriculum Unit. The candidates were required to design an integrated (Language Arts, Math, Social Studies, Science, Art, PE) developmentally appropriate thematic unit following the Teaching for Understanding framework. The candidates' task was to determine the grade level and select an attractive theme for children, to brainstorm all the possible outcomes that can emerge from this theme, decide to what degree they have clear, guiding, overarching questions which are central to a domain, connect the theme with goals for the year and standards, decide what is worth understanding, decide to what degree their understanding goals are clear and unique within each generative question, determine which specific understandings that they wanted to develop, decide what students should learn, decide to what degree they develop performances in which students are making their thinking visible and are developing their understandings, decide to what degree they are engaging students in cycles of formal and informal feedback with themselves, others, and the teacher around their actions to develop their understandings over time, decide how they would assess children's understanding; and decide the standards that would be covered in the unit.

Data Collection and Analysis Procedures

The authors triangulated the data from the performances of understanding listed above which were collected and analyzed through thematic analysis. Each author read all data, searching for meaningful categories, or recurring themes and patterns, in teachers' discourse that emerged to answer their research question (Pane, 2009). Upon combining and indexing both authors' analyses, two emergent themes were agreed upon: (a) shifts in participants' philosophies and (b) shifts in participants' discourse.

Shifts in Teachers/Master's Degree Candidates' Philosophies

The participants' stories of teaching and learning experiences reflected their philosophies about teaching and learning coming into the course. Interestingly, these stories were in many cases similar to our examples of children's and teachers' common responses to didactic teaching and learning philosophies in many schools (see Appendix 8.1). The participants' self-reflected about how they saw themselves before learning the philosophies, teaching approaches, and reflective tools inherent in the three inter-related frameworks (i.e., HoM, Visible Thinking, and Teaching for Understanding), and the shift in their teaching and learning philosophies as reflected in their practices and as they engaged in self-awareness and valuing dimensions of self-growth. As strong believers in social constructivist approaches that engage children cognitively, we created the story of a learning experience in a group of teachers/master's degree candidates, who are practitioners in different fields. A representative sample of the participants' (note each participant's name is a pseudonym) stories/self-reflections about their teaching philosophies follow:

Adela: "My philosophy has been influenced in that I now believe that I can engage students in substantive discussion and make their thinking visible by the things they produce. My new routines make it easier for me to discover incorrect perceptions of content and promote a deeper learning experience. Visible thinking enables me to ask questions that expose how my students are thinking, assimilating ideas thus interpreting the new information. This helps me to make connections."

Cassidy: "Constructivist approach...is now a part of all the lessons that I teach. I have my students doing problem solving and working collaboratively with each other. They are now learning about the big picture and transferring their skills and understanding to the other disciplines. I am no longer a drill master but a facilitator."

Varenia: "The language of cognition is at the center stage of my teaching learning programs in order to create an ambience or classroom culture that positions meta-cognitive skills at the fore to make thinking become visible."

Germaine: "I now strive to be more self-reflective more attuned to situations in my classroom and I am generally more skillful and strategic in solving problems particularly in my professional practice."

Verona: "I am now able to focus on ways to nurture my students' thinking skills and improve their level of understanding....now that I know that thinking can be taught, I try to identify the types of thinking I want my students to engage in and plan my class activities accordingly."

Sabel: "My philosophy was, "I teach, you learn." When students did not learn it was because they were lazy and it was no fault of mine....The VT routines and HoM engendered partnerships that enhanced students' understanding of concepts, confidence levels and respect for each other. I now witness pleasant, eager and animated faces that suggest renewed interest in the subject by the students. My methodology took on added dimensions in that, I do not engage in 'telling' anymore, instead I make an effort to formulate questions that I use to provoke the students' thinking process during their responses."

Shifts in Teachers/Master's Degree Candidates' Discourse

Each candidate reflected on her teacher discourse. A representative sample of reflections are as follows:

Marina: "Data collected in the form my teacher's journal, interviews with teachers and pupils supported that my discourse in the classroom was not geared towards students' understanding and student autonomy. It was, however, overwhelmingly focused on student motivation to complete the content of the prescribed curriculum in the time allotted. This resulted in instances of self-handicapping by the pupils because they said that they sometimes felt overwhelmed by my efforts at curriculum coverage. The data regarding also revealed that students were generally not encouraged to be very reflective and to critically evaluate knowledge acquired. It also provided limited opportunity for my pupils to examine how meaning was constructed and negotiated. Furthermore, language did not play in pivotal role in this constructed knowledge. Additionally, students did not assume the primary responsibility for solving their problems. They were instead asked to mostly supply answers to discrete steps and questions. They were also not given the occasion to verbalize their thinking."

Marina: "After internalizing the Habits of mind and Visible thinking my teaching and learning philosophy has changed. I have gained insight into the enhancement of children's cognitive development. I now know that posing more significant questions that probe pupils' thinking, and using specific jargon or new labels to tailor their perceptions will effect positive change or generate success in my teaching and learning programs."

Amelia: "My discourse is now one the language of cognition is at center stage of my teaching learning programs in order to create an ambience or classroom culture that positions meta-cognitive skills at the fore to make thinking become visible. I now practice to pose critical questions, use precise terminology, and provide data and not solutions to make pupils assume the initiative for taking the required action which will lead them being more responsible for solving their own academic problems. Through the habits of mind I have changed my approach in treating situations. I now strive to be more self-reflective more attuned to situations in my classroom and I am generally more skillful and strategic in solving problems particularly in my professional life. Before learning about the habits of mind and visual thinking I was easily discouraged and frustrated when my students encountered difficulty understanding concepts being taught. I would sometimes just stand and look at them or ask firmly "*What is it that you don't understand?*""

Nancy: "Now, I think this course should be offered to all teachers in training as it content thereof is quite powerful and critical to the effective functioning of the teaching learning process to be explored only at the master degree level. The content of this course has enriched my life as an educator in so many ways. I think the knowledge and understanding regarding the approaches of teaching for students understanding, fostering visible thinking in students and teaching them to use the habit of mind to develop flexible approaches to solve problem and monitor their understanding has empowered me as an educator. I am now able to teach and relate to my students with more confidence. The knowledge I have gained makes me more conscious of the needs of the children I teach, particularly in preparing lessons instruction, helping them to become critical thinkers and craft understanding of content. This I believe, will help to determine successful end results as I am more proficient in structuring my lessons to suit my students varied learning styles. My level of maturity has also been improved as I have develop a higher level of cognition in order to understand most of the content I am given. It makes me more analytical, reflective and evaluative of the teaching discourse I employed in my classroom."

Some of the teachers' reflections provided evidence to us that they seemed to be beginning to internalize the HoM by providing justification for their actions, thoughts, and discourse in their classrooms. It is also interesting that the participants' student responses, which are not included in this chapter due to space limitations, showed that they seemed to recognize some of their teachers' shifts in discourse and practices.

Conclusions

Based upon our analysis of the data and conversations with the participants in the study, a growth pattern was emerging for participants away from didactic teaching toward dialogical and dialectical thinking and teaching approaches. Our implementation of Habits of Mind (HoM), using Visible Thinking (VT) and the Teaching for Understanding (TfU) frameworks in EDE 6205 seemed to provide not only awareness for candidates to try out the approaches we modeled, but the candidates' reflections provided evidence of their building commitment to the values of teaching dialogical and dialectical thinking and discourse. One of the participants said that it was a life-changing experience. There was a pattern in teachers' reflections that they had become more aware that they could teach children to think. Furthermore, candidates reflected on the dialogical and dialectical thinking model that they were now using to view both their students and themselves as learners and thinkers. One of the candidates said, "How can teachers teach students how to think if they are not thinkers themselves?"

Candidates appeared to be in a process of changing their perspectives about teachers' and students' roles in the teaching and learning process. Participants revisited their core values and shifted the focus away from their role in the education process (as knowledge givers) to the importance of the learners' role (as problem finders, posers, and solvers) in the education process. One candidate said, "I became aware of my role in the classroom as an instructor who guides pupils to be more engaged in the performances of their own understanding."

Participants were engaged in a process toward internalization of the knowledge, skills, and dispositions inherent in HoM, VT, and TfU frameworks and our instructional approaches in EDE 6205. Evidence indicated that our course was influential in helping the candidates' build commitment to begin the process of shifting in their philosophies of teaching and learning away from didactic to dialogical and dialectical approaches. In the captured data, the participants expectations about their students were changing and their students were able to notice some of the changes. One of the candidates reflected, "My expectations of the students have changed and they are able to live up to this expectation. The response from my students is that the topics are more exciting because they are allowed to participate more." Candidates saw changes from a teacher-centered to a student-centered approach. They recognized the importance of teaching children to think by modeling. Another candidate reflected: "The way we think, interact, model, assess the opportunities we use, the documentation we do, the expectations, the role we take on, the culture we create, the way we plan, the theories we use, and the way we think shapes the discourse in our classroom. Students normally imitate and behave according to their environment (culture)."

The authors strongly believe that good practices do not require complicated methodologies but an understanding of the essence of human beings and their ability to think and act intelligently. Thus, most of the performances of understanding used for this study led to a collaborative construction of meaning where all participants' thoughts were valued and respected.. Giving participants the opportunity to experience how thinking can be taught through HoM and theVT approach within the TfU framework also provided them with a strong foundation for understanding how thinking about thinking can create powerful learning. The story told in this course revealed how the students began to build thinking dispositions and create a culture of thinking that eventually, as they bring them to practice, they can internalize it and set the mantra of their classroom. The shift toward a dialogical and dialectical thinking perspective will enhance teaching and learning and increases students' self-esteem. As a consequence, students will be more intrinsically engaged and challenged to learn in depth and, most of all, develop a joy for learning.

References

Blyte, B., & Associates. (1998). *The Teaching for Understanding Guide*. San Francisco, CA: Jossey-Bass.

Chase, S. E. (2011). Narrative inquiry: Still a field in the making. In N. K. Denzin & Y. S. Lincoln (Eds.). *The Sage handbook of qualitative research* (4th ed.) (pp. 421-434). Los Angeles, CA: Sage.

Costa, A. (2001). *Developing minds: A resource book for teaching thinking*. Alexandria: Virginia. Association for Supervision and Curriculum Development.

Costa, A., & Kallick, B. (Eds.). (2008*). Learning and leading with habits of mind: 16 essential characteristics for success*. Alexandria: Virginia. Association for Supervision and Curriculum Development.

Costa, A., & Kallick, B. (Eds.). (2009). *Habits of mind across the curriculum: Practical and creative strategies for teachers*. Alexandria: Virginia, Association for Supervision and Curriculum Development.

Denzin, N. K., & Lincoln, Y. S. (Eds.) (2011). Introduction: The discipline and practice of qualitative research. In N. K. Denzin & Y. S. Lincoln, *The Sage handbook of qualitative research* (4th ed.) (pp. 1-19). Los Angeles, CA: Sage.

Dottin, E. (2010). Dispositions as Habits of Mind: Making Professional Conduct More Intelligent. New York: University Press of America.

Flyvbjerg, B. (2011). Case study. In N. K. Denzin & Y. S. Lincoln (Eds.). The Sage handbook of qualitative research (4th ed.) (pp. 301-316). Los Angeles, CA: Sage.

Fogarty, R. (2001). Our changing perspective of intelligence: Master architects of the intellect. In In Costa, A. (Ed.) (2001). *Developing minds: A resource book for teaching thinking* (pp. 427-436). Alexandria: Virginia. Association for Supervision and Curriculum Development.

Freire, P. (2000). *Pedagogy of the oppressed*. New York, NY: Continuum.

Holstein, J. A., & Gubrium, J. F. (2011). The constructionist analytics of interpretive practice. In N. K. Denzin & Y. S. Lincoln (Eds.). *The Sage handbook of qualitative research* (4th ed.) (pp. 341-355). Los Angeles, CA: Sage.

National Council for Teachers of English. (2012). *Position statement on the definition of 21st century literacies*. Retrieved from http://www.ncte.org/positions/statements/21stcentdefinition.

Pane, D. M. (2009). *The relationship between classroom interactions and exclusionary discipline as a social practice: A critical microethnography*. FIU Electronic Theses and Dissertations. Paper 109. Available at http://digitalcommons.fiu.edu/etd/109

Paul, R. (2001). Dialogic and dialectical thinking. In Costa, A. (Ed.) (2001). *Developing minds: A resource book for teaching thinking* (pp. 427-436). Alexandria: Virginia. Association for Supervision and Curriculum Development.

Perkins, D. (1992). *Smart schools: From training memories to educating minds*. New York: Free Press.

Perkins, D. (2001). Thinking for understanding. In Costa, A. (Ed.) (2001). *Developing minds: A resource book for teaching thinking* (pp. 446-450). Alexandria: Virginia. Association for Supervision and Curriculum Development.

Perkins, D. (2009). *Making learning whole: How seven principles of teaching can transform education*. San Francisco, Jossey-Bass.

Rex. L. A. (Ed.). (2006). *Discourse of opportunity: How talk in learning situations creates and constrains*. Cresskill, NJ: Hampton Press.

Rex, L. A., & Schiller, L. (2009). *Using discourse analysis to improve classroom interaction*. New York, NY: Routledge.

Ritchhart, R. (2002). Intellectual character. What it is, why it matters, and how to get it. San Francisco, CA: Jossey-Bass.

Ritchhart, R., Church, M. & Morrison, K. (2011). *Making thinking visible: How to promote engagement, understanding, and independence for all learners.* San Francisco: Jossey-Bass.

Ritchhart, R. (2011). *Creating Powerful Learning Opportunities.* Keynote address presented to the Clarice Smith National Teacher Institute, Smithsonian American Art Museum. Retrieved from http://ronritchhart.com/Presentations_files /Smithsonian_Opportunities2_2.pdf

Ritchhart, R., & Perkins, D. N. (2008). Making thinking visible. *Educational Leadership,* *65*(5), 57-61.

Ritchhart, R., Turner, T., & Hadar, L. (2009). Uncovering students' thinking about thinking using concept maps. *Metacognition Learning* (2009) *4,* 145–159. DOI 10.1007/s11409-009-9040-x. Retrieved from http://edci6304fa2010learning cognition.pbworks.com/f/Ritchart%2Bet%2Bal%2B2009%2Bmetacognition%2Bins truction.pdf

Salmon, A. & Lucas, T. (2011). Exploring young children's conceptions about thinking. *Journal of Research in Childhood Education, 25,* 364-375. DOI: 10.1080/02568543.2011.605206

The Critical Thinking Community. (2012). *Glossary of critical thinking terms.* Retrieved from http://www.criticalthinking.org/pages/glossary-of-critical-thinking-terms/496

Tishman, S., Perkins, D. & Jay, E. (1995). *The thinking classroom: Learning and thinking in a culture of thinking.* Boston: Allyn and Bacon.

Vygotsky, L. (1978). Mind in society: *The development of psychological processes.* Cambridge, MA, Harvard University Press.

Visible Thinking (VT). (2012). Retrieved from http://pzweb.harvard.edu/vt/Visible Thinking_html_files/03_ThinkingRoutines/03a_ThinkingRoutines.html

Appendix 8.1

EDE 6205 Stories from the Authors' Personal Experiences Reflecting Didactic Teaching Theory

We provide four stories from the authors' personal experiences to illustrate the implications of a didactic teaching approach. The first is a common story in many settings where teachers deliver content through methods courses. Upon completing a unit lesson about matter, the first author had a conversation with her seven-year-old daughter, Nichole, asking her what she understood about this topic. With great pride, Nicole took the book and recited all the information that she had memorized while pointing to the images. In her telling, she mentioned that solids cannot adapt to any shape. When asked her to explain why solids cannot take a container's shape, Nicole's response was, "Because solids are solids." Then the first author asked Nicole, "What makes you say that?" And she replied a little bit reluctantly, "This question is not in the book."

A different way of seeing didactic teaching is the teaching-as-transmission view. This view plays out in our language when we talk about teacher training, which usually means training in new methods (Ritchhart, Church, & Morrison, 2011). In this case, the message that children get from the teacher is that learning is getting facts that they can retain in their short term memory. The rest of the story about the unit lesson about matter illustrates this message. Two months after getting an "A" in this lesson, the first author asked Nichole to explain what she understood about matter, but this time she was only able to tell me that there are three types of matter—solid, liquid, and gas—without understanding or being able to transfer knowledge from one context to another. When students are not cognitively challenged to be curious and to pose and solve problems using their imagination and creativity, learning is neither attractive nor retained.

Another story of learning (that results from didactic teaching) was told by Athena, a four-year-old who was the "Student of the "Month" in her preschool. While she was preparing a cardboard illustrating her portrait and her favorite things, her grandmother asked her, "Why do you think you were awarded the "Student of the Month?" The child's answer was, "Because I don't talk anymore." Teachers' common complaint about children is that they are always talking. Isn't talking important in the learning process?

As children grow, they become more talkative and teachers spend a lot of time and energy trying to control the students' participation (Ritchhart, 2011). A fourth story drawn from a research study conducted by Debora Pane reveals the implications of didactic teaching from two language arts classrooms in an alternative education secondary school. When asked to share a typical day in school, both teachers' mere discourse was about their ongoing struggle to control students' academic and social behavior (Pane, 2009). Ms. Gomez explained:

I have to come up with some way to trick these kids into learning something new that day because most of the time, you know, they just fight me on it or they want to sleep or they want to talk or they just don't want to do it so but you know, I've gone through in the three years that I've been teaching, I've tried pretty much everything. I've tried bribing them, I've tried threatening them, I've tried babying them, you know, anything that I can, sometimes with some kids certain tactics work, but with most of them, I still don't know how to get through to them. A lot of them.

Mr. Glass stressed that alternative education students only come to school to socialize, they come to hang out, they do not come with a mindset to study, or to do conceptual academic work . . . They love busywork or what I would call handouts that do that do not require them to do much more than fill in the blanks, copy material from the board, that they consider I did my work I should get an A or I should get a B . . . . This is my personal opinion to this entitlement mentality, that the kid or the student can dictate to you what they will do and how they will do it and I don't accept that so they then are forced to either adopt my expectations or fight me on it and a lot of kids will choose to fight me on it and so we will wind up with kids going to detention.

Both teachers' discourse revealed preconceptions of alternative education students as poorly behaved and academically challenged. Teachers' discourse revealed educational practices that provided few spaces for students' conceptual understandings to emerge and develop over time in a culture of thinking (Ritchart, 2011). For example, to maintain control in the classroom, Ms. Gomez took rigorous anecdotal notes on students' behavior and filled out referral forms regularly while trying to get students to practice for the high-stakes test. She anticipated disruptive behavior and, thus, planned to either use her psychology background knowledge to rehabilitate students or to issue written referrals to suspend students from class (exclusionary discipline) when she ran out of options. On the other hand, Mr. Glass controlled his classroom by first ridding the classroom of disruptive students (suspension, exclusionary discipline) who he felt did not care about learning that day. Then, he lectured continuously to the remaining student(s) about the lives and works of great authors and helped them fill in one-word answers or select the correct multiple choice answers on tests based on his lectures.

Both teachers' discourse and practices abided strictly by didactic views of teaching and learning that sustained the mainstream ideology about alternative education students as those who need to be disciplined or cured of their social and academic deficiencies (Freire, 2000). However, each teacher's discourse differed in how and why he or she focused solely on gaining control in the classroom. Ms. Gomez used language arts requirements for passing the high-stakes test as a backdrop for listening to students talk among each other in order to figure out ways to reduce hostility among her students. Mr. Glass used his expertise in lecturing about great authors and their works of literature as a backdrop for keeping his students compliant and quiet. Even though each classroom sounded (i.e., loud versus quiet) different, both teachers endorsed didactic teaching and learning practices that required passive students and used exclusionary discipline to control student behavior. Neither teacher's discourse considered thinking as the mantra of the class. As a result, both teachers strived continually for more control, ultimately removing (suspending) students to stop conflicts and discord in their classrooms.

Appendix 8.2

Interpretation of the close relationship between TRs and the HoM

SEE/THINK/WONDER. This routine encourages students to make careful observations and thoughtful interpretations; it sets the stage for inquiry, using the following questions:
- What do you see?
- What do you think? and
- What do you wonder?
    HoM that are present in the *SEE/THINK/WONDER* routine include but are not limited to the following:
- Persisting—going back to an image over and over again;
- Listening to others—as people share their observations, thoughts and inquiries, others listen and try to understand with empathy;
- Thinking flexibly—while sharing observations, thoughts and inquiries, people have the capacity to change their minds;
- Questioning and posing problems—upon observing and thinking, people ask questions about what they know and they don't know;
- Applying past knowledge to new situations—while observing, people connect images with prior knowledge or experiences;
- Gathering data though all senses—using any type of prop (e.g., artwork, science experiment, photograph, essay, music piece, dance), people can collect data with any of their senses (e.g., what do you feel/smell/hear/taste?); and
- Thinking interdependently—since people have different perspectives, they can interpret things differently when they are prompted to think or wonder about things.

WHAT MAKES YOU SAY THAT? This routine encourages interpretation with justification, using the following questions:
- What is going on? and
- What do you see that makes you say that?
    HoM that are present in the *WHAT MAKES YOU SAY THAT?* routine include but are not limited to the following:
- Thinking with clarity and thinking about thinking—with these questions, people have to plan what they want to say and reflect on their thoughts. They have to use their ability to know what they know and what they don't know.
- Gathering data though all senses—people have to gather data to justify any claim with evidence;

- Taking responsible risks—people take the opportunity to get a message through, based on prior knowledge and experience;
- Striving for accuracy—people have to check over their messages for accuracy, they have to invest more thinking;
- Managing impulsivity—when people know that they will be asked these types of questions, they think before they act or say something.
- Learning continuously— when people are allowed to revisit their thoughts before saying something, they are always modifying and improving themselves; and
- Applying past knowledge to new situations—people learn from experience. When confronted with these questions they have to make connections with past experiences.

I USED TO THINK . . . BUT NOW I THINK. This routine is used to reflect on how and why our thinking has changed, by reminding students of the topic that is being considered and having students write a response using the following sentences stems:
- I used to think,
- Now I think.
  HoM that are present in the *I USED TO THINK . . . BUT NOW I THINK* routine include but are not limited to the following:
- Metacognition—people have to reflect on their thinking and see changes;
- Apply past knowledge—people assess prior conceptions and see the evolution of their thoughts; and
- Question & posing problems—people examine an old problem from a new angle.

CONNECT/EXTEND/CHALLENGE. This routine is used for connecting new ideas to prior knowledge by using the following questions:
- Connect—How are these ideas and information presented connected to what you already knew?
- Extend—What ideas did you get that extended or pushed your thinking in new directions?
- Challenge—What is still challenging or confusing for you to get your mind around?
  What questions, wondering or puzzles do you now have?
  HoM that are present in the *CONNECT/EXTEND/CHALLENGE* routine include but are not limited to the following:
- Applying past knowledge to new situations—when confronting to a new problem, people have to draw from prior experiences;
- Responding with wonderment and awe—when trying to find solutions to problems, people are delighted to solve problems on their own and request enigmas from others;

- Creating, imagining and innovating—by identifying problems and seeing their thoughts taking new directions, people are innovating themselves;
- Learning continuously—by asking these questions with new ideas, people learn continuously;
- Questions & posing problems—when people identify a challenge, they are developing the ability to find problems to solve, look for evidence, find reliable data sources;
- Thinking flexibly—flexible people can make shifts as they extend their thoughts; and
- Taking responsible risks—by making connections, extending thoughts and finding challenges, people are self-reflecting before taking risks to adventure new areas of their thinking.

CIRCLE OF VIEWPOINTS. This routine is used for exploring diverse perspectives by brainstorming a list of different perspectives, then exploring each one with the following script skeleton:
- I am thinking of . . . the topic . . . From the point of view of . . . the viewpoint you've chosen;
- I think . . . describe the topic from your viewpoint. Be an actor—take on the character of your viewpoint ;
- A question I have from this viewpoint is . . . ask a question from this viewpoint; and
- Wrap up: What new ideas do you have about the topic that you didn't have before? What new questions do you have?
  HoM that are present in the *CIRCLE OF VIEWPOINTS* routine include but are not limited to the following:
- Listening with understanding and empathy—by exploring the view point of others, people are able to appreciate diverse perspectives;
- Thinking flexibly— by exploring the view point of others, people's minds are open to change based on additional information and data or reasoning, which contradicts their beliefs;
- Questioning and posing problems—by exploring the view point of others, people pose questions about alternative points of view;
- Applying past knowledge to new situations—when confronted with a new point of view, people will often draw forth experience from their past;
- Creating, imagining, innovating—creative human beings try to conceive problem solutions differently, examining alternative possibilities from many points of view;
- Remaining open to continuous learning—by adopting a new perspective, people seize problems, situations, tensions, conflicts and circumstances as valuable opportunities to learn; and
- Thinking interdependently—by adopting others' view points, people can have access to new data to make critical decisions.

Table 8.2
A Summary of the Relationship Between the Habits of Mind and Thinking Routines

Habits of Mind	Thinking Routines			
	2	3	4	5
Persisting				
Managing Impulsivity	X			
Listening with Understanding and Empathy				X
Thinking Flexibly			X	X
Thinking about Thinking; Metacognition	X	X		
Striving for Accuracy	X			
Questioning and Posing Problems		X	X	X
Applying Past Knowledge to New Situations	X	X	X	X
Thinking and Communicating with Clarity and Precision	X			

Thinking Routines
1. See/Think/Wonder
2. What Makes You Say That?
3. I Used To Think…But Now I Think
4. Connect/Extend/Challenge
5. Circle of Viewpoints

Within the process of making connections between HoM and RTs, it was important to highlight the type of thinking that was taking place. We strongly believe that the Thinking Routines are excellent strategies to cultivate Habits of Mind and engage children in deep thinking and understanding.

CHAPTER NINE

Physical Activity, Sports, and the Habits of Mind

By

Charmaine DeFrancesco

According to the National Association for Sport and Physical Education (NASPE), the purpose of any physical education program is to assist individuals in developing the knowledge, skills and dispositions to take pleasure in participating in physical activity throughout their lifespan (NASPE, 2004). This purpose is directly aligned with one of the primary charges in the mission statement of the College of Education at Florida International University: "…to prepare professionals who have the knowledge, abilities, and dispositions to facilitate and enhance learning and development within diverse settings" ("The Conceptual Framework of the College of Education," n.d., p.4). Seasoned professors of sport and physical education will agree that most students (referred to as candidates in teacher education) will learn content knowledge and physical skills without too much difficulty; however, helping them to develop mindful behaviors is a different story all together.

This chapter will focus on how the Habits of Mind (HoM) as described by Costa and Kallick (2000) can be embedded into physical education and coaching programs to help students and other participants become more mindful in their professional practices. A general overview of the environmental influences and the unique opportunities that make physical education and sport natural venues to teach students and professionals how to be aware of, value and internalize the HoM will be presented, followed by an applied course-related example used to facilitate positive behavioral and intellectual changes among candidates. The final discussion will focus on improvement strategies that could be used to further promote the development of the HoM in candidates.

Environmental Influences. Over 55 years ago, Benjamin Bloom and his colleagues (Bloom & Krathwohl, 1956) identified three domains or categories in which learning occurs. These consist of the cognitive, affective and psychomotor domains. Educational institutions at all levels within the United States focus consistently on the cognitive domain because it is "knowledge-based". The affective domain is attitudinally-based, and it is typically related to developing appropriate classroom behaviors within school-based settings. The slogan *"Behavior Counts"* can be seen on bulletin boards and office doors in many educational institutions. In its purest sense, the psychomotor domain spotlights the development of motor skills, although lately, physical educators have included the development of health-related fitness components into it. It is the forgotten domain because other than early child professionals, most educators seldom recognize the importance of its relationship to the other domains in the holistic development of individuals across their lifetime.

Unfortunately, and due in part to the emergence of high-stakes testing, reduced school budgets and the limited interdisciplinary knowledge of educational administrators and classroom teachers, learning and development within the psychomotor domain (i.e., physical education) has all but been eliminated from educational requirements. NASPE (2006) reported that most school-based physical education courses have over 40 students participating in each class because school districts choose to reduce the number and quality of "periphery" classes rather than "academically relevant" classes (i.e., those essential to the performance of high-stakes testing) when economic conditions plunge. Currently, most elementary students across the country participate in physical education only one or two days a week. Furthermore, because of these reduced educational requirements and limited athletic budgets, the average adolescent receives more than 80% of his or her physical activity participating in out of school programs (Parker, 2012). The most adverse aspect of out of school sport and physical activity programs is that many of the coaches and program leaders do not have any formal training in teaching, coaching or physical education (Wiersma & Sherman, 2005), and fewer still have had no experiences teaching or coaching students with diverse needs (Moran & Block, 2010). Entry-level candidates, therefore, have developed their beliefs and knowledge about teaching physical education and coaching from individuals who are self-trained or who model their teaching and coaching behaviors from what they have witnessed from media outlets. Teacher education candidates frequently come into the program with ideas and behaviors that are at best, void of anything related to "best practices" in teaching physical education and coaching.

Uniqueness. As stated previously, many individuals receive much of their physical activity in non-school sponsored activities, but that does not negate the fact that over 7.5 million students participate in sponsored high school sport programs, including those for students with disabilities (National Federation of State High School Associations, 2011). The United States is one of the few countries across the globe that chooses to incorporate sport programs and athletic development into its educational system. The goodness of fit of this strategy is debatable, but it does provide a unique environment to introduce individuals to the HoM. Moreover, most student-athletes will tend to value the HoM once they become aware of them because they can readily apply the behaviors to accelerate their skill development and improve competition outcomes. Several of the HoM are critical for athletic development. For example, any time an individual begins to learn a new motor skill or sport-related performance strategy, he or she will fail considerably at performing it correctly for a prolonged period of time. Persistence is required during the learning process until the skill or strategy becomes automatic. While this is true for learning across domains, in sport there are more losers than winners (e.g., a baseball player with a excellent batting average will fail approximately 65-70% of the time) and as such, the capability for individuals to continue after significant failures is critical for skill improvement to occur.

Coaches can also work with classroom teachers to promote the HoM during their subject-area lessons. Students interested in developing their sport skills may be less enthusiastic when it comes to "academic" learning let alone practicing the HoM in regular classroom environments, and this is particularly true in urban school districts and areas that are economically depressed (McCaughtry, Barnard, Martin, Shen & Kulinna, 2006; Messner, 2009). But, if students realize that practicing the HoM to improve sport performance can be accomplished in different contexts, they may become more committed to using them within the classroom too. This assumes however, that there will be interdisciplinary dialogue among teachers and coaches across subject areas. It is paramount to begin the journey of developing habits by getting students to be mindful and think about their own thinking (Dottin, 2010).

Physical Activity, Sport & the Habits of Mind. The College of Education at Florida International University, has three general student-learning outcomes. We want our candidates to become "stewards of the discipline" who possess the appropriate content knowledge needed to teach physical education and coach individuals appropriately. We also want our students to become "reflective practitioners" who can think critically and insightfully and who are sensitive to cultural differences. We want our students to develop into "mindful educators" who are disposed toward improving the condition of all learners within the communities in which they serve. These outcomes are not developed independently. In the college, full and part-time faculty have worked together to develop consistent teaching platforms that promote the successful attainment and inter-connectiveness of student learning outcomes with emphasis on making the conduct of teacher education candidates more intelligent.

The College of Education has identified 12 of the 16 HoM described by Costa and Kallick (2000) as being crucial to its learning outcome for candidates to be mindful educators (The Conceptual Framework of the College of Education," n.d.). These HoM are also critical to physical activity and sport participant outcomes. The faculty in the college has the freedom to independently decide on which of the 12 HoM to focus in each of their courses. I choose to focus on six HoM, as I believe that most of our candidates, regardless of if they want to teach physical education within the schools or coach (or do both) will embrace the importance of developing these habits within themselves and have the willingness to assist their students and athletes to do the same. The habits on which I focus are:

1. Persistence
2. Managing impulsivity
3. Thinking flexibly

4. Striving for accuracy and precision
5. Applying past knowledge to new situations (transfer)
6. Thinking and communicating with clarity and precision

Most physical educators and athletic coaches will agree that these HoM are significantly relevant to the learning and performance of motor skills. More important to this discussion, most individuals who lack formal training in coaching would also be inclined to believe that these attributes are necessary for high level athletic performance, and this makes it fairly simple to get our candidates to value these HoM. Motor Learning and Development is an upper division core course for our K-12 Physical Education teacher certification program and the Sports and Fitness track that focuses on developing professionals to work as coaches or fitness leaders. It is not a methods (i.e., how to teach) course per se. It is content-based and conceptual, and it challenges students to think reflectively and with purpose. This course addresses and evaluates how well our candidates meet the three learning outcomes of the College. I teach this course, and embed HoM into course lectures, discussions and assignments.

An Applied Course-related Example. The Motor Learning and Development (MLD) course focuses on introducing candidates to the basic concepts involved with learning and performing motor skills. We examine foundational influences behind the study of motor development (i.e., what individuals "should" be able to do based on their cognitive, affective and physical development across the lifespan) and motor learning (i.e., the "personal" and "situational" factors that impact how quickly and how well one learns motor skills and sport-related strategies). MLD emphasizes the interrelatedness of learning and development within the cognitive, affective and psychomotor domains (see Figure 9.1), although initially, we review what comprises each domain independently. We review related research and theoretical aspects of each domain before we examine the interconnectedness of learning and development. Each domain-related discussion has a practical, field-based observational component attached to it and when combined, these observations help students develop their final projects (See Appendices 9.1 and 9.2). The field observations are conducted in small groups, and the exercise directs the candidates' attention to focus on relevant aspects of previous class discussions. Field placements are approved by the instructor to ensure that the candidates are observing seasoned and formally trained teachers and coaches. Many of the field observations take place at schools where our part-time faculty hold full-time teaching positions. This arrangement is particularly helpful in assisting our candidates bridge the gap between theory and practice.

In this class, each domain is addressed and discussed in terms of its practical importance. For instance, when focusing on the cognitive domain, we examine Piaget's Theory of Cognitive Development (as cited in Payne & Isaacs, 2010) and we discuss how the four-stage theory impacts the scope and sequence of our teaching and coaching practices. Candidates also learn about what they can expect students and young athletes to achieve. For example, if the students' cognitive level has been assessed at the Concrete Operational Stage, they will have difficulty thinking hypothetically, which means teachers and coaches must communicate with clarity and precision (HoM) and not expect that the students will be able to comprehend elaborate sport-related strategies. During field observations, candidates are asked to evaluate and hypothesize which stage of Piaget's Theory the participants seem to have achieved so that they may better develop their lesson and coaching plans to meet the needs and abilities of the learners to improve their success rate which in turn, will increase their enjoyment.

When we discuss the affective domain, we study the importance of social interactions and cultural diversity. Candidates learn about the socialization process, social roles, expectations and individual differences. It is during this part of the course that students are challenged to manage their impulsivity and think flexibly. For example, questions such as "Should a female coach a boy's football team?" or "Why are there so many Hispanic baseball players?" or "Should there be separate categories in the Olympics for disabled athletes"? typically ignite serious discussions that are primarily opinion-based. At the start of these discussions, the arguments from students are offered spontaneously with only their past experiences serving as their supporting evidence. By the time students finish their assigned learning experiences and observations, they become more reflective and thoughtful, especially after being required to observe physical activities and social interactions from a different perspective than what was required from them previously.

Class discussions regarding the psychomotor domain begin with candidates learning about physical growth and maturation, and the process in which individuals learn motor skills using the three-phase model developed by Fitts and Posner (1967). The process involved with learning motor skills is very similar to the three phase progression of developing HoM as suggested by Costa and Kallick (2000). The first phase of the Fitts-Posner model (1967) is described as the cognitive phase. During this phase, learners form an understanding or awareness of what needs to be done to perform the skill. Learners will make considerable cognitive and movement errors during this phase and social reinforcement from teachers and coaches is a must to develop the student's persistence. The second phase requires the learner to practice the skill using internal and external feedback from teachers and coaches to help develop accuracy and precision. The final phase is the automatic phase where the learner performs the skill effortlessly without having to think about it. Costa and Kallick (2000) refer to this process as "internalization" and it occurs when the desired behavior becomes a habit.

Another concept that is a basic tenet of motor skill learning is transfer. The rate in which individuals learn and automate skills is enhanced if they see the value and connections of using information previously learned and applying it to new situations. In most educational contexts, this is referred to as the transfer of learning. In many sport situations, game strategies and basic concepts are transferable to many situations. For example, the skill of defending an opposing player may be transferred from the basketball court to the soccer field quite easily. The movements involved with performing an over arm throw are the same movements that are needed to successfully serve a tennis ball or complete a volleyball serve. If teachers and coaches can effectively communicate to their students and athletes that it is useful to apply past knowledge and skills to new situations, the chance for transfer to occur will be greatly improved. Transfer is a concept that our students become very familiar with during the MLD course.

Once our candidates have completed their related readings and observations, they are ready to utilize their understandings, skills and dispositions gained throughout the MLD course to create their practice or lesson plans (See Appendix 9.2). This project serves as the artifact for this course. The majority of the candidates do quite well in this assignment even though there is considerable content and off-campus time involvement required for its satisfactory completion. Students become aware of the related HoM because as their instructor, I reference them regularly and provide them with related and relevant feedback each time they turn in an observational task. Quite frequently, students and I share discussions outside of the classroom too.

Although there are strong and seemingly inherent connections among several of the HoM and student learning outcomes related to the preparation of physical education teachers and coaches, it has been naïve of me and our faculty to assume that by embedding the HoM into courses that candidates would grasp the framework and develop the HoM that cultivate consistent intelligent professional behavior. Thanks to a professional development workshop facilitated by Drs. Arthur Costa and bena Kallick that I attended, I learned some strategies that will assist me, my colleagues and our students to embrace and better "work" the HoM.

Lessons Learned from a HoM Workshop. In February 2012, the College of Education sponsored a workshop entitled *Discovering and Exploring the Habits of Mind.* The workshop was organized by members of the Faculty Learning Community on Habits of Mind, of which I am a member, and was open to faculty members as well as to teachers and administrators from the local school district. One of ideas that I took away from that workshop was that neither I nor my content area colleagues were doing enough to make the HoM truly visible or workable for our candidates. Like transfer, there is more chance for students to recognize connections if they are instructed to do so. Demonstrating the HoM will not happen automatically, and these dispositions are too important in the holistic development of our students to leave acquisition to chance.

Program faculty must make the HoM outcomes clear to candidates. We cannot just hope that they develop the HoM. One of my senior colleagues once said to me during a discussion about the process of teaching and learning that "...hope is not a strategy..." As we work to revise our courses and activities we will need to intentionally include the HoM into our course syllabi, our lessons, assignments and our rubrics. We also need to follow the strategies identified on the HoM webpage (http://www.instituteforhabitsofmind.com/) and use the educational materials provided there to enhance our classes, program and candidate outcomes.

Additionally, we need, in the College, and our programs, to focus more on the 12 habits of mind articulated in the college's Conceptual Framework, and make certain that each of the HoM are addressed throughout the program as all are important to the holistic development and intellectual behaviors of our students. For example, since all physical activities include thinking proficiency, it makes sense to purposefully teach individuals critical thinking strategies by prompting them to them to be reflective in evaluating their own thoughts and movement outcomes. This practice facilitates the development of their metacognition (Rovegno & Bandhauer, 2013).

While I chose to embed six of the 12 HoM into the MLD, in the near future, there will be revisions made to deliberately make candidates more aware of them, and the remaining 6 HoM will also be infused into program courses with intent to overtly introduce them to our candidates. They will be included within the syllabi and students will have experiences that assist them see value in developing the HoM as personal attributes and establish connections to the content related to physical education, sport and physical activity. In each course, and similar to the process of learning motor skills, they will practice the HoM until they are able to apply them automatically within their professional and other daily activities.

As mentioned earlier, many of the HoM are critical to learning, performance and personal satisfaction gained from participating in sport and exercise activities. Sport psychology consultants refer to the systematic and consistent practice of mental skills as psychological skills training or PST (Weinberg & Gould, 2010). Several of the methods we use in PST were adopted from cognitive psychology which involves examining the perceptions, memory, thinking, speaking and problem-solving skills of individuals (Anderson, 2009). Because of this, HoM instruction would seem to be a natural and excellent addition to our physical education and sport curricula. The ultimate goal of PST is for athletes and exercisers to be able to self regulate their thoughts, feelings and behaviors to effectively and intelligently cope, adapt and perform in the vibrant world in which they compete (Weinberg & Gould, 2010) and this of course, is also the fundamental goal HoM development.

One method of teaching PST to athletes is to use a strategy known in the educational field as scaffolding. Scaffolding is an instructional approach where special prompts (e.g., images, reminders) and techniques (e.g., modeling, providing various types of instructional or performance feedback) are used by an expert (e.g., a teacher, coach, sport psychology consultant, or a talented student or athlete) to assist novices grasp the importance of what needs to be done to complete a movement successfully, improve their thinking skills and ultimately, increase their performance. Systematically and gradually, instructional prompts and guidance from the expert are removed during automatization of the skill. The scaffolding technique can also be readily employed to enhance education candidates' awareness, value of and internalization of the HoM.

Once it became clear to me that our candidates could be introduced, practice and internalize the HoM using sport and exercise discussions and activities, I made a commitment to revise my materials to reflect that decision. However, and like in most disciplines, not all faculty have agreed to make appropriate modifications in their course materials or their instructional methods and this is quite problematic when we conduct program and candidate assessments. As pointed out by Dottin (2010), "… candidates must be provided opportunities to see the habits of mind, practice them, and receive feedback about their performance" (p. 120) if the unit truly embraces the disposition outcome included in our conceptual framework.

Similar to PST, there are probably a few main reasons that three of my colleagues in my program are resistant to changing what they do and how they do it. A primary reason for them not to change their instructional practices may be due to the scientifically-based content of their courses where students are expected to memorize body parts, energy systems and related functions. Some faculty are unwilling to change their pedagogical or coaching methods, and remain fairly rigid in their approaches to teaching. Not having enough instructional time or knowledge about the HoM are two other reasons some faculty colleagues have communicated and opposition to adding the HoM into their syllabi, and perhaps the most significant reason why faculty are hesitant to address the HoM in their classes centers on the fact that they have not internalized the HoM which may result in reduced confidence to assist their students in the process. Weinberg and Gould (2010) suggested that the implementation of a PST program can be enhanced with excellent planning, commitment and using mindful strategies to address predicted challenges that may arise. Given the foregoing, I would speculate that more college-wide HoM workshops may help to encourage change within our programs. I will continue to work the HoM and encourage my students to do the same. As a collective, we must work toward making our professional conduct more intelligent and effective.

Appendix 9.1

MOTOR LEARNING & DEVELOPMENT

OBSERVATIONAL TASKS TO HELP DEVELOP YOUR LESSON

1. Select either a youth sport program that practices regularly throughout the semester or a physical education class from a public or private school. Students or youth sport athletes must not be older than 13 years of age.
2. Obtain permission from administrators, teachers or coaches to observe instructional sessions or practices for at least 10 hours during this semester. Have administrators, teachers or coaches fill out the permission form attached to this document, make two copies. Give the original to your instructor and give one copy to the program administrator. Keep one copy for your records.
3. You must observe instructional or practice sessions with your group members.
4. Complete the following questions throughout the semester to help you develop your lesson:

a. What are the demographics of the individuals you will be observing? Include: average age, grade level, sex, cultural backgrounds, and other variables to better describe the participants.

b. According to Piaget, what is the typical cognitive level of these individuals? Have the majority of participants obtained this level? How was your assessment determined? Did you observe any variations among participants? If so, explain.
c. What types of behaviors did you observe related to the self-esteem of these participants? What kinds of activities promoted the development of a positive self-esteem in participants? Explain. What types of experiences were detrimental to the social development of the participants? Did the participants seem like they were having fun? Describe other types of emotions that you observed among the participants. What could you do make their experiences more positive? What types of social interactions did you observe? Did you notice any cultural or gender differences among the participants?
d. Where do these participants range in terms of their growth and maturation? What did you observe about the physical characteristics of the participants? What types of cultural and gender-based influences do you think effected the physical characteristics of the participants?
e. What have you observed about the development of the fundamental motor skills, object control skills and sport skills of the participants? Assess the development of these skills during your observations using your text as a reference. Are the participants really ready to learn specific sport skills? Explain.
f. What do you believe are the main reasons individuals that you observe participate? Is this objective achieved? How did you make this assessment?

What percentages of participants seem to have positive experiences? What can instructors/coaches do to make physical activities more positive for everyone? How would you increase the motivation of the participants to get involved in these activities?

Appendix 9.2

MOTOR LEARNING & DEVELOPMENT PROJECT

Each small group of students will design a physical education or sport-related movement lesson (skill development). The lesson/practice plan <u>must</u> include rationale that explains "why" certain activities were chosen. The activities of the lesson/practice must be developed to address several of the Sunshine State Standards (i.e., objectives) intended for the chosen student/athlete population. Developmental and situational aspects of the teaching and learning process must be identified and presented. You will be expected to present your project to class using related technologies. You will also be expected to submit a written report complete with references other than those cited in the course textbook.

LESSON/PRACTICE PLAN FORMAT

The following is the most important aspect of your project regarding motor development & learning. If your group does not express itself clearly and provide both documented research (i.e., where students /athletes "should be") compared with your field observations (i.e., students/athletes actual development) your group will not receive full credit for the project. The focus here is on the why" rather than the "what" and "how".

Age & Developmental Level
(Describe your students/athletes)
Cognitive level ▶ How do you know this? (List research and describe your field observations)
Social development ▶ How do you know this? (List research and describe your observations)
Physical development ▶ Skill-wise and fitness-wise. (Be sure to compare your observations to related research.)

1. Outcomes: (Select from Sunshine State Standards)
Identify at least 4 SSS – one for the cognitive and affective domains and two for the psychomotor (include a fitness and motor skill objective). Make a list numbered 1-4. Identify which domain is addressed by each outcome. Begin each SSS with: "At the completion of this lesson, students/athletes will be able to".... Identify SSS (e.g., P.E.6.2.1)
2. Introduction:
Discuss how you will motivate your students/athletes and help them to persist
Describe how you will set the focus for the teaching/coaching/learning session

Discuss what previous learned concepts and skills can be applied to facilitate learning (transfer)

This part of your paper is important – but not as important as the first section. Transfer your knowledge and skills gained from your other classes (i.e., skills and practice; coaching, teaching methods etc.) to help guide the development of this section. In this class, we are more concerned with "why" we choose to teach/coach students/athletes what we do rather than "how we do it.

3.   Lesson Focus/Guided Practice:

Discuss what skills you will be teaching/practicing

Discuss how you will organized your students/athletes and the practice area

Discuss what the most relevant cues/key teaching points are needed to perform successfully

Discuss how you will evaluate the progress of your students/athletes (task sheets, observations, rubrics etc. – also include a completed task-sheet/rubric)

Provide examples of related feedback that you might give your students/athletes to enhance learning and performance.

4.   Closure:

Review & reflect about what you tried to accomplish

Explain how you will offer general and specific praise to your students and athletes

Offer a general evaluation of student/athlete progress and the lesson/practice in general

5.   Equipment/Materials

Include a list of items you will need to implement your lesson. Also include a drawing of the field - layout

References

Anderson, J. R. (2009). *Cognitive psychology and its implications* (7th ed.). New York, Worth.

Bloom, B. S. & D. R. Krathwohl. (1956). *Taxonomy of educational objectives: The classification of educational goals,by a committee of college and university examiners. Handbook 1: Cognitive domain.* New York, Longmans.

Costa, A. & Kallick, B (2000). *Discovering and exploring habits of mind.* Alexandria, VA: Association for Supervision and Curriculum Development.

Dottin, E. S. (2010). *Dispostions as habits of mind: Making professional conduct more intelligent.* Lanham, MD., University Press of America.

Fitts, P. M., & Posner, M. I. (1967) *Human performance.* Oxford, England: Brooks and Cole.

McCaughtry, N., Barnard, S., Martin, J., Shen, B., & Kulinna, P.H. (2006). Teachers perspectives on the challenges of teaching physical education in urban schools: The student emotional filter. *Research Quarterly for Exercise and Sport,* 77 (4), 486-97.

Messner, M. A. (2009). Boyhood, organized sports, and the construction of masculinities, In D. S. Eitzen (Ed.)(8th ed.) *Sport in contemporary society: An anthology (pp. 50-66).* Boulder, CO: Paradigm.

Moran, T.E, & Block, M.E. (2010). Barriers to Participation of Children with Disabilities in Youth Sports. *TEACHING Exceptional Children Plus,* 6(3) Article 5. Retrieved on June 30, 2012 from http://escholarship.bc.edu/education/tecplus/vol6/iss3/art5

National Association for Sport and Physical Education (2008). *Comprehensive school physical activity programs.* Reston, VA.

National Association for Sport and Physical Education (2006). *Teaching large class sizes in physical education: Guidelines and strategies.* Retrieved on June 30, 2012 from http://www.aahperd.org/naspe/publications/teachingTools/upload/Teaching-Large-Class-Sizes-in-PE-2006.pdf

National Association for Sport and Physical Education (2004). *Moving into the future: National standards for physical education* (2nd ed.). Reston, VA.

National Federation of State High School Associations (August, 2011). *High school sports participation continues upward climb.* Retrieved on June 30 2012 from http://www.nfhs.org/content.aspx?id=5752

Payne, V. G., & Isaacs, L. D. (2010). *Human motor development: A lifespan approach* (8th ed.). Mountain View, CA: Mayfield.

Parker, S (2012). *Physical fitness and exercise: The Facts.* Retrieved on June 30, 2012 from http://www.healthguidance.org/entry/6299/1/Physical-Fitness-and-Exercise-The-Facts.html

Rovegno, I., & Bandhaurer, D. (2013). *Elementary physical education: Curriculum and instruction.* Burlington, MA, Jones and Bartlett Learning.

The Conceptual Framework of the College of Education (The Professional Education Unit) (2006). Florida International University, Miami, FL. http://education.fiu.edu /docs/Conceptual%20Framework%2006-19-09.pdf

Weinberg, R. S., & Gould, D. *Foundations of sport and exercise psychology (5th ed).* (2010). Champaign, IL., Human Kinetics.

Wiersma, L.D., & Sherman, C. P. (2005). Volunteer youth sport coaches' perspectives of coaching education/certification and parental codes of conduct. *Research Quarterly for Exercise and Sport,* 76 (3), pp. 324-338.

CHAPTER TEN

Elementary Education Candidates Valuing Dispositions in a Supervised Clinical Practicum in Reading: Applying Past Knowledge to New Situations

By

Lynne D. Miller
Helen Robbins
Maria Alvarez Tsalikis
Lynn Yribarren

The BS in Elementary Education K-6 (with ESOL Endorsement) program at Florida International University consists of 19 upper division courses taken prior to the final set of courses, EDE 4936, Student Teaching Internship, and EDE 4943, Senior Seminar in Elementary Education. These courses build on candidates' learning from two years of lower division coursework that include three pre-requisite education courses required by the Department of Education in our state: Introduction to Education, Teaching Diverse Populations and Educational Technology. In conjunction with the three lower division and 19 upper-division program courses, each of our 300 plus candidates participates in over 200 hours of field experiences prior to student teaching. This translates to a contribution by our pre-service teachers of over 15,000 hours per term to the education of elementary school students and to the support of teachers in local South Florida communities. Even prior to graduation, our candidates are contributing much to local school districts, and this places a huge responsibility on our program to carefully support the quality preparation of each of our candidates.

Throughout our comprehensive undergraduate teacher preparation program, candidates have multiple opportunities to develop and apply knowledge, skills and dispositions that prepare them to work effectively with diverse learners in a variety of contexts, including urban schools. Their preparation grows out of our college's conceptual framework. As per our college's vision, "We seek a desired future in which the emphasis on inquiry is the means-ends connection to enhancing reflective intelligence" (Conceptual Framework, n. d., p. 4). We seek to prepare our candidates as Stewards of the Discipline, in this case, having knowledge of content areas and pedagogy associated with Elementary Education. We then strive to support their development of skills so that as Reflective Inquirers candidates are able to support the learning of all students, regardless of their diverse learning needs. Additionally, we design experiences to nurture candidates' Habits of Mind (HoM) (Conceptual Framework, n. d., p. 9-11), or professional dispositions, so that as Mindful Educators they may use reflective intelligence to approach their work as educators, as well as nurture the use of similar Habits of Mind by their students.

While Costa and Kallick (n. d.) have identified 16 habits of mind, we include 12 of these in our program: (1) Adopting a critical eye toward ideas and actions (Being Analytical); (2) Withholding judgment until understanding is achieved by being thoughtful in his/her actions (Managing Impulsivity); (3) Working to see things through by employing systematic methods of analyzing problems (Persisting); (4) Thinking about his/her own thinking (Reflective Thoughtfulness); (5) Thinking and communicating with clarity and precision (Communicating Accurately); (6) Showing curiosity and passion about learning through inquiry (Being Inquisitive); (7) Showing a sense of being comfortable in situations where the outcomes are not immediately known by acting on the basis of his/her initiative and not from needing a script (Taking Responsible Risks); (8) Recognizing the wholeness and distinctiveness of other people's ways of experiencing and making meaning by being open-minded (Being Open-minded); (9) Taking time to check over work because of his/her being more interested in excellent work than in expediency (Striving for Accuracy); (10) Abstracting meaning from one experience and carrying it forward and applying it to a new situation by calling on his/her store of past knowledge as a source of data to solve new challenges (Applying Past Knowledge to New Situations); (11) Showing sensitivity to the needs of others and to being a cooperative team member (Thinking Interdependently); and, (12) Showing a sense of care for others and an interest in listening well to others (Empathic Understanding).

Until recently, in each of our Elementary Education program courses, we nurture several of the HoM in conjunction with candidates' development of knowledge and skills related to the subject area focus of the given course. However, beginning with the 2011 fall term, we decided to implement a different approach in one of the program's reading courses, RED 4110. We shifted focus to addressed only one disposition, HoM, with the intent of helping to nurture it in our candidates in a more focused, in depth manner. This chapter will describe how we approached this task, and it will provide several examples of how we nurtured candidate's development of the targeted disposition.

Selecting One Course, Selecting One Disposition

Our BS in Elementary Education K-6 (with ESOL Endorsement) program contains four required reading courses that candidates must take in order, with each being a prerequisite for the next one in sequence: (1) RED 3313, Language and Literacy Development; (2) RED 4150, Content and Methods of Teaching

Beginning Literacy; (3) RED 4311, Content and Methods of Teaching Intermediate Literacy; and, (4) RED 4110, Content and Methods of Teaching Literacy in Schools. RED 3313 examines the relationship between young children's oral language and reading development. It also helps candidates develop an understanding of phonological awareness, phonemic awareness and other basic concepts related to phonics instruction. RED 4150 facilitates candidates' understanding of knowledge related to emergent reading and writing in young, school-aged children and helps candidates develop knowledge and skills that support literacy development through the third grade. RED 4311 places an emphasis on literacy assessment, as well as on candidate's knowledge and skill that will help him/her facilitate literacy learning in the upper elementary grades, including content area reading. Finally, RED 4110 is a supervised clinical practicum. In this course, candidates and the professors meet biweekly at local public elementary schools usually located in underserved, low socio-economic areas. Each academic year Memorandums of Agreement are signed by FIU and local public school district officials that give permission for our faculty and candidates to work with students at elementary school sites. Four different elementary school sites are used in both the fall and spring terms, and one is used in the summer term. In the fall and spring terms, we typically offer four sections of RED 4110, each section containing 35 candidates. We offer two sections of RED 4110 in the summer, with a total enrollment of 40 candidates. Once paired with students, our candidates provide service to over 180 struggling readers annually. Each student, most often second and third graders, receives approximately 20 hours of (free to students) quality, one-on-one literacy tutoring over a 16 weeks period. The elementary schools we serve recognize the benefit of the literacy tutoring for their students as they welcome our faculty and candidates back from year after year.

Professors Miller, Robbins, Tsalikis, and Yribarren teach reading courses in the program, and Dr. Miller is the Program Director for the BS in Elementary Education K-6 (with ESOL Endorsement) program. After considering each of the reading courses, we decided to implement the one-course, one-disposition trial in the fourth reading course, Content and Methods of Teaching Literacy in Schools (RED 4110). While thinking about this supervised clinical practicum, we concurrently reviewed each of the 12 HoM to determine which had the best fit. In RED 4110, we expect candidates to apply learning from the other three prerequisite reading courses, as well as from other courses in the program, as they work for the first time, in a sustained manner during the period of 16 weeks, with a struggling reader. Therefore, the disposition that stood out was each candidate' "abstracting meaning from one experience and carrying it forward and applying it to a new situation by calling on his/her store of past knowledge as a source of data   to solve new challenges (Applying Past Knowledge to New Situations) (Conceptual Framework, n. d., p. 16)."

Implementing the One-Course, One-Disposition Trial

Prior to the start of the fall 2011 term, the course materials (syllabus, assignments and rubrics) were reviewed and revised to clearly reflect the selected HoM, Applying Past Knowledge to New Situations. We wanted the syllabus, assignments, and rubrics to reveal what the course instructors would be emphasizing orally in course lectures, discussions and targeted feedback. As the term began, each of the three instructors, Dr. Tsalikis and Dr. Yribarren, who taught one section of RED 4110 and Dr. Robbins teaching two sections of RED 4110, helped candidates develop an awareness of the HoM, using the prepared materials as a start.

The instructors helped candidates develop deeper understanding s, using information from Describing 16 Habits of Mind, in which Arthur Costa and Bena Kallick elaborate on the HoM of Applying Past Knowledge to New Situations (n. d.). Through a brief presentation candidates learned that humans may refer back to previous learning and experiences when grappling with a new, challenging situation. However, many individuals approach new situations as though they are encountering them with no prior knowledge or experiences that could help to inform their thinking. We then engaged candidates in a discussion in which they shared personall experiences related to Applying Past Knowledge to New Situations. We extended this discussion to help them identify learning from the three prerequisite reading courses and the other, typically by this point in the candidates' program of studies 14 or more, Elementary Education program courses taken prior to the practicum may be used to approach learning experiences in the RED 4110. We wanted them to grasp that they had a large foundation of knowledge upon which they could draw to facilitate the literacy development of the struggling reader with whom each candidate is working.

In the following examples, we describe three different aspects of the fourth reading course, RED 4110, that highlight the benefit of our candidates' applying past knowledge to new situations (HoM). As presented earlier, instructors begin nurturing this HoM from the very beginning of the sequence of four courses. The examples that follow show how the HoM is integral to specific instructional experiences. As an aside, each example was written by one instructor of RED 4110 and shows how the instructor approaches a particular aspect of the course (data driven instruction, literacy niche and reflections). While we all teach to common ends, with a shared syllabus, we believe it is more authentic to speak from our individual experiences regarding the selected aspects of the course than speaking as a collective.

Data-Driven Instruction (Dr. Tsalikis)

Our program includes teaching more than just good pedagogical skills. As a quality teacher preparation program we create opportunities for candidates to develop Habits of Mind (Conceptual Framework, n. d., p. 9-11) that align with and enhance current educational practices. In RED 4110, it is critical that candidates refine their abilities to continuously align grades K-6 student progress information with planning and instruction. The development of this ability, related to reading, begins with our first reading class, continues through the second and third, and is polished in the fourth. In RED 4110, we help our candidates recall what they have learned in previous courses and apply those knowledge skills and dispositions to their current charge, providing data-driven literacy instruction to a struggling reader.

Our candidates come to appreciate that as our schools and districts strive to maintain their accountability to the state and the many stakeholders of our education system, teachers are seeing more and more the importance and impact of data-driven instruction. Data-driven instruction poses that educators base both short and long term goals on student need. Further, student need is identified not only by Individual Education Plans (IEPs) or other "traditional" documentation, but also by the consistent and systematic gathering of student data through student progress monitoring. For example, test results like those obtained from the Stanford Achievement Test (SAT), in lower grades, and from the Florida Assessment for Instruction in Reading (FAIR) (Florida Department of Education, n. d.) are used as part of a series of input sources to determine student grouping placement. In turn, this specific student placement is intended to support each child's learning so that ideally, individual student success will translate into classroom success, school level progress, and higher district ratings. It is essential that our candidates understand how data-driven instruction benefits student learning, as well as how assessments, followed by appropriate instruction, have farther reaching impacts on schools and school districts.

In our sequenced four reading courses, we engage candidates in linking lesson planning with instructional decisions based on student need (assessment data). In fact, in most cases, candidates are required to document directly into their course assignments specific information that shows how their lessons support their learners and, furthermore, how their lessons specifically support student learning needs based on student data. In the reading courses this is achieved through a steady progression of infusing this thinking throughout the sequentially and structured reading classes. While, as a literacy faculty, we clearly understand how the content of the four reading courses build one upon the other, our candidates are in the process of learning and understanding the connections. Our aim in our team approach and sequenced building up of candidate experiences, knowledge, skills, and dispositions (HoM) is to challenge the candidates to value constructivist thinking and inquiry-based learning in order to help make prior knowledge from other courses more accessible in new experiences and learning environments. Many of our undergraduate candidates view assignments in a course as isolated experiences. Then, once they receive a grade for a course, those experiences may fade even further into compartmentalized memory related to that specific course.

In my view, the fourth reading course, RED 4110 is truly the masterpiece of the reading sequels. This supervised, clinical, hands-on experience forms the nexus between theory and practice. And, to be successful in tutoring their student, candidates must apply assessment and instruction knowledge and skills learned in previous courses. Therefore, the candidates and I spend time talking on a regular basis about the value of applying past knowledge to new situations (HoM). We systematically identify learning from each of the other reading courses, as well as from some of the other program courses that support data-driven instruction. Each candidate recalls different types of assessments and lessons that may be useful for working with his/her student. While candidates know that activating students' prior knowledge is an important instructional step, our discussions related to their applying past knowledge to new situations (HoM) brings them to new levels of understanding this principle and valuing its importance for teaching and learning. They realize that what they learned about literacy in the other three reading classes will enable them to participate successfully in the fourth reading class and will be valuable as they move forward in their careers as elementary school teachers who are well prepared to support data-driven literacy development. During the entire term in RED 4110, candidates identify, in discussions and written reflections, where they have applied past knowledge to new situations (HoM) as they deliver assessments and plan and deliver instructional experiences. As instructor, I continuously provide oral and written feedback to nurture and reinforce the HoM. By the end of the course, they realize that the HoM is not only of value to them, but to their students.

Literacy Niche (Dr. Yribarren)

Though I believe that each aspect of RED 4110 is interrelated, I will isolate the Literacy Niche assignment for the purposes of an example of how we help candidates apply past knowledge to new situations (HoM). The literacy niche is a purposeful, functional, and organized collection of materials displayed on a tri-fold board (like those used in Science Fair displays), as well as a variety and range of quality children's texts and writing materials. Each candidate in the fourth reading course develops a literacy niche for and with the student being tutored. A well-developed literacy niche should inspire and motivate learning, yet it functions primarily to provide on-going and developing support for each student's literacy development.

At the beginning of the term, all of my candidates must bring a blank tri-fold board to class. This board will become the literacy niche for the elementary school student. The blank tri-fold board is symbolic of the bare walls of their future classrooms that the teacher and students will build collaboratively so it will reflect everyone in the class, not just the teacher. In RED 4110, the literacy niche provides an opportunity to build a print-rich environment that will serve as the candidate's and student's private instructional space for tutoring, then be relinquished to the child at the end of the term to signify the student's ownership or his or her literacy development. As each candidate and student pair builds the niche together, it mostly displays student work. Additionally, projects that the candidate and student do together are displayed on the board, and there are some candidate-made displays, such as a word wall. Both the front and back of the tri-fold board are used.

Before the candidate meets his/her student, the candidate puts a border on the tri-fold to make it pleasing in appearance. Then, as the candidate begins work with his/her student, other materials begin to be posted. Even at the beginning of the term, I see how much background knowledge and understanding my candidates have about effective literacy learning environments. I am able to discern which candidates use the literacy niche to post purposeful material and which attempt to fill the board with "decorative" or generic, filler activities. For me, this serves as an informal assessment of what knowledge candidates' are applying from past learning (HoM) from the other three reading courses.

The concept of providing students with a print rich environment is introduced to candidates in the second reading course, RED 4150. The idea is to recreate the experience that the pre-service teacher will have to face when presented with his or her first classroom. The soon-to-be teacher will need to construct a print rich environment that reflects the culture and abilities of his or her students, as well as inspire and motivate the students to learn. The work that "decorates" the niche is produced by the student and becomes motivational and inspirational because of quantity and eventually quality. In RED 4150, candidates develop a photo journal. In this assignment, candidates take pictures of ideas-too-good-to-miss related to print-rich classrooms. They take these pictures in their field experience classrooms; however, there are not photos of the students. They organize and present their photos with an explanation about what is in the photo, why they chose to photograph it, and how it relates to the explanation in their textbook of a print-rich environment.

When we begin our discussion about the literacy niche assignment, the candidates often do not spontaneously bring forward what they learned about print-rich environments in RED 4150. This provides an opportunity to talk with candidates about the usefulness of applying past knowledge to new situations (HoM). We discuss the HoM, including reasons why individuals tend to compartmentalize past learning. I help candidates understand that their students will do this as well and that it is incumbent on them, as teachers, to use strategies, and help their students use strategies, to access past learning.

After this discussion, the candidates remember that they do know about different types of texts, the purpose of different types of texts and how to choose texts that are functional, inspirational, related to student interest, and of quality. They realize, happily, that they have much foundational knowledge upon which to build their literacy niche. Candidates remember that the materials should represent the student's instructional and independent reading and writing levels. Further, they eventually recall and build on a genre study assignment, related to children's literature, that they completed in the first reading course, RED 3313. In the genre study assignment, candidates read and reviewed books from each of ten genre or book formats. They learned to use criteria to select quality books and to use guidelines to determine the reading level of those books. Then, from the third reading class, RED 4311, candidates' remember that they shifted focus from children's literature to informational texts. They learn to select appropriate texts based on results from several literacy assessments.   Candidates are reminded that how to use quality texts to support the literacy development of his/her student. Once again, we process the importance of applying past knowledge to new situations (HoM).

Building on these experiences, in RED 4110 each candidate shares with others 10-20 books that s/he has selected for his/her elementary student. Each candidate tells why the books were chosen for his/her student. Eventually, candidates bring the selected books to tutoring and display them inside their niche area as part of the print-rich environment that surrounds the elementary student. One of my candidates expressed how she connected to her background knowledge in her book share explanation: "depending on the story they can actually love or hate reading, I know I did. When searching for reading material, I thought of what I learned in previous classes about finding literature that engages students and teaches at the same time."

There are some required items posted on the niches, such as a daily agenda and a fluency monitoring charts that show student progress daily. The niches also include instructional supports, such as word walls, vocabulary charts, and how-to charts.   Bookmarks comprise another section of the niche. The bookmarks provide a visual record of many books read by and with the student across the tutoring sessions. As the student sees his/her literacy niche becoming a record of his/her work, he/she is inspired and motivated to continue working. As the student observes growth in his or her ability, it helps the candidate to support the student's positive self-efficacy as a reader and writer.

The pre-service teacher needs to refer to past knowledge and previous courses to help decide what is appropriate for the student. At first they do not seem to realize the wealth of knowledge and skills they have already developed. However, through discussing the value of applying past knowledge to new situations, by having candidates apply past knowledge and then by having them reflect on their use of past knowledge, candidates begin to internalize the HoM and access this type of thinking without my prompting them to do so. In a written reflection one candidate expressed the following, "NOW I understand the point of the four extensive reading courses required for an elementary education major. The first three courses help prepare us for this final RED 4110 course."

At different times, I teach all four of the required reading courses. I see the importance and the connection of assignments and knowledge development, and I am very pleased when my students make those connections. I have read many of my students' reflections that exemplify this concept of relating and building on prior knowledge. While related to lesson planning, one last quote that I really like tells of one of my student's ability to transfer from our reading course to other content area method courses. She stated, even though the lesson plan is time consuming, I know exactly what I need to say and do which makes the lesson flow smoothly. It is interesting that other classes do not follow this format. I have been able to apply what I learned in this course to those classes. For example, applying the advance organizer, transfer, and detailed ESE and ESL modifications are things that I have incorporated in my other classes.

As the instructor, I am able to use the niche as a representation of my candidates' and their students' growth. And, I am able to use it to help candidates value and begin to internalize applying past knowledge to new situations (HoM).

Reflections (Dr. Robbins)

I teach each of the four reading education courses required in the Elementary Education program. The reading education courses present information and experiences that help candidates learn to teach reading in an incremental way; each course builds upon the previous and each sets the stage to help candidates connect past learning to new situations encountered throughout each course. The four reading courses combine a mix of theory and practice with large amounts of field experiences that link to what is learned in class.

Exploring Prior Knowledge and Experiences. Candidates, in the first reading course, bring some level of background knowledge as to how reading is taught to young children, and how they themselves learned how to read. Candidates' background knowledge related to teaching reading is somewhat limited, and many candidates have misconceptions about how reading is taught. Further, many cannot remember how they learned to read. Typical comments are "I think we worked in a small group" or "I wrote book reports" or "We took turns reading in class." I engage candidates in a discussion and encourage them to elaborate on their responses. From these first, personal experiences, I want candidates to make connections with past knowledge and experiences. And, these discussions provide me a glimpse of into candidates' prior knowledge related to reading and reading instruction. I realize that the candidates and I have a lot of work ahead of us towards their growth as literacy professionals, and I am pleased that I am already beginning to nurture their disposition to apply past knowledge, some still in the form of experiences, to new situations (HoM).

Since candidates enter the first reading course with limited knowledge of how to teach reading, it is not difficult to observe change and growth in candidates' knowledge, skills and dispositions related to literacy teaching and learning. One part of the course is teaching candidates how to develop a lesson to teach a phonemic awareness skill. The direct instruction model is taught and candidates learn to write a detailed lesson plan related to phonemic awareness. After writing the lesson plan and delivering the lesson in their field placement class, candidates are asked to write a reflection.

Using Reflections to Make Connections. In the reading courses, we use written reflections strategically to, in part, help candidates make connections among what they already know (past knowledge), what transpired in the lesson and what they identify as still needing to be learned. The reflections are called

"Three-Level Reflections" and prompt candidates to think and write descriptively and analytically, as well as identify what they learned through the experience. I help candidates understand that there is an expectation that they will carry forward what they learned and apply it, when appropriate, to new situations (HoM). It is hoped that the process of candidates' thinking about what they learned and committing this thinking to paper in the form of a reflection will help make this new learning more accessible in the future. In our program, reflections are an integral part of candidates' learning process. The following shows how I structure Three-Level Reflections for my candidates. The example pertains to the phonemic awareness lesson, but the prompts are similar for each different lesson candidates teach, with the term "phonemic awareness" changing depending on the lesson. Candidates write in response to prompts for each level:

Level One: Descriptive

- Describe the type of lesson you taught.
- Describe the strategy you used to teach the phonemic awareness.
- Explain how you prepared for the lesson.
- Describe the kinds of materials you used to teach the lesson and why you selected those materials.
- Explain how the students responded to the lesson. What are some examples of the students' responses?
- Were your goals for the students' learning met?
- Do you think the students understood what you taught them? Why? Why not?

Level Two: Analytical

- Explain why or why not your lesson was successful.
- What did you learn from writing this lesson plan?
- How did the lesson plan help you teach a phonemic awareness lesson?
- What did you learn from implementing the lesson plan with the students?
- What would you do the same next time you teach a phonemic awareness lesson? (This pertains to your teaching)
- What would you do differently next time you teach a phonemic awareness lesson based on what you learned from teaching this lesson?

Level Three: Self-Reflection

- Explain how teaching this phonemic awareness lesson has increased your knowledge of how reading is taught.
- Explain what you knew about teaching phonemic awareness before you wrote and implemented the lesson.
- Explain what you now know about teaching phonemic awareness after you implemented the lesson.

- What were the specific modifications you provided for the ESOL and ESE student that made learning accessible to them? What were the specific modifications you provided?
- Provide reasons why it is important to teach phonemic awareness to students.
- Explain how you would teach phonemic awareness in your classroom when you begin teaching.

Although I meticulously work through each part of the reflection with the candidates emphasizing the need to think critically about what they did and what they learned, the first reflection is almost always eye opening. Candidates address the reflection prompts by conveying what they did, but most fall short of any insights about what they learned. After I receive and read what they have written, I use this opportunity to go back over each part of the reflection to fine-tune candidates' understandings and help them crystallize their thinking about what they did and what they learned. The carefully constructed reflection prompts are essential elements in helping candidates think about what they did and what they learned. The prompts provide a framework, a guide for their thinking. From my experience, without this framework, candidates more than likely use descriptive writing and do not take their reflections further.

The Three-Level Reflection follows candidates through their second, third and fourth reading courses. After each lesson planning or assessment assignment, candidates are asked to write a Three-Level Reflection. At times, adjustments are made to the guiding prompts to match the criteria of the assignment. Reflecting helps candidates to clarify thinking and enables them to be aware of what they are learning and have learned. They are an important part of the cycle of applying past knowledge to new situations (HoM).

Building to the Grand Reflection. Upon completion of the first three reading courses candidates participate in their fourth and final reading course, just prior to their student teaching internship. In this supervised clinical practicum, candidates link what they have learned in their previous three reading courses and use that background knowledge to begin to more fully understand the complexities of teaching reading. Each candidate assesses a student's reading abilities and identifies specific reading and teaching needs for the student based on assessments. Each candidate is assigned to teach a student who either cannot read or is one or two years below grade level in reading. In order to gain understanding of what it takes to teach reading effectively, they must now use background knowledge from previous reading classes, as well as other courses in the Elementary Education program, and continue to construct new knowledge and skills through their participation in the clinical practicum.

Throughout the fourth reading course, candidates reflect upon each of the nine reading comprehension lesson they teach. The reflections follow the Three-Level Reflections model. The specific reflection prompts are adapted to refocus on the comprehension lessons. Although the candidates have written reflections throughout the previous three reading courses, the first reflection they write in this course tends to contain superficial, surface-level responses to the questions that guide their thinking. Perhaps this is because one-on-one reading tutoring is a different situation than candidates have experiences previously in their completion of field experiences in local school. Regardless, I revisit the reflective prompts frequently throughout the term to continue to encourage candidates to think deeply; to help them recognize that their learning from the previous classes may be used to approach learning experiences in this supervised clinical practicum. Through these reflections, I am able to observe candidates thinking evolve from those superficial observations about themselves, to a deeper understanding about what they learned about themselves as teachers of reading, and what they learned about their student's progress in reading. A typical comment on beginning reflections would be "I learned I have to have patience." A typical reflection later in the term would be, "I learned my student learns best when she is engaged in meaningful activities based on what her needs are." Candidates, over time, begin to draw from what they learned from previous reading courses, without my prompting, to continue to learn and apply what they are currently learning in the clinical practicum. Candidates ultimately realize that their knowledge about how to teach reading has a direct impact on their students' reading achievement, as evidenced through a Grand Reflection, the overarching final reflection for the course.

The last reflection asked of candidates in the supervised clinical practicum is a "Grand Reflection." Its name signifies its importance. Its scope and sequence does not solely rely upon candidates' experiences in the clinical practicum, but it also asks them to tie in their previous experiences from other reading classes and discuss how those experiences contributed to their learning. Carefully constructed guiding prompts help candidates deeply reflect upon what they learned through their experiences. The Grand Reflection is not limited to the guiding prompts; candidates are encouraged to discuss any other aspect of their learning. They are encouraged to refer to any experiences throughout the clinical practicum and, where applicable, to show how these experiences are connected to other background knowledge gained from previous reading classes.

It is through this Grand Reflection process that candidates crystallize their thinking about what they learned and applied in this fourth reading course with what they brought forward from the previous three reading courses. These are typical of candidates' reflections:

> Without the knowledge about the importance of assessments I have gained from a previous class, I would not have been able to properly instruct my student in this practicum.
> My other three reading classes prepared me by helping me understand the theory behind reading instruction. I now know how to put theory and research into practice. The research about reading instruction does work, because it was successful with the student I tutored.
> I brought forward that we should have books from different cultures; the student learned about their culture and others as well.

Even though I did not have much experience in teaching literacy, the knowledge and practice within a college classroom helped immensely. Without those previous classes I would have struggled in my preparation, and my student would have suffered due to my lack of insight.

Some knowledge and elements I already knew came from previous reading courses, like writing lesson plans and assessing using the *Basic Reading Inventory*. What I gained from this last class is different than just learning about reading from textbooks. Here we used what we learned and actually put it to use. I went from knowing that a student should be exposed to reading and writing, to actually having the books and materials to help the student make progress in reading.

My three previous reading courses have contributed to my preparation in my clinical practicum and to my growth as a teacher. They have strengthened my understanding in the reading process. If I didn't already understand the steps in the reading process, I would have been unsuccessful during my clinical practicum. I learned very early on in this course that its purpose was to place things that I have learned into action. I applied all that I learned from the first three courses and had I not understood what I was doing, I would have been very unsuccessful.

My experiences in teaching the fourth reading course, RED 4110 have shown me that that it is possible to help candidates de-compartmentalize their learning from previous courses so that they become adept at applying past knowledge to new situations (HoM). However, to do so, candidates need multiple, meaningful experiences Thinking about experiences through written reflections is one such type of experience. When faced with a new teaching situation, I want my candidates to pause, think and ask themselves, "What have I already learned and what do I already know from previous situations that may inform my thinking about the current one?" Based on candidate performance and written reflections, it seems that candidates are using this HoM without my external prompting in relation to literacy teaching and learning.

In Conclusion

We are pleased with the results of our one-course, one-disposition trial and plan to continue to use the model in RED 4110. We were able to tighten concepts in our written materials (e.g., syllabus, assignment sheets, reflection prompts, rubrics), and we were able to involve candidates in a variety of different types of discussions related to applying past knowledge to new situations (HoM). We saw, first-hand, that to change habits, including Habits of mind, requires a collaboration among instructors and students, multiple opportunities to experience the HoM, and ample time to actively process learning, inclusive of the HoM, both orally and in writing. Hopefully, the candidates will carry forward the value of applying HoM in their work with students as they support them in their literacy development and other elementary education subject areas. While time and effort intensive for professors and candidates, we are committed to this supervised clinical practicum, RED 4110. In our view, this course, inclusive of Habits of Mind, reflects the best of a community of practice in which the local school district, teachers, administrators, Florida International University, professors, pre-service teacher education candidates and children are working together for the benefit of all.

References

Florida Assessment for Instruction in Reading (FAIR), & Stanford Achievement Test (SAT) (n. d.) (n. d.) Retrieved from http://www.fldoe.org

Conceptual Framework, College of Education. (n. d.).Retrieved from http://education.fiu .edu/docs/Conceptual%20Framework%2006-19-09.pdf

Costa, A., & Kallick, B. (n. d.). Describing 16 habits of mind. Retrieved June 22, 2012 from http://www.instituteforhabitsofmind.com/resources/pdf/16HOM.pdf .

CHAPTER ELEVEN

Microteaching Lesson Study (MLS) for Promoting Habits of Mind in Courses for Learning to Teach Mathematics

By

Maria L. Fernandez
Roxanne V. Molina
Esther F. Joseph
Leslie Nisbet

The development of teachers as reflective practitioners is a construct pervasive in conversations about teacher education. This construct is of central importance in the conceptual framework undergirding the work of the faculty in the College of Education (COE) at Florida International University (FIU) as manifested in the learning outcomes for the college's graduates to be "reflective inquirers" and "mindful educators" ("The Conceptual Framework," n.d.). Educating teachers to be reflective and mindful "students-of-teaching" seems imperative if teachers are to be adequately prepared to teach future generations of students. Teachers, like other professionals, will need to be critical thinkers, analyzing, evaluating and exploring possibilities, guided by integrity and ethical standards (Yost, Sentner, and Forlenza-Bailey, 2000). Teacher education programs are unable to address all current and future situations encountered by prospective teachers. Thus, just focusing on the application of effective strategies in teaching will not suffice. Societal developments, for example, growth in population diversity and technological advances, will undoubtedly influence classrooms. To meet the needs of all their students, we believe that teachers will need to take into account social and ethical considerations in their professional conduct, and will need to develop dispositions (that is, habits of mind) "toward behaving intelligently when confronted with problems, the answers to which are not immediately known" (Costa & Kallick, 2000a, p.1). From this perspective, the development of reflective intelligence is important in the preparation of teachers. Reflection has the potential to limit the impulsive nature of teaching and enable teachers to act with intention and deliberation (Dewey, 1933).

Guidance about how to help graduates in the College of Education become reflective inquirers and mindful educators and act with intention and deliberation, is provided in the college's conceptual framework; we should help them to develop and be "able to apply the dispositions or, that is, habits of mind (intellectual and social) that render professional actions and conduct more intelligent" ("The Conceptual Framework," n.d., p. 2). In an effort to promote our students' development as reflective and mindful educators acting purposefully and applying habits of mind, it has been important that we, as a college faculty, act with a common goal, communicating and co-constructing our evolving understanding of ways to achieve that goal.

When the first author, a mathematics educator, joined the COE faculty five years ago, she was introduced to the faculty community that helped her to understand the College goals for its students. Then, over the five years that followed, the other authors participated in the work of the college as doctoral teaching assistants in mathematics education, and were mentored by the first author. The authors collaborated with one another, and took on responsibilities for teaching or co-teaching mathematics education courses. Through the first author's continued collaboration with other COE faculty members, and leadership in directing the mathematics education group in the academic work of the College, the authors co-constructed student goals for the mathematics education courses that fit within the overarching goals and learning outcomes for COE students. We endeavoured to develop and implement approaches to teaching students enrolled in mathematics education courses in ways that foster their development of dispositions (habits of mind). One approach, developed by the first author, that all the authors began to implement in various mathematics education courses was Microteaching Lesson Study (Fernandez, 2005, 2010).

Microteaching Lesson Study (MLS) is a pedagogical approach that strategically builds on collaborative, continuous improvement aspects of lesson study, and the simplified environment associated with microteaching to foster active learning and the development of knowledge and practices aligned with recent reforms (Fernandez, 2005, 2010). We feel that practices promoted by MLS can also include habits of mind (or dispositions) appropriate for the development of reflective practitioners and mindful educators sought across the work of the College. MLS involves groups of three teachers or pre-service teachers working cooperatively on a research lesson, for a given topic and overarching student learning goal, over three repeated cycles of (1) planning, (2) teaching and observing (through video or in person), (3) analyzing with a mentor or other observers and (4) revising the research lesson; and creating an MLS reflective report of the process. During MLS, the research lesson is taught to three different small groups (classes) of peers or K-12 students (approximately 5 to 10 per reduced-size class) over the cycles. The lesson topics are not understood by the individuals taught and may be selected to teach within a shortened lesson length (e.g., 20 to 30 minutes); this is particularly the case when teaching small groups of peers within college courses.

According to Dewey (1944), "In learning one act, methods are developed good for use in other situations....The human being acquires a habit of learning" (p. 45). Dottin (2010) suggests that "fostering habits or growing habits comes, therefore, from 'doing' and reflecting on experience" (p. 14). Based on these ideas, the structure of MLS suggests the "doing" and "reflecting on experience" and the "one act" with potential to support pre-service teachers' development of habits of mind appropriate for our COE graduates to teach mathematics effectively and conscientiously.

MLS for Developing Reflective Practitioners and Mindful Educators

Prior to joining FIU, the first author developed, and began to study the implementation of MLS with pre-service secondary school mathematics teachers (Fernandez, 2005; Fernandez & Robinson, 2006). Her intent was to develop a practical experience for pre-service teachers to complement their field experiences, and provide them with opportunities to connect theory and practice, by developing knowledge and practices for teaching mathematics, in a systematic way, distinct from the typical idiosyncratic and particular nature of individual field experiences referred to by Ball and Cohen (1999). Through her research, she found that MLS helped pre-service secondary mathematics teachers move away from teaching mathematics as "telling" to their developing "pedagogical content strategies used to create lessons engaging students in discovery and construction of mathematics relationships and concepts" (Fernandez, 2005, p. 42). These strategies were aligned with recent reforms for teaching mathematics (National Council of Teachers of Mathematics [NCTM], 2000). In investigating seventy-four pre-service teachers' perceptions of MLS, she found that they overwhelmingly felt the experience was a worthwhile learning experience, and that it provided opportunities for them to put into practice what they were learning in the course and allowed them to recognize the value of reflection, alternate points of view and feedback in teaching resulting from collaboration with peers (Fernandez & Robinson, 2006).

Once she joined FIU, the first author became familiar with the COE Conceptual Framework through collaboration with other faculty, and through college-wide academic meetings and workshops that were focused on the college's continuous improvement in order to maintain national accreditation through The National Council for Accreditation of Teacher Education, and State Program Approval through the Florida Department of Education. As part of this process, she reviewed the main portfolio task in an introductory course on teaching secondary school mathematics used to collect evidence of meeting select accreditation standards. The task required pre-service teachers to individually plan, teach and reflect on a mathematics lesson during an individual field experience, an experience thought of as idiosyncratic, in particular by Ball and Cohen (1999). In order to limit the individual, idiosyncratic nature of the main portfolio task in the course, and expand the potential learning of the pre-service teachers as reflective practitioners and mindful educators, she replaced the existing portfolio task with MLS (and the MLS report), where the MLS groups of pre-service teachers teach either small groups of secondary school students or small groups of peers. She felt that MLS could help foster some of the habits of mind sought among graduates of the college. Although she did not directly study habits of mind in relation to MLS, her research on MLS suggested its potential for promoting habits of mind (HoM) as identified by Costa and Callick (2000a, 2000b). For example, in relation to the HoM "applying past knowledge to new situations," she found that MLS helped the pre-service teachers draw on and apply their developing pedagogical mathematical knowledge to new lessons, determined by a pre- and post-assessment of individually developed lesson plans by the participants (Fernandez, 2010). Also, with respect to the HoM "listening to others with understanding and empathy," she has repeatedly found that MLS helps foster pre-srvice teachers' valuing of others' points of view in teaching mathematics through the collaboration taking place within the MLS group cycles (Fernandez, 2008, 2010; Fernandez & Robinson, 2006; Fernandez & Zilliox, 2011). Another example is the HoM "thinking about our thinking (metacognition)" which seems to be intrinsically connected to the process of reflection or "deliberation-in-process" (Fernandez, 2010) that has been evidenced to be of central importance in learning through MLS as part of the repeated process of framing and reframing events or problems within their lessons over the repeated MLS cycles (i.e., planning, teaching and observing, reflecting, and revising) (Fernandez, 2010; Fernandez & Zilliox, 2011).

While revising the introductory course on learning to teach secondary school mathematics to include MLS and alignment with the goals and curriculum of the College for pre-service teacher development, the first author also began to explore ways of revising the introductory course for learning to teach elementary school mathematics. During that time, the second and fourth authors joined Florida International University as doctoral students in mathematics education. The first, second and fourth authors, decided to investigate the implementation of MLS with pre-service elementary school teachers in an introductory content and methods course for elementary school mathematics. We felt that the pre-service elementary school teachers would benefit from the experience in ways similar to that of the pre-service secondary school mathematics teachers. Our MLS research with the pre-service elementary school teachers has revealed findings similar to those of the pre-service secondary school mathematics teachers (Molina, 2012; Molina, Fernandez, Nisbet, 2011). For example, as with the secondary pre-service teachers, the elementary pre-service teachers have been found to value the opportunity for learning from others' points of view through the MLS process, a finding aligned somewhat with the HoM "listening to others with understanding and empathy." Another example is related to the HoM "applying past knowledge to new situations," which was evidenced in part by Molina (2012) using a pre- and post-assessment that demonstrated significant difference among MLS pre-service teachers in comparison to a non-MLS control group with respect to growth in mathematics and mathematics pedagogical knowledge. Also, the HoM of "thinking about our thinking (metacognition)" seems to be aligned with the finding among pre-service teachers about the importance of reflection through MLS and the pre-service teachers' deepening of ways to think about teaching, both their own and that of their group members (Molina, Fernandez, Nisbet, 2011).

The literature (Fernandez, 2005, 2010; Molina, 2012; Molina, Fernandez, Nisbet, 2011), shows that participation in MLS results in multiple positive benefits including improved content and pedagogical content knowledge, increased ability to plan lessons. While the aforementioned research findings suggest that MLS may be aligned with the habits of mind desired of FIU COE graduates, previous research has not directly examined pre-service teachers' habits of mind in relation to participation in MLS. Given the potential of MLS for fostering habits of mind among pre-service teachers, we became interested in and conducted a study to understand our pre-service teachers' perspectives on habits of mind in relation to MLS. The remainder of this chapter is devoted to discussing our study, findings and further remarks.

Methods

In this investigation, as is typical of our implementation of MLS within our introductory courses on learning to teach mathematics (Fernandez, 2005, 2010; Molina, Fernandez, Nisbet, 2011; Molina, 2012), the pre-service teachers engaged in MLS during the latter part of the semester after the requisite course ideas and theory had been studied and developed. Participants were placed in MLS groups, of at most three, in such a way that members were mixed in terms of pedagogical disposition and mathematical understanding and ability. The formation of MLS groups was based on results of pre-assessment instruments and the instructors' understanding of the pre-service teachers' mathematics thinking. Each MLS group was then assigned a topic related to ideas not fully developed during the earlier part of the semester along with an overarching student learning goal for their MLS research lesson.

Next, MLS groups were allotted time in class (and as homework out of class) to collaborate on the development of their initial lesson. During this time, the instructors, who acted as MLS mentors, interacted with the groups and posed questions intended to help the pre-service teachers develop both their content and pedagogical knowledge for teaching mathematics. This allowed the instructors to model, as well as to potentially foster the habits of mind among pre-service teachers.

A member of each MLS group then taught a first version of their MLS lesson to a portion of the class who served as their students, while their MLS group-mates acted as observers and videotaped the lesson, later watched by the

MLS group members and, at times, the mentor. Following the first teach, MLS group members engaged in a debriefing session in conjunction with their MLS mentor to discuss the effectiveness of the lesson in terms of student learning. After engaging in the initial debriefing session, each MLS group revised and taught the lesson again. This cycle of planning, teaching, and debriefing was completed three times. This allowed each group member the opportunity to teach a version of the lesson. The elementary pre-service teachers received feedback from the MLS mentor during the first and second debriefing sessions with no feedback for the third debriefing session.

In order to understand pre-service teachers' perceptions of how MLS helps develop the habits of mind in their introductory course on teaching mathematics, a Likert-type survey was administered to participants after completion of the MLS process. The survey contained statements related to ten HoMs (Costa & Kallick, 2000a, 200b), and one overarching learning goal (reflective intelligence), (see Table 11.1 in the Findings section), aligned with the dispositions that we as a College want to nurture among our students ("The Conceptual Framework," n.d.). A total of 42 undergraduate elementary pre-service teachers enrolled in two sections of a course on teaching mathematics were asked to complete the survey after completing three cycles of MLS. The elementary pre-service teachers rated eleven statements on a scale from 1 to 5 where 1 meant Strongly Disagree and 5 meant Strongly Agree; three statements were reverse response items. Means and standard deviations for all the HoM-related statements were computed (see Table 11.1).

Discussion of Findings

Results from the HoM MLS Feedback Survey indicated that the pre-service teachers found the process helpful in developing multiple habits of mind (see Table 11.1 for mean ratings). The survey ratings revealed the highest scores were for statements related to managing impulsivity, and thinking about thinking. The pre-service teachers found participation in MLS most helpful to developing their proclivity and ability to carefully plan in preparation of a lesson (managing impulsivity) and to reflect on, become more conscious of, and evaluate strategies for teaching mathematical ideas (thinking about thinking). The mean values corresponding to each of these two statements were 4.69 and 4.55 with standard deviations of 0.47 and 0.55, respectively. The next highest scores were for statements related to their perceptions of the value of MLS in helping them to develop an understanding of the importance of learning continuously through the process of teaching, supporting their development of knowledge that would be useful to apply in the future, and recognizing the importance of considering alternate points of view in teaching (a reverse response statement). The mean values corresponding to each of these three statements were 4.45, 4.43, and 4.43 with standard deviations of 0.80, 0.86, and 0.83, respectively.

Corresponding explanations related to the mean ratings of the Likert-type items in Table 11.1 were also investigated. Through analyses of the participants' explanations about their ratings for each item, several themes emerged for each statement that elucidated participants' perspectives on MLS as an approach supporting pre-service teachers' development and implementation of habits of mind. Qualitative analysis revealed from one, two (most prevalent), or at most three major themes for each HoM statement arising through the coding of participants' explanations for their ratings. These themes will be discussed below.

Mean and Standard Deviations for HoM MLS Feedback Survey

Item	Habit of Mind	Statement	Mean & Standard Deviation
1	Managing Impulsivity	MLS helped me to understand the importance of careful planning in preparation to teach a lesson.	4.69, 0.47
2	Listening to Others	MLS helped me develop my ability to listen to others with care in order to understand their point of view.	4.26, 0.73
3	Thinking Flexibly	MLS **did not** help me recognize the value of considering alternative points of view in planning and teaching mathematics.	4.43[R] 0.83
4	Thinking about own Thinking	MLS helped me to reflect on, become more conscious of, and evaluate strategies for teaching mathematical ideas	4.55, 0.55
5	Questioning and Posing Problems	MLS helped me develop my ability to ask questions and pose problems when planning or teaching a mathematics lesson.	4.29, 0.74

6	Applying Past Knowledge to New Situations	MLS helped me to develop knowledge that I will be able to apply in the future.	4.43, 0.86
7	Thinking and Communicating with Clarity and Precision	MLS did not help me recognize the value of clear and precise communication when discussing and teaching mathematical ideas.	4.34 (R) 0.88
8	Thinking Interdependently	MLS did not help me develop my ability to work interdependently with other teachers in planning and reflecting on lessons	3.88 (R) 1.25
9	Learning Continuously	MLS helped support the importance of learning continuously from teaching, developing capabilities for effective and thoughtful action and exploration of alternatives.	4.45, 0.80
10	Gathering Data through All Senses	MLS has helped me understand the benefits of systematically observing and discussing observations in learning from teaching.	4.31, 0.81
11	Reflective Intelligence	My course instructor, working as our MLS group mentor, helped us to use reflective intelligence in planning and revising our MLS lesson in light of our teaching of the lesson	4.36, 1.00

Notes: (R) indicates reverse response item. Response ratings based on (1) Strongly Disagree, (2) Disagree, (3) Neutral, (4) Agree, (5) Strongly Agree.

With respect to Managing Impulsivity (Item 1, Mean=4.69, SD=0.47), all of the participants' strongly agreed or agreed that MLS helped them to understand the importance of careful planning. One of the major themes that emerged from the analysis of their explanations was the importance of planning the details of a lesson in preparation to teach. Carefully planning the details of lessons will bode well in these pre-service teachers' managing impulsivity in teaching. For example, as one participant explained, "I learned that it takes time and patience to have a successful lesson. You need to analyze every single part of your lesson and make sure you think of everything that could happen." Another commented, "I felt that I really learned that planning a lesson requires preparation. I had to research and carefully demonstrate how to use manipulatives as I never have before."

A second major theme that arose from analysis of participants' explanations for their ratings to this item was recognizing the importance of planning for student understanding. Participants' responses supporting this theme included, "I realized that you have to be prepared to answer any questions your students may have;" and "You have to make sure you cover every component of a lesson so that the student understands, by preparing you ensure you cover every aspect."

In relation to Listening to Others (Item 2, Mean=4.26, SD=0.73), the majority of the participants strongly agreed or agreed (except six neutral ratings) that MLS influenced them positively in this area. Many reported valuing others' perspectives as they can lead to new ideas for practice. This theme was evidenced in statements such as, "I needed to learn others' ideas so I can improve my work and make it better for further work," and "With my group members we were able to come up with a really well done lesson on our third teach by listening to each others' ideas." Another major theme related to this HoM was the value of constructive criticism for improving their practice. For instance, one participant stated, "MLS helped me listen because when we debriefed I had to listen to constructive criticism to better our lesson and our teach." Another stated, "Others can tell you things you didn't think of before and help you grow." This finding is aligned with prior research findings related to pre-service teachers (both secondary and elementary) recognizing the value of considering others' points of view in teaching (Fernandez, 2010; Fernandez & Robinson, 2006; Molina, 2012; Molina, Fernandez, Nisbet, 2011).

The item related to Thinking Flexibly (Item 3, Mean=4.43, SD=0.83) was a reverse response item. Based on the reserved ratings, the elementary pre-service teachers indicated overwhelmingly that they strongly agreed or agreed (except three neutral ratings) with this statement. From analyses of their explanations for their ratings, MLS helped the pre-service teachers open up to and develop different approaches to teaching. This theme was most prevalent amongst all others for this HoM given participant explanations such as, "It did help me consider different views because the groups taught lessons in a different way than I learned them as a kid;" "It helped me consider others' points of views in order to better my teaching;" and "We are used to traditional ways of solving problems and this helped us see different ways of using hands-on manipulatives." An inclination toward thinking flexibly will benefit participants in their continued growth as teachers. Findings from pre- and post-assessments of pre-service teachers involved in MLS have shown that pre-service teachers' thinking about approaches to teaching has become more flexible and open to alternative more student-centered approaches to teaching mathematics through participation in MLS (Fernandez, 2010; Molina, 2012).

When it comes to Thinking about Thinking (Item 4, Mean=4.55, SD=0.55), all of the participants, except one neutral, strongly agreed or agreed on the support MLS provided them for reflecting on, becoming more conscious of, and evaluating strategies for teaching mathematics. A major theme arising from their responses was their observed value of reflecting on lessons. For example, one participant responded, "By reflecting on our presentations we were able to evaluate if what we were teaching and how we were teaching is effective." In agreement with this idea, another mentioned, "I really liked that we were videotaped; it helped me reflect in a completely different way. I was able to really see the mistakes I made and reflect on what went well [in the lesson]." In the literature, the importance of reflection and thinking about their thinking about teaching through MLS and, in particular, the use of videotaped MLS lessons for reflection and deliberation among group members has been found to be a key aspect of learning through MLS (Fernandez, 2005, 2010; Fernandez & Robinson, 2006).

Another most important theme that emerged from the analysis of participants' responses to item 4 was their ability to recognize growth in their thinking about teaching mathematics through the MLS process. Evidence of this theme includes the following responses: "Reflecting, yes, I used a lot of different strategies that we never used before;" "Prior to this class and MLS assignment, I always turned to traditional strategies. I now understand that I can teach my students to better understand math by using nontraditional strategies;" and finally, "I was able to finally think outside of my box. I learned to use nontraditional ways to teach math (and I am a very traditional thinker)."

Participants' ratings of the Questioning and Posing Problems HoM related statement (Item 5, Mean=4.29, SD=0.74) were primarily agree and then strongly agree with three neutrals and one disagree. The explanations corresponding to participants' ratings revealed one major theme for this item: participants valued learning to ask questions during a mathematics lesson. For example, one participant commented, "I had to think of what students might say and I also had to think about questions to probe them." Another wrote, "I had to come up with questions to see if the students were grasping the content." A third responded, "It did make me think of questions and problems that will help my students understand the concept of the subject." Prior research has demonstrated actual growth in the participants' development and posing of questions and problems through analysis of the developing MLS lessons over the three cycles (Fernandez, 2010; Molina 2012; Molina, Fernandez, & Nisbet, 2011), as well as through pre- and post-assessment lesson plans (Fernandez, 2010).

Of particular importance to this study were the participants' perspectives about developing knowledge that will be applicable in the future. This idea is connected to the Applying Past Knowledge to New Situations HoM (Item 6, Mean=4.43, SD=0.86). Participants' ratings of this item were overwhelmingly strongly agree and agree with one neutral. Two major themes emerged from analysis of the participants' explanations of their ratings for this item. First, many participants highlighted the value of learning new mathematics teaching strategies to use with their future students. As one participant emphasized, "Completely! I am now aware of manipulatives and other strategies I can use to explain math problems." Another participant explained, "With MLS I learned that there are so many ways to teach a concept and math can be made easy and fun. I will definitely use the knowledge I gained in my own classroom." Second, participation in MLS improved elementary pre-service teachers' ability to plan mathematics lessons. Responses elucidating this theme included, "MLS helped on getting an idea on how it will be teaching and the things I need to do prior to teaching;" and "Yes this will help me for planning math lessons in the future." Fernandez (2010) and Molina (2012) have demonstrated pre-service teachers involved in MLS actually drawing on knowledge developed through the process and applying it to a new situation.

With respect to the Thinking and Communicating with Clarity and Precision reverse response statement (Item 7, Mean=4.34, SD=.88), the pre-service teachers primarily strongly agreed and agreed (except for four neutrals) that MLS helped them recognize that communicating about mathematical ideas with clarity and precision was important and valuable.

A major theme from analysis of the participants' explanations for their ratings was their understanding that clear and precise communication helped improve their students' understanding. For example, one participant stated "It did help me recognize how clear you must be when teaching a lesson and how open communication between you and your students helps them ask questions and ultimately understand." Another stated, "The students need to recognize a specific idea. Learning and teaching is the ability to communicate a message. For instance, division means to share equally; the students need to know that and the teacher needs to communicate that." A second major theme that arose was participants' realization that clear and precise communication was important for effective peer communication. Some participants' explanations referred to both major themes for example, "This assignment reinforced my belief in the value of clear communication without clear communication students and colleagues cannot understand your ideas and points of views." Others focused solely on communication with their group members, for instance, "Communication was the key to our success. We were able to resolve any problems that came up in our lessons;" and "It's very important to communicate with your group members and listen for different ideas that can be valuable to the students and their learning."

The reverse response item related to Thinking Interdependently had the lowest mean and highest standard deviation of all the items (Item 8, Mean=3.88,

SD=1.25). All except 12 of the participants (who rated the item neutral to strongly disagree) felt strongly agree or agree that MLS helped them develop ability to work interdependently with colleagues. A major theme in the responses for those with positive ratings was the value of collaboration. These participants credited the use of effective collaboration as a principal influence for improvement in their lessons. Those who viewed collaboration as highly important and valuable stated, "This project did help me develop my ability to work with others because I continually worked with my partner and my professors to make my lesson better". Another shared "MLS helped me develop my ability to work with other teachers in my school." Many of the pre-service teachers found their peers ideas to be valuable. For instance, these reported, "MLS has expanded my way of thinking like the saying two heads are better than one. Using your resources like other teachers is a great way for teaching. Teachers should work together and get ideas from each other." For those that rated this item in a negative way, their explanations revealed a theme of ineffective collaboration. For example, some commented, "I hate group projects! There is always someone irresponsible and the rest must carry their weight in order to pass. NOT FAIR." Some of our previous work has found some negative experiences with collaboration among our elementary pre-service teachers (Molina, 2012); such negative experiences have been more limited with the secondary pre-service teachers (Fernandez, 2005).

In relation to the Learning Continuously HOM (Item 9, Mean=4.45, SD=.80), all of the pre-service teachers, except three, strongly agreed or agreed that MLS helped them understand the importance of learning continuously from teaching. One major theme that arose was participants crediting the repeated revision of their MLS research lessons as continuous learning. For instance, one participant stated, "The MLS process helped me in learning how to develop and modify lessons and ideas for future lessons," while another participant commented that "Lessons can always be made better - even good ones. Taking advice, listening to others, and observing how students perform with a task can help make lessons better." Another major theme that surfaced was learning continuously through new teaching strategies and multiple representations utilized during MLS. Examples of explanations supporting this theme include, "MLS helps us to look to other alternatives when our first teach did not go as planned, therefore we learn to explore other alternatives in order to teach it better;" "I learned that I can learn from my teaching experiences. I also learned that through my research I can find alternative methods and ways of teaching:" and, finally, "I agree it helped me to think about different strategies that maybe I wouldn't have thought about before."

With respect to Gathering Data through All Senses (Item 10, Mean=4.31, SD=.81), all the participants (except for three neutral and two disagree) strongly agreed or agreed on the benefits of learning through systematic observations and related discussions offered through MLS. One major theme revealed in the participants' explanations of their ratings to this item was the value of observing and discussing other's teaching. Participants repeatedly commented on how watching others helped them learn. For instance, one participant stated, "Yes. Observing, discussing, being able to take criticism and give criticism so that after teachers don't feel discouraged when you go over your lesson." Another responded, "Through my observations and discussions with group members and instructors. I learned that it is essential to carefully observe what occurs in a classroom when you are teaching. This helps to make changes & improvements." According to our participants' explanations, reflection was another major theme and a vital part to systematically gathering data through all sense. Participants reported reflecting on their past teaches and reflecting on how to improve their future teaches. As one participant stated, "Yes by teaching math I learned the importance of discussing/reviewing info with the class as well as observing your students to ensure that they understand the topic." Another participant commented, "Watching [our] videos and reflecting on those videos helped to understand and further observe what was going on and what needed to be improved." The data collected during MLS including the video of MLS lessons (which has been thought to provide a more complete record of the lessons) has been found to be important in participants' discussions and self-reflections on their MLS lessons for learning through the experience (Fernandez, 2005,; Fernandez & Robinson, 2006; Molina, 2012).

According to their responses to Item 11 (Mean=4.36, SD=1), the pre-service teachers felt participation in MLS increased their levels of reflective intelligence. Participants attributed this increase in reflective intelligence to MLS mentors' facilitation of reflections and the MLS mentors' feedback. Participants found the MLS mentor helpful in improving their lesson, "The course instructor facilitated the entire process; she helped me to understand how to better communicate my ideas to my students." Another participant stated, "Meeting with our instructor, after our teach, was really helpful, and because of that my group progressed and did better in the last lesson than the first which was the point of MLS." Participants also found the mentors' feedback valuable: "The instructor was very helpful and there to give insightful ideas to improve our lessons and teaching approach." Another participant stated, "Our instructor gave us valuable feedback that helped us reflect on our previous lesson in order to improve the following." According to Fernandez (2010), Fernandez & Zilliox (2011) and Molina (2012), the role of the MLS mentor (or knowledgeable advisor) in supporting MLS groups' reflection on and deliberation about the lessons within the MLS cycles has been found to be an important one for both secondary and elementary pre-service teachers' learning. These studies suggest that the MLS mentor should engage in at least one of the first or second MLS lesson debriefing sessions with each group within the three MLS cycles.

Further Remarks

Based on this investigation, elementary pre-service teachers perceive MLS as a worthwhile and beneficial learning experience with respect to their development and use of habits of mind. According to Dottin (2010),

Experimentation with deliberation and direction is intelligent action (thinking or reflection). We aquire new habits in those situations in which the organism-environment transaction is interrupted-we encounter a problem. Reflective experimental problem solving is consequently an inquiry process (p. 15).

MLS provides an environment for experimentation with deliberation and direction for pre-service teachers to develop their knowledge and practices for teaching. Through this investigation, MLS can be seen as an inquiry process that supports elementary pre-service teachers' acquisition of habits of mind, as suggested by Dottin (2010). Given the similarities in our prior work between the learning of secondary and elementary pre-service teachers of mathematics, it is likely that MLS will also foster habits of mind among secondary school pre-service teachers. Data on this will be collected in the future to continue to inform our efforts to foster habits of mind across our FIU COE graduates. Additionally, we will further study elementary and secondary pre-service teachers' use of habits of mind beyond the course where they complete MLS to better understand the long-term impact of MLS on pre-service teachers habits of mind.

References

Ball, D. L., & Cohen, D. (1999). Developing practice, developing practitioners: Toward a practice-based theory of professional education. In L. Darling-Hammond & G. Sykes (Eds.), *Teaching as the learning profession: Handbook of policy and practice* (pp. 3-32). San Francisco: Jossey-Bass.

Costa, A. L. & Kallick, B. (2000a). *Describing 16 habits of mind*. Retrieved July 15, 2012 from http://instituteforhabitsofmind.com/resources/pdf/16HOM.pdf.

Costa, A and Kallick, B (2000b). *Discovering and exploring habits of mind*. Alexandria, VA: Association for Supervision and Curriculum Development.

Dewey, J. (1933). *How we think: A restatement of the relation of reflective thinking to the educative process*. Boston, MA: Heath.

Dewey, J. (1944). Democracy and education: An introduction to the philosophy of education. New York: The Free Press.

Dottin, E. (2010). *Dispositions as habits of mind*. Lanham, MD: University Press of America:.

Fernandez, M. L. (2005). Learning through microteaching lesson study in teacher preparation. *Action in Teacher Education*, 26(4), 37–47.

Fernandez, M. L. & Robinson, M. (2006). Prospective teachers' perceptions of microteaching lesson study. *Education, 127*(2), 203-215

Fernandez, M. L. (2008). Developing knowledge of teaching mathematics through cooperation and inquiry. *Mathematics Teacher, 101* (7), 534-538.

Fernandez, M. L. (2010). Investigating how and what prospective teachers learn through microteaching lesson study. *Teaching and Teacher Education*, 26(4), 351-362.

Fernandez, M. L., & Robinson, M. (2006). Prospective teachers' perspectives on microteaching lesson study. *Education*, 127(2), 203–215.

Fernandez, M. L. & Zilliox, J. (2011). Investigating approaches to lesson study in prospective mathematics teacher education. In L. C. Hart, A. S. Alston, A. Murata

(Eds.), *Lesson study research and practice in mathematics education.* Norwell, MA: Springer.

Molina, R. (2012). *Microteaching lesson study: Mentor interaction structure and its relation to elementary preservice mathematics teacher knowledge development.* (Unpublished doctoral dissertation). Florida International University, Miami, FL.

Molina, R., Fernandez, M. L., & Nisbet, L. (2011). Analyzing elementary preservice teachers' development of content and pedagogical content knowledge in mathematics through microteaching lesson study. In M. S. Plakhotnik, S. M.. Nielsen, & D. M. Pane (Eds.). *Proceedings of the tenth annual college of education and graduate student network research conference,* 162-169. Miami, FL: Florida International University.

National Council of Teachers of Mathematics. (2000). *Principles* and *standards for school mathematics.* Reston, VA: Author.

The Conceptual Framework of the College of Education. (n.d.). Retrieved on July 11, 2011 from http://education.fiu.edu/docs/Conceptual%20Framework%2006-19-09.pdf

Yost, D. S., Sentner, S. M., & Forlenza-Bailey, A. (2000). An examination of the construct of critical reflection: Implications for teacher education programming in the 21st Century. *Journal of Teacher Education, 51*(1), 39-49.

CHAPTER TWELVE

Using an Historical Lens and Reflection to Establish Our Vision of Teaching Pre-Service Elementary Teachers Content and Methods of Science

By

George E. O'Brien
Kathleen G. Sparrow

Backdrop

Florida International University (FIU), which opened classes in 1972 in Miami, Florida, is one of the largest and most diverse institutions of higher education in the United States, with over 83% of its 48,000 students being minorities and nearly 40% the first generation in their families to earn a college degree (FIU, 2012a.). The B.S. in Elementary Education K-6 (with ESOL Endorsement) program is housed in the Teaching and Learning Department in the College of Education (COE). The program (129 semester hours) can be described as traditional and is designed to be completed by candidates after finishing general education and major required components in a four year full-time enrollment plan of study.

In this chapter, we will provide the story of the course SCE 4310. SCE 4310 is the elementary education content and methods course designed to provide the knowledge and experiences necessary for pre-service teachers to be disposed toward teaching science in their classrooms. It provides for the development of knowledge, skills, and dispositions as Habits of Mind (HoM) necessary to prepare students to assume the role of teachers of science in elementary school. Such a course is supported by the National Science Teachers Association (NSTA) in its Standards for the Preparation of Science Teachers (NSTA, 2011), and in its Standards for the Preparation of Science Teachers, *Recommendations for Elementary Generalists* (NSTA, 2003), and supports the College of Education's vision "to seek a desired future in which the emphasis on inquiry is the means-end connection to enhancing reflective intelligence" ("The College of Education Conceptual Framework, n.d., p. 4).

Our objectives are to describe 1) the SCE 4310 course, including expectations for its candidates and lessons learned from its origins until 2012, 2) how we have studied, planned, and designed the SCE 4310 course to develop purposefully candidates' dispositions as Habits of Mind (HoM), through the building of awareness and conceptualization, 3) how we structured our learning environments to enhance dispositions as HoM, 4) how we have encouraged candidates' self-reflection and meta-cognition, while documenting their dispositions during engaging, interactive science investigations by use of various problem solving strategies and tools, including reflective discourse (Roychoudhury & Rice, 2009; Sadler, 2006), writing in journals/science notebooks, development portfolios, inventories, and *TaskStream* web-based electronic portfolio artifacts (Dana & Tippins, 2003), 5) how we have introduced to the candidates opportunities to apply the modeled approaches and experiences, as they demonstrate "dispositions in action" (Eick & Stewart, 2010; Thornton, 2006) in K-6 learning environments, 6) how we have piloted innovative science education resources during 2011-2012 to create the design and implementation of a second, in what is to be a series of two, sequenced, pre-service elementary teacher content and methods science courses beginning in spring, 2013, and 7) our vision for creating a more comprehensive, longitudinal multi-staged sequence of pre-service elementary, early childhood, and exceptional student education teachers' science experiences.

In writing to these objectives, that address both retrospective and contemporary thoughts related to pre-service teacher science education in our college, we want to share each author's personal voice when describing personal contexts, reflections and analysis, and, where appropriate, in using an historical lens. However, in the descriptive elements of the chapter, although sometimes referring to only one of the authors, we use the plural voice. The authors' working relationship began in 2008, although Dr. O'Brien has been at FIU since 1988, a shared perspective and common reflective outcomes are frequent in our thinking about the recent developments at FIU.

SCE 4310 – Constructing New Dimensions from a Competency-based Approach

The main body of SCE 4310, that one author, Dr. O'Brien, taught for the first time during spring 1989, had been created by Senior Professors Richard Campbell and Luis Martinez-Perez, and it was consistent with a technological conceptual orientation (Feiman-Nemser, 1990 see also the Introduction chapter in this book). Campbell had focused on a process and product research agenda (Gage, 1978). Campbell (1979, p. 123) described SCE 4310 as a course with a competency-based approach which centered on pre-service teachers' development of basic and integrated science process skills. He had adapted this approach from his graduate teaching and research experiences at the University of Indiana (Howey & Zimpher, 1989; Andersen & Gabel, 1981). During this period, he and his colleagues were studying the effectiveness of process skill instruction in relation to self-concept, attitudes, planning, and reading comprehension (Campbell & Okey, 1977), while working with pre-service and in-service teachers placed in elementary schools with diverse populations in urban settings (Campbell, 1978; Campbell, 1981).

Before receiving his first teaching assignment, lead author (O'Brien) had an essential (benchmark) learning experience to complement his professional preparation, including his culminating academic preparation at The University of Iowa in 1985, and professional development and other professional experiences in elementary and science teacher education, most recently at the University of Pittsburgh. FIU, a longtime partner with Miami-Dade County Public Schools (MDCPS), the fourth largest school district in the US, placed most of its student teachers from the elementary education program in public schools across the vast district. During fall 1988, he had the privilege of supervising thirteen student teachers in eight elementary schools in very diverse ethnic and cultural communities in geographical areas ranging from the inner city to more suburban neighborhoods. The wealth of languages and dialects spoken in the communities which housed the schools was astonishing. His observations of the student teachers, cooperating teachers, and children in the various classrooms during that sixteen week semester provided a very contextualized and rich learning experience for him and added tremendously to his knowledge and understanding of science education and student diversity, including race/ethnicity, language, culture, and socioeconomic status (Lee & Luykx, 2007; Lee, Lewis, Adamson, Maerten-Rivera, & Secada, 2007; Barton, 2007).

Important lessons that he took away from his sixteen weeks of supervising student teachers in elementary schools included: 1) science as hands on, minds-on and activities-based was not common practice in these particular schools, 2) observations of practitioners' isolation, at least with respect to assistance with science preparation and teaching, was the norm, 3) there would be challenges moving forward to change this scenario in schools, when the FIU intern experiences offered so little focus on science education, and 4) I would need to begin establishing professional partnerships with members of the FIU and MDCPS communities and with other local educational institutions including science museums and the Metro Zoo. With partners, we would then need to find funding to sponsor opportunities for pre-service and in-service teachers to help as many teachers as possible in such a vast school district. Based on these first-hand observations, coupled with studies supported by the National Science Foundation (NSF) that concluded that the classroom teacher was the key to successful science education opportunities in elementary classrooms (DeRose, Lockard, & Paldy, 1979), The lead author felt an intense desire to help provide pre-service and in-service elementary teachers the best science education experiences possible in the upcoming semesters. Further, he was encouraged by several of the FIU student teachers and MDCPS cooperating teachers who expressed genuine interest in receiving more science education professional development and told me that they would be visiting with me in the near future.

1988: The Calm before the Storm of Science Reform

In 1988, the backdrop and landscape of science education were beginning to suggest comprehensive changes to come in science teacher education and K-12 school science. At this time, a plethora of national reports and other influential publications, such as *A Nation at Risk* elaborated on the crisis in science education and declining performance of pre-collegiate students in school science (Victor & Kellough, 2000). In the state of Florida, the Department of Education teamed with the Florida Chamber of Commerce and the Florida Education and Industry Coalition and was poised to publish and release *A Comprehensive Plan: Improving Mathematics, Science, and Computer Education in Florida* (Florida Department of Education, 1989, April), yet nationally there were no recognized national science education standards per se. *Project 2061 Science for All Americans* (American Association for the Advancement of Science, 1989) *and Benchmarks for Science Literacy* (American Association for the Advancement of Science, 1993, 2009) had not yet been published. The lead author found that one of the most helpful publications related to teaching SCE 4310 was The National Science Teachers Association's (NSTA) *Standards for the Preparation and Certification of Elementary Teachers of Science* (1987, July), to be continuously revised through 2011. The document provided insights into the practical development and management of pre-secondary science education programs for initial teacher preparation and in-service teachers. During this time, he selected three primary resources for preparing to teach SCE 4310: 1) the NSTA Standards (1987, July), 2) science education syllabi and curriculum materials created by the senior faculty at FIU, and 3) his academic preparation and personal history.

SCE 4310: Changes 1989 – 1994

*1989-1990. S*tarting in spring, 1989, the lead author, taught at least one class of SCE 4310 every year through 2012. What did he change (i.e., add and/or modify) during the first couple of semesters of teaching SCE 4310? With what he had been learning about constructivism specifically, and learning theories more broadly, he had come to understand more than ever that learning and effective teaching are mindful and challenging processes. He intended to approach the teaching of SCE 4310 as a constructivist, with full and active pre-service teacher participation in science learning. By 1989, constructivist learning theories (Duit & Treagust, 2003) and increasingly social constructivism (Vygotsky, 1978) had become the dominant theoretical paradigm in teacher education. In an analysis of syllabi and textbooks of the period, the co-authors found that there were several added topics and teaching approaches modified for SCE 4310, including: curriculum and teaching for the topic of cognitive science and the constructivist concept of knowledge (Reilly, 1989; Glaser, 1988; Norman, 1978; Rumelhart & Norman, 1978); an interactive view of teaching; an inquiry-centered approach to teaching (Collins & Stevens, 1982); added

Piagetian activities (Oregon Department of Education, 1989) infused Science/Technology/Society curriculum and teaching (Penick & Meinhard-Pellens, 1984); and an increased number of school-based experiences, computer-based activities, and modifications, including a readings and study booklet for pre-service teachers created by the instructor (Yager & Penick, 1990). Although we cite these aspects as added on or modifications in the curriculum, SCE 4310 still focused on teaching candidates' science via activities, while nurturing development of science process skills. The lead author's personal history, preparation, and prior career opportunities weighed heavily on the changes made early on in his teaching, research, and service at FIU.

We wanted to help the pre-service teachers to construct their own understanding of content and pedagogical content knowledge (PCK) by doing inquiry lessons focused on questioning and thinking skills (Von Glasersfeld, 1989, Shulman, 1986; Briscoe, Peters,, & O'Brien, 1993; O'Brien & Korth, 1991). These lessons were activity-based, but in each successive semester the activities were expanding in depth and scope. We referred to these longitudinal activities as investigations., The nature of these inquiry-based methods helped the pre-service teachers to develop not only content knowledge and PCK, (e.g., local ecosystems, force and motion), but additionally science process skills linked to the subject matter, and leading to higher confidence in doing science (O'Brien & Peters, 1994). In SCE 4310, we sought to find out if the approaches we were modeling for pre-service teachers helped them gain knowledge and skills. Additionally, we sought to improve the affective domains of learning, including attitudes and self-efficacy (Yager, 1987). Our experiences in MDCPS schools helped to integrate teaching and learning for understanding in multicultural contexts (O'Brien, 1991a), while adding more computer-based hands-on experiences with probe-ware and simulations (O'Brien, 1991b).

1991-1994

During the early 1990s, we were able to build a team of full-time faculty and adjunct faculty to teach regularly in SCE 4310. The Elementary Education program was still of the same size, but tenure-earning faculty were productive in earning grant funding from several agencies, and, therefore, in some cases had reduced teaching loads which made room for adjunct faculty. We had not established a high number of full-time doctorate students and graduate TA opportunities at the time, and adjunct faculty were recruited at a fixed stipend range of about $1600-2000 per 3 semester hour course per semester. The quality of new faculty adjuncts teaching SCE 4310 during the period was outstanding. Their "characteristics of the instructor included: 1) engages students interactively in instruction; 2) takes student prior knowledge into account when planning the instruction; 3) promotes a sense that all students can succeed in the course; 4) models thinking and study skills important for succeeding in the course; 5) emphasizes the value of science, mathematics and technology for all people of all ages; 6) models an enthusiasm for an inquiry orientation in learning; and 7) is familiar with K-12 classrooms and teachers" (Flick, 2006, p. 23).

1995-2005 NCATE, National Science Education Standards, Florida Curriculum Frameworks, Florida Sunshine State Standards, and other reform-based activities

The prior science educational experiences of candidates before enrolling in SCE 4310 were often not effective. A major development in the 1990s was the *National Science Education Standards'* (National Research Council, 1996) call for elementary school teachers to "develop a broad knowledge of science content in addition to some in-depth experiences in at least one science subject" (p.60). Although there was debate in the 1990s about how to improve science education for pre-service elementary teachers, the demands from standards reform pointed to a societal need for more understanding of the nature of science, inquiry-based learning experiences, and understanding of conceptual linkages of one subject matter domain to another.

During 1995-1996, at FIU, two efforts were made independently of each other to provide more standards-based, reform science experiences for pre-service elementary teachers. For a short period of time, lasting only several months, when the faculty was restructuring the components of the new BS degree program, an added upper division science education content and methods course was proposed and accepted by faculty for development. However, other statewide factors related to needing other subject areas in the Elementary Education program resulted in a reversal of faculty votes, and the program was left with one content and methods of science course, i.e., SCE 4310. Another happening at FIU led to a nomination for a joint appointment of a COE and College of Arts and Sciences (CAS) faculty member in science/environmental education. The search was conducted and an appointment eminent, but both deans withdrew their offer to support a new two-college joint hire. The result, if followed up on, would have meant creating a required lower division course, replacing one of the science courses offered in a tradition style, and not limited to K-6 pre-service teacher candidates with a science and environmental education content and methods blend. Both of the reform options did not succeed.

During the 1990s, the B.S. Elementary Education program was housed in its own Department of Elementary Education. The number of tenure-earning faculty in this department averaged about 17 during the decade of the 1990s. Members of this department worked in developing a structure and programs that the college administrators would be comfortable in managing. The process of administrative change was ongoing for several years, but the payoff for the department's faculty came when the College of Education, in pursuit of national accreditation, began its development of its mission, theme, and conceptual framework. One outcome was the faculty in the Elementary Education Department were geared up and ready to be strong contributors to creating and then living the purposeful and meaningful charge based upon reform standards and guidance from the NCATE Accreditation journey. The improved changes to the program concurrently with the NCATE process was one of the most critical successes for faculty members and candidates in the BS in Elementary Education 1-6 (with ESOL Endorsement) program. The science education course and program framework components were very innovative (O'Brien, Lewis, & Williams, 1999) (see figures and information in Appendices 12.1, 12.2, and 12.3).

The science component addressed the conceptual framework, mission, theme, and goals of the college's Institutional Report and six-phase pre-service Elementary Education Program. The program was designed to prepare more highly skilled, motivated and knowledgeable beginning teachers. The program was a result of collaboration among faculty members and representatives from FIU's feeder community colleges and FIU's two major school partners, i.e., MDCPS and Broward County Public Schools. The faculty was guided by the following principles (Loucks-Horsley et al., 1990) in developing the model: 1) make science basic; 2) build a curriculum that nurtures conceptual understanding; 3) view science learning from a constructivist perspective; 4) connect curriculum, instruction, and assessment; 5) use a variety of assessment strategies; 6) relate curriculum frameworks and instruction to the National Science Education Standards (National Research Council, 1996); and 7) use a wealth of local community resources.

Also, the lead author felt fortunate to return to his role of supervising student teachers during 2001-2002, when a team of faculty from FIU and a corps of seasoned professional K-12 school teachers from MDCPS, working with state of Florida Department of Education funding, created opportunities for pre-service teachers and in-service teachers to collaborate in a mathematics and science integrated project-based approach (O'Brien et al., 2002; Krajcik, Czerniak, & Berger, 20043; Lewis et al., 2002; Alacaci et al., 2002). This partnership, an innovative effort, came as MDCPS was ten years along in its urban systemic mathematics and science teacher education (enhancement) initiative, with intense in-service professional development opportunities for K-12 teachers of mathematics and science. The climate in elementary schools had definitely changed, with more and more elementary teachers teaching science lessons on a regular basis and with more equipment, materials and resources in science than in the schools the lead author had visited regularly in 1988.

In 2003, the National Science Teachers Association created a new version of the Standards for Science Teacher Preparation (NSTA, 2003, pp. 6-9) which defined ten areas of standards: Content, Nature of Science, Inquiry, Issues, General Skills of Teaching, Curriculum, Science in the Community, Assessment, Safety and Welfare, and Professional Growth. From the start of our careers in teacher education, we believed these standard areas were each valuable and essential to the teachers of science in K-6 schools.

2008-2011 Professor Kathy Sparrow Brings Tremendous Professional Experience to SCE 4310

The story moves ahead a few years when Kathy Sparrow took on a role as an adjunct faculty member at FIU. She joined the university to teach SCE 4310 in 2008, and she brought with her 15 years experiences of working as the Science Learning Specialist, K-12 in a large urban district in Akron, Ohio. Her background in working with science teachers and on state science committees (e.g., Advisory Board for Science Curriculum Model, Review Committee for the Ohio Graduation Test) focused her experience on science curriculum and how science was taught in the classroom. During her tenure as science specialist, she was able to provide much professional development (i.e., funding was available) to Akron K-12 teachers in science content and pedagogy.

Based on her previous experience with elementary teachers, she realized that: (a) Elementary teachers needed instruction in inquiry and science process skills; (b) Elementary teachers needed to learn science content and pedagogical content knowledge; (c) Elementary teachers needed to feel confident that they could teach science; (d) Elementary teachers needed to realize the importance of teaching science in addition to reading and mathematics and in a way that students learned science.

SCE 4310 (2010-2011) Exploratory Study

The authors had been working in planning and development of SCE 4310 for two years, and wanted to know more about the effect of nested learning objectives (Costa & Garmston, 1998; Skerritt, Hard, & Edlund, 2008) in our classes, so we set up two components of an exploratory study project. The conceptual framework of our study used the landscape of the Costa and Kallick (2008) Four Levels of Educational Outcomes (see also Chapter by Angela Salmon and Debra Mayes Pane in this book). We wanted the candidates to come to be aware that dispositions as Habits of Mind (HoM) (The College of Education Conceptual Framework, n. d., p. 11) are linked to other constructs. In SCE 4310 attitudes, values, processes, problem solving abilities, thinking tasks, and dispositions are all valued ideas. Benchmarks for Science Literacy (AAAS, 1993, 2009) established Habits of Mind, and are presented in the authors' (Settlege & Southerland, 2007) presentation of Scientific Habits of Mind (value system).

The context of the next descriptions are the activities and investigations that take place primarily inside a classroom. The candidates were assigned readings in each of the three foregoing references and brought to awareness of the meanings of each individual HoM as they are presented in relationships to the different cultures including our COE UNIT and the various programs represented by candidates in SCE 4310 (elementary, early childhood, and exceptional student education). Discourse was facilitated concerning differences in the culture of schools and communities, and culture of science (values), and concerning differences and similarities of ideas presented by the three sources and particularly three habits of mind, curiosity, openness to new ideas, and skepticism.

The following represent class descriptions by Professor Sparrow during the semester of the exploratory study.

> SCE 4310 is a learner-centered class and models the constructivist/inquiry learning approach. This approach values the following: (1) Active learning: active participation of the students in the earning process. (2) An emphasis on higher-order thinking skills, e.g., judgment, evaluation. (3) Group-based activities and interaction. (4) Use of hands-on, minds-on investigative activities. The underlying foundation of this course embodies the 12 dispositions as Habits of Mind (HoM) of the College of Education and a resolve that students will leave the course with an understanding of the importance of elementary science education and a confidence to teach science.

We structured our learning environments to enhance dispositions, and a directed effort was made to engage students in activities that modeled the 5Es (Engage, Explore, Explain, Extend, Evaluate) Learning Cycle Model Approach (Bybee, 2002) and inquiry learning. Specifically, some of the first encounters with inquiry in the classroom were with problem solving activities such as designing a vehicle, Footprint Mystery (National Academies Press, 1998), Black Box Mystery and the Cube Activity NAP, (1998), which all help candidates explore the nature of science (NOS) (Lederman, 2007).

The first day of class, after the candidate's had read the professor's (Sparrow's) Philosophy of Education espousing a constructivist, collaborative and inquiry-oriented approach to teaching science, the students were presented with a problem: in their groups of four or five, they were to construct a "vehicle" that would travel across their lab table without their touching it. They were given specific materials which they could use to design their vehicle or car, including two drinking straws, four life savers, an index card, two sheets of paper, tape, and two large paper clips. The pre-service teachers had to collaborate, exchange ideas for the best design, and then construct their car using only the materials that were given to them. Needless to say, at first they were skeptical that they could accomplish the task they had been given. However, slowly students started talking together, listening to each other's ideas–both new ideas and prior knowledge–and together, with some trial and error and design testing, they created their car that met the criteria that they had been given. At the end of class, each table displayed the design of its car and demonstrated how it travelled across their table without their touching it. Students used mathematics, developed some knowledge about technology principles, and did science process skills, not the least of which was communicating to develop a collaborative Habit of Mind, fostering team work. This first activity set the tone for the subsequent classes during the semester, with students being unaware of how this first class experience mirrored not only science Habits of Mind, but also related to several of the College of Education's 12 dispositions as HoM.

We want HoM to be a meaningful, seamless part of SCE 4310. We found that a four step process facilitated our ability to effectively integrate HoM, as well as other important characteristics for approaching science (i.e. thinking, behavioral skills, and cultural values). First, we, as instructors needed to be clear in our understanding of specific HoM and other characteristics. We developed this clarity through discussions, planning sessions, visiting each other's classes, and sharing reading and other curriculum and teaching information. Next, we reflected on our own teaching, identifying where we made visible, or could make visible, HoM through our own behaviors. HoM must be modeled with awareness by the professor and observed with awareness by candidates. We then examined specific ways that our candidates could use and demonstrate HoM through course experiences. These identified ways would enable us to draw candidates into targeted reflection and discussion related to their development, use and refinement of HoM. Finally, by looking ahead, we identified what candidates should be seeking to do with their students related to HoM during student teaching and beyond. Again, by our being clear about ways candidates could incorporate HoM into their teaching and learning contexts, we were better able to support our candidates' in transferring the use of HoM to work with children.

Our thinking processes include the following element (see Figure 12.1).

HoM and other important characteristic (thinking behavioral skills, cultural values)	Examples of Instructors' method/approach toward candidate's awareness/valuing/internalization	Examples of Candidates' Qualities as Learners during SCE 4310 class sessions (as future teachers of science)	SCE 4310 Outcome: Looking ahead-- What candidates should be seeking to do as student teachers?

Figure 12.1 Four Step Planning Component for Integration COE's Dispositions as Habits of Mind (HoM)

In the following class activities, the students engaged in probably what one would call "classic" inquiry activities which introduced the candidates to inquiry processes and the 5E Learning Cycle approach. Each of the activities engaged them in collaborative inquiry and discussion. In The Footprint Mystery, students needed to propose hypotheses about the diagram of the footprints, and then re-think their hypotheses when a second diagram (additional data) was presented.

Similar activities included a version of the Black-box Mystery. They were given a canister that was taped closed and contained an unknown object or objects. Candidates worked together to make observations regarding the contents of the canister and distinguish their observations and inferences. In the Cube Activity, they were first presented with a paper cube with one side taped down to a card. On each side of the cube was a number from 1–6. The number 2 was hidden from view. Students worked together making observations and were encouraged to identify patterns among the arrangement of the visible numbers. From their observations, their data, they proposed which number was taped down and not visible. Students were then presented another cube, similarly with one side not visible to them. This time the cube was more complex. Instead of one number, each side had a male or female name, a number in the upper right and a number in the lower left. This cube was more of a challenge for the students because the answer was not as readily obtainable. The students worked together and needed to show more persistence (HoM) in analyzing the cube, finding patterns, and logically deducing the name and numbers that were on the side of the cube tape down.

A major inquiry investigation was presented with the earthworm investigation which followed the 5E approach. Students made observations and created their own questions and designed an appropriate investigation. Initially, the students were presented with a dehydrated earthworm (one unfortunate worm found baked to death on the sidewalk) as part of Engage. Then the professor read part of the book, *Wiggly Worms at Work* (Pfeffer & Jenkins, 2003), to further introduce earthworms. Students were then asked to write in their Journals the following words: habitat, food chain, body, internal organs, respiration, movement and reproduction. Students were asked to write down what they knew about these terms. Working in table groups, students each received one or two live worms. Students were to make observations of their worms. Suggestions of qualitative and quantitative observations were given by the professor. Students recorded their observations in their Journal. They also constructed a My Worm Wonderings (Ansbury & Morgan, 2007) chart in their Journal to be completed. As a homework assignment, students were to consult several websites (given to them by the professor) and supplement their prior knowledge from the terms they wrote down initially. Students also considered what they want to know about earthworms that they could investigate in the classroom, as a precedent for their open inquiry investigation. The activities engage the students in constructing content (subject matter knowledge) in this case about earthworms and all of the critical ideas important in understanding this living organism and its natural habitats. In this example, the components of Costa and Kallick's (2008) Four Levels of Educational Outcomes include:

1. Content Domain–knowledge of facts, generalizations, terminology concerning the earthworm (Cochran & Jones, 2003); PCK which has many elements linked to the general pedagogy, knowledge of the students, and science PCK for various dimensions of learning in development of teacher of science such as Science PCK for Unit Planning, Science PCK for lesson planning, and Science PCK for implementation, as examples (Appleton, 2006)

2. Thinking Skills–Some of these skills during the lessons include: Focusing skills, Information Gathering Skills, Organizing Skills, Analyzing Skills,

Generating Skills, Integrating Skills, and Evaluating Skills. The thinking skills will align with various structure components of the lessons including: Problem Finding/Refining, Research Designing, Data Collecting, Data Analyzing, and Evaluating (Pizzini, 1991; Pizzini, Shepardson, & Abell, 1989).

3. Cognitive Tasks That Demand Skillful Thinking–The investigation that is described in the investigation of earthworms is challenging to the SCE 4310 students with rich cognitive tasks requiring strategic thinking, making decisions, clarifying ambiguities, and testing ideas (Costa & Kallick, 2008).

4. Habits of Mind (HoM)–During the earthworm activities and investigations, the discourse among students and the instructor provide opportunities to assess the dimensions of the Habits of Mind present in the small groups and individuals working on finding out answers to their questions. What was the commitment of individuals in groups to organizing their study, using the various thinking skills during various aspects of the lesson structures? What capabilities do the students exhibit? How do students value various aspects of the science processes in which they are actively engaged? The classroom culture that develops during each week of a semester will provide opportunities for students to become analytical, manage impulsivity, persist, reflect thoughtfully, communicate accurately, and become curious and possibly passionate about the investigations like the earthworm investigation.

The following class students worked as a table group. Starting the Explore phase, students identified their problem and set up a lab report for their earthworm investigation. Students used available resources in the classroom or materials they brought in to conduct their study. Students were reminded of the previous activities (e.g., cube activity) where the more data they collected, the more evidence they had and the more support they had to see if their hypothesis was supported or not supported. Students wrote their procedure, and proceeded to conduct their investigations. They wrote their data as they collected it in their Journals. After they wrote their conclusions, they reflected on their investigation and data, then wrote what they learned from the entire investigation.

When the investigations were completed, the class participated in a Worm Conference. Representatives from each investigative group presented their problem, the experimental design, an overview of their collected data, and the conclusions that the group developed.

The modeling of inquiry throughout the class time and having the students actually participate in inquiry activities is the prelude to students reading about inquiry and the 5E Learning Cycle and subsequently implementing the processes in the classroom with their table mates. For background information students read "The Many Levels of Inquiry" (Banchi & Bell, 2008), "BSCS 5E Instructional Model" (Ansberry & Morgan, 2007), "The Nature of Science and Science Inquiry," (Brunsell, 2008) from their NSTA Collections. Students were also provided with step-by-step instructions for an inquiry lesson plan and a rubric describing an Inquiry/5E Learning Cycle Lesson.

The design of the set of activities and investigations are constructed as nested learning objectives where the instructor plans carefully to raise students consciousness of the complexity of the various lesson components containing content (i.e., science related facts, laws, theories, generalizations, concepts/ideas; PCK; NOS), thinking skills, cognitive tasks that demand skillful thinking, and habits of mind. The instructor sets up the activities so that students learn how the dimensions of the outcomes have the quality defined by the contextual setting either inside the classroom or during outdoor investigations. The curriculum, resources, assessment, classroom management, environment, multiculturalism, and languages help determine the nature of the class experience during the semester.

The next set of experiences took place after the worm study. Students were assigned an activity from the Exploratorium (http://www.exploratorium.edu/science_explorer/). Students' challenge was to use their assigned activity to develop an inquiry lesson. Intermittently, Dr. Sparrow modeled the inquiry activity "Dancing Raisins" with the class. ["Dancing Raisins" is activity where raisins are added to a glass of tap water and a glass of club soda. Students are to make deductions from their observations of the activity of the raisins in each of the glasses. Bubbles form around the raisins in the soda, float to the top of the glass, subsequently the bubbles break and the raisins sink to the bottom of the glass. Students try to explain what happens in terms of mass, volume and density (Bianchi & Bell, 2008)]. With these experiences as examples and explanations, each student developed an inquiry lesson that he or she would teach to his or her table mates. For our students, this was the first time that they had written a science lesson, which was totally different than the lesson plans they had written before for other content areas. Although, the students were apprehensive at first, they worked through the demands of the inquiry lesson plan and the 5Es. The following class, the students took turns teaching their lesson to their table. After each student taught his/her lesson to his/her tablemates, the ''teacher'' completed a self-assessment on his/her teaching and lesson. The "students" also completed an assessment of the teaching and the lesson of the "teacher." Subsequently, the professor also read each lesson and provided written feedback to the student. Therefore, each student received feedback from three different sources.

The following class students regrouped by the learning activity they had taught, i.e., all the students that taught the Black Magic lesson to their tables were a group, etc. Using the information in the background reading of "Inquirize Your Lesson" (Everett & Moyer, 2007) that students had done previously, students together shared and analyzed their lessons. As a group, they collaboratively rewrote their inquiry-5E lesson plan for the activity they had taught. By the students' thinking interdependently, being open-minded to each other's ideas, and analyzing their various strategies (3 HoM), they collaboratively rewrote an inquiry lesson together.

Although all of our students experience doing science indoors and outdoors, the set of activities and learning experiences provide a visual representation of the 5E Learning Cycle Approach in operation inside a classroom. The context to visualize the description of component 1 of the exploratory study can be best visualized by the descriptions of the classroom experiences (see Results A. Component 1 below). Now, think of a warm and balmy Miami, and you are outdoors in a nature preserve on campus, and the instructor has worked with you for several weeks with the 5E activities and investigations indoors and outdoors, but for a few weeks a major component of learning is centered on the biodiversity of three habitats (wetlands, pine rocklands, and hardwood tropical hammock) in a nine acre "living classroom" just a few blocks from the COE, but still on-campus. Just like the experiences described for indoors, our candidates are novice in exploring the outside habitats. We gradually work from earthworm studies, pond studies, to the FIU Nature Preserve and the FIU Organic Garden together on the 9-acre site.

Nationally, elementary teachers are reporting use of environmental settings to teach science (Schepige et al., 2010). Since 1988, we have used inquiry-based teaching, frequently in the outdoors such as at the FIU Nature Preserve (Lewis, Alacaci, O'Brien, & Jiang, 2002). The teaching strategies including Search-Create-Solve-Share (SCSS) (Pizzini, 1991; Pizzini, Shepardson, & Abell, 1989) and Project-based Science (Krajcik, Czerniak, & Berger, 1999) have motivated and interested teachers and children for years. What knowledge, skills, and dispositions, as Habits of Mind (HoM) do pre-service teachers develop doing inquiry in these settings? Results in B. Component 2 provide a frame of reference for analysis of the question.

Results of the Exploratory Study

Component 1: Pre-service Elementary Teachers' Understanding and Use of the Learning Cycle during a Science Methods Course Using Culture and Reflection Orientation as a Starting Point

Introduction. The study examined the factors involved in the understanding and use of the 5E Learning Cycle Model of science teaching (Bybee, 1997; Bybee, 2002; Settlage & Southerland, 2007). The participants were 50 pre-service elementary teachers enrolled in multiple sections of SCE 4310, our science content and methods course, taught by one of the authors of this chapter. We have followed the lead of the national reform movements to prepare future teachers to engage their students in inquiry as part of their science instruction (AAAS, 1989; Interstate New Teachers Assessment Consortium (INTASC), 1992; National Research Council, 1996). The course included most of the elements and major topics found in science methods courses for pre-service urban elementary teachers (Moscovici & Osisioma, 2008, fall). The course used culture and scientific habits of mind (e.g., curiosity, openness, skepticism) (Settlage & Southerland, 2007; AAAS, 1989) and reflection orientation (Abell & Bryan, 1997) as starting points in the study of content and methods of teaching elementary grades science. Pre-/Post-tests, survey data, in-class and school-based artifacts including participant reflections/journal entries, and classroom activities during the 16-week course show the success and challenges for pre-service elementary teachers developing knowledge and applications of the 5E (Engage, Explore, Explain, Extend, Evaluate) Learning Cycle Model.

The study will be informative to colleagues developing and teaching science content and methods courses, particularly in the USA. The next phase of study for the researchers will be to follow a sample from our population of pre-service elementary teachers longitudinally through student teaching and their early teaching careers to better identify and understand long-term outcomes of the content and methods science course and other program courses (e.g., see chapter in this book by Lynne Miller, Helen Robbins, Maria Tsalikis, & Lynn Yribarren).

The Learning Cycle Teaching and Learning Model. The learning cycle (TLC) has been embraced as a teaching approach that is consistent with the goals of the National Science Education Standards (NRC, 1996; Hanuscin & Lee, 2008). TLC is an early inquiry-oriented science teaching strategy that can be traced back to 1959 as an evolving teaching method (Barman & Shedd, 1992; Lawson, 2004). Lawson (2004, 2010) has classified the learning cycle into three types: descriptive, empirical-abductive, and hypothetico-predictive. For this study, we have selected the use of the learning cycle teaching model adapted by both the class textbook (Settlage & Southerland, 2007) and one of FIU's local partnering school district's Miami-Dade County Public Schools. The five phases of the learning cycle teaching model for our study include: Engage, Explore, Explain, Extend, and Evaluate.

Methods and Procedures

We collected data through the following methods:
1. Pre-and Post-tests (Second and last class of the semester).
2. Surveys at the beginning and end of the semester.
3. 2010 Florida Comprehensive Achievement Test–Grade 5 FCAT Science (13 Sample Questions) (Florida Department of Education, 2009).
4. Collection of students' assignments. These included journal reflections, lesson plans, in-class, homework, and school-based (or field-based) assignments.

We conducted research minimally invasive to the process of the course. All artifacts that were collected were produced by the participants as a normal component of the course. All participants supplied informed consent. Change in the pre-service teachers' understanding of the learning cycle was measured by the pre-and post-administration of the Learning Cycle Test (Odum & Settlage, 1996). The 13-item (with two responses per each item) multiple choice test measures students' understanding of the learning cycle. Odum and Settlage (1996), reported a Kuder-Richardson-20 reliability coefficient of 0.76 for the instrument, and Lindgren and Bleicher (2005) reported 0.87.

Component 1 Results

Table 12.1

Descriptive Statistics for pre- and post-TLC (N=50)

		Mean	SD	Median	Mode
Pretest items	(21	6.02	2.32	7	6
Posttest items	(21	8.68	3.60	9	19
Posttest items	(26	11.02	4.58	11	11

*Note, there was a mistake (5 missing items) on copies of LCT when administrating the pre-test (i.e., 2 class sections) and post-test in one class section of SCE 4310. Therefore, further data analysis was not available.

Information for Selected Questions/Responses from the post survey (N=50)
Questions

1. Describe what you gained from the SCE course.
A sample of participants' responses to question 1:
"I think the most significant thing I learned was to let students come up with their own ideas before explaining someone else's ideas to them." "I gained a lot of experience on how to teach science effectively. Being very hands-on and letting students explore are both major way of getting them to learn about new things." "I gained a new perspective on the teaching and learning of science. I learned that students learn best when they are allowed to explore, discover and learn with hands-on activities. I also gained confidence about myself as a future science teacher." "I gained a huge amount of confidence about teaching science. I am so grateful for taking this course because of what I gained." "I think the most significant thing I learned was to let students come up with their own ideas before explaining someone else's ideas to them." "I gained a different perspective of how science should be taught. I had my own preconceptions but now I understand how to implement my instruction with hands-on inquiry activities that foster learning. I gained insight, instructional resources, and experience." "I learned inquiry based questions allow students to better understand and grasp a concept."
2. How confident are you about learning science?
Students reported more positive feelings about learning science or a favorable changed attitude since the beginning of the course. Very Confident √32 Somewhat Confident √18 Not at all confident 0.
3. After completing this course, do you feel differently about teaching science? (Sample of comments from different pre-service teachers): "Yes, I

have more confidence in learning science. I now know that it can be fun to do." "Yes, before this class I really disliked science. However, this class showed me that through inquiry lesson plans science can be enjoyable."
4. After completing the course, do you feel differently about teaching science? Most pre-service teachers responded that they felt more confident and more prepared to teach science. (Sample of comments from different pre-service teachers): "I feel more prepared, passionate, and energetic about teaching science in my classroom." "The lesson plans are intense. I think teaching science at an elementary level will be more difficult than expected." "Yes, I used to think of it as a downside to teaching elementary students, but now I'm excited to do future experiments in class."

Reflections written in Development Portfolio (N=50)

Pre-service teachers stated the following: that micro-teaching was the most meaningful in-class activity (40%); their teaching inquiry lessons in schools was most the meaningful field [K-6 school] assignment (37%); pre-service teachers' interviews of children in schools concerning concept development of living things was the most meaningful field [K-6 school] assignment (33%).

Analysis/Discussion

Our observations of the candidates doing the investigations, creating reflections and numerous artifacts, and completing challenging science work showed a steady progression of development of science process skills, subject matter knowledge, PCK, and thinking as the semester moved along. The instructors collected various artifacts concerning reflection of the development of knowledge, skills, and dispositions during the semester. These artifacts became a professional development portfolio during the semester, and particularly focused on assessments for three areas curiosity, openness, and skepticism each represented in three aspects of the SCE 4310 framework: 1) dispositions, as HoM ("The College of Education Conceptual Framework," n.d., p. 11) 2) the Settlage and Southerland (2007) study as part of "Culture of Science," and 3) the AAAS (1993) aspects of values, attitudes, and traits as dimensions of scientific thinking. Pre-service elementary teachers in general gained confidence and reflected in context to comfort and acculturation to the "doing" science (i.e., Victor and Kellough (2000) would frame these ideas as part of the cyclic sciencing processes or culture that was created in the course.

Candidates were very successful and exhibited in some way or form through our observations an awareness of the HoM and often exhibited curiosity, openness, skepticism, cooperation, and numerous other "dispositions in learning science" and as outcomes expressed some values and inclinations toward internalization. The microteaching was valued by candidates, but did not carry the weight of Eick & Stewart, 2010; Thornton, 2006) "dispositions in action" in the professional environment of a K-6 elementary school classroom. The candidates showed awareness and in many cases provided evidence of the caring and values that may continue to grow professionally.

The scores from the questions in the Learning Cycle Test (LCT) showed modest gains. It is not clear if each candidate had adequate conceptualization of the knowledge, skills, thinking, HoM that in considerable time could develop. The LCT for other national samples of testing showed other populations of candidates from around the country having a challenge with this test. We think the literacy skill set and other factors on the scale may make this a very challenging test for our candidates. More research and data would need to be collected for follow-up and comparison of this sample.

Reflection/Discussion

One of the author's (Sparrow's) background and experience was as a science supervisor of a large urban school district, K-12, including 40 elementary schools. Especially in the elementary schools, the focus was on reading and mathematics, because that is what was tested both for No Child Left Behind and state assessments. Knowing that science would start being assessed in 2005, a more aggressive approach was taken toward elementary teachers to include and teach science in their classes. The focus was on inquiry and using science kits that were purchased as part of a new science adoption in 2000. In her experience, many teachers were receptive to teaching science, but did not feel qualified or confident.

In planning for this pre-service elementary methods course, there were two major objectives: One was to have candidates experience collaborative inquiry and hands-on science and to have positive experiences and enjoy the class; and the second objective was to instill in the candidates a sense of confidence-not that they would know a lot of new science content-but that they could plan and conduct good inquiry science lessons. From the results of the post-survey, an overwhelming majority of the students did identify a sense of being "very confident" to teach elementary science. Many of the students also realized the importance of teaching science to young children starting in kindergarten.

Component 2. Study - Promoting the Use of Outdoor Learning Spaces by Elementary Pre-service Teachers in a Science Methods Course

We have designed several learner-centered activities which encompass place-based inquiry (Sarkar & Frazier, 2010; Sobel, 2004). Place-based pedagogy uses a particular place for the context of the investigation where the integration of a variety of scientific and environmental concepts occur (Sarkar & Frazier 2010, p. 160). The integrated environmental and science education approach encourages active participation by pre-service teachers in real-world contexts and issues from which concepts and skills can be learned (Sarkar & Frazier, 2010). Although the FIU Nature Preserve was established in 1978 and has been introduced in our science content and methods courses for many years, a new initiative (2010) at FIU "GO Green" (online resources at http://gogreen.fiu.edu/initiatives/nature-preserve/index.html) has provided multiple facets of building and integrating sustainability and environmental education in our learner-centered approach. In addition to study of big ideas such as pond ecology, South Florida ecosystems, and plant-animal interactions, in previous semesters, new activities in gardening/food, solid waste and recycling, and energy systems have been developed by faculty.

Component 2 Results

We conducted the research minimally invasive of the process of the course. All artifacts that were collected were produced by the participants as a normal component of the course. All participants supplied informed consent. Concept maps were scored by a referent-free approach (Novak & Gowin, 1984). The method considers hierarchy (H), propositions (P), cross-links (Cl), and examples (E) important for scoring. A convenient sample of five pre-service teacher's concept maps focusing on activities at the Preserve from each class were scored, while *TaskStream e-folio* artifacts concerning responses to "open" questions concerning the habits of mind (OQ-T), curiosity, skepticism, and openness to new ideas were evaluated on a four scale rubric (0, 1, 2, 3, 4) concerning quality and accuracy to ideas presented. A third aspect of comparisons for each of the sampled pre-service teachers was the responses to inventory questions concerning concept mapping and overall development in Scientific Habits of Mind (SHM). All scoring was done by the instructor of the class. No other scorers were used in this study. Data are presented for two courses in Table 12.1 for the methods described here.

Table 12.2 Results of Scoring Pre-service Teachers (PT)
Science Methods Course 1 (n=5)
Scores Course 1

PT	P	H	CL	E	W	TS-CM	OQ-T	SHM
PT1	19	10	20	7	-1	55	2 1 1	HF F
PT2	4	10	0	11	-1	24	NoR	HF F
PT3	3	5	0	2	0	10	NoR	HF F
PT4	2	10	0	8	0	20	NoR	Hf F
PT5	9	5	0	6	-1	19	2 2 2	F F

Science Methods Course 2 (n=5)

Scores Course 2 (* Added Preserve, Inquiry, Investigation)

PT	P	H	CL	E	W	TS-CM	OQ-T	SHM
PT6	13	10	10	0	-2	31	NoR	HF F
PT7	6	5	0	0	0	11	1 1 1	HF F
PT8	18	5	0	15	0	38	2 2 2	HF F
PT9	10	10	0	8	0	20	1 1 1	F F
PT10	18	5	0	15	0	38	3 3 3	HF F

1. Concept Map (CM): 2. Responses to "Open" Questions - *TaskStream* Assignment: 3. Responses to Selected Questions [Focus: A. Concept Mapping; B. Outdoor-based Activities from the Habits of Mind Inventory / HF = Highly Favorable; F = Favorable; No res = No responses: Scoring for the Concept Maps = 1 point for each correct component (P, H, Cl, and E) and each wrong (W) component was deducted 1 point: TS-CM = Total Score, where higher scores represent higher quality of presentation of ideas.

Instructor's Analysis/Discussion

Some factors to consider about the scoring results of the 10 participants in two SCE 4310 sections: 1) The instructor asks candidates at the beginning of the semester about their prior experiences and prior knowledge about concept mapping and the science activities they would be doing during the semester. Before attending the first SCE 4310 class of the semester, candidates typically have not experienced doing concept maps and/or doing concept maps (CM) using a concept mapping electronic tool such as *Inspiration*. Candidates are provided readings and examples of concept maps related to learning science starting the second week of classes, and then each candidate uses her/his understanding of concept mapping to develop her/his own CM related to science concepts associated with activities/investigations at least two-three times during the semester. The CMs are completed in the candidates' science notebooks/journals. Candidates share CMs in small group as part of learning the science concepts by doing science work together (e.g., Earthworm Investigation, various investigations working with plants, outdoor observation studies). Candidates get to evaluate and try to understand the other person's use and understanding of CMs. In essence, they begin to score or at least assess the quality of each other's understanding of science concepts (vis-à-vis learning in a constructivist learning environment). The CM process takes adjustments and time to learn for most candidates (just as all real world problem solving does) and the process is more open ended than traditional science labs have been for the candidates. For the candidates, it is a real change of paradigm, and they are put in the world and culture of scientists. The first concept mapping experience follows activities such as writing science autobiographies (Koch, 1997), draw-a-scientists, and viewing videos such as "Search for Solutions, Conoco Phillips" where the class views the real scientists speaking about what science means to them. The candidates are asked to think about what the scientists do in the culture of science? Thinking skills and communicating skills are practiced and developed as a regular feature of the course. Candidates frequently confuse other cognitive tasks such as webbing [for brainstorming ideas] that are different than concept mapping. Webbing, which is used for lateral and more divergent thinking is very different, but is more frequently used by many K-12 school teachers and colleagues in other college level courses. Although candidates are asked to develop/construct her/his own concept map, the final assignment (e-folio, TaskStream) is most frequently completed outside class time. Candidates select her/his own concepts that she/he thought most appropriate and representative of her/his understanding of activities and concepts learned while doing science at the FIU Preserve. All scores of CMs are representative of novice learners in the content domain of studies and the particular concepts studied in the semester. Taken in context and consideration of the educational backgrounds and personal histories of the candidates with the nature of activities completed during the semester and the relative inexperience of the candidates in doing inquiry-based science, scores of 30 and higher for a CM represent novice learners, but making progress in the processing of CMs and learning science content. CM scores were similar, for both groups however, it is noted that the best CM score was achieved by a participant in the section without an added inquiry investigation. All participants completed the Scientific Habits of Mind (SHM) Inventory and responded favorably or highly favorably in her/his self-development and understanding of the featured the HoM aspects of the study.

Additional survey information from participating SCE 4310 pre-service teachers

Pre-service elementary (K-6) teachers (N=54) completed/stated the following: 89% - Visits and study at the preserve were very meaningful and valued course activities. 91% - completed a concept map (CM) using a CM-electronic tool, such as Inspiration (for the first time). 73% - either taught a lesson for elementary children or intended to do so in the future using outdoor locations and approaches used by the instructors.

*Selected Scientific Habits of Mind Question in study

Reflect on your conduct after each of the following learning Objectives in the course, and provide written responses to the questions below:

State the situation during the respective Learning Objective that caused *you* to be aware of your demonstrating or not demonstrating the scientific habit of mind. Provide locations (e.g., dates, specific activities) within your scientific notebook, portfolio, and/or *TaskStream* artifacts that show evidence demonstrating or not demonstrating the scientific habit of mind. Note: Where indicated √ and if applicable show for a particular scientific habit of mind and learning objective, if one or more of your science lessons in a school this semester had a focus or a teaching component that clearly related to this particular scientific habit of mind (indicate evidence from the lesson planning and/or reflection/assessment).

Learning Objective (from Chapter #10, Settlage & Southerland, 2007)
Concept mapping is one of the ways in which students can use writing to solidify their science ideas. Concept maps provide a visual way to represent understandings. Concept maps represent an individual's understandings about a concept and its relationship to other concepts. During SCE 4310 class activities, were there learning experiences that provided opportunities for you to use supportive evidence to accept or reject claims or propositions? Elaborate: *As a tool to support your conceptual learning and development, did you find concept mapping valuable? Summarize your experiences with concept mapping in SCE 4310. √Did your science lessons in your school placement provide opportunities for students to use supportive evidence to accept or reject claims or propositions? Elaborate:

Sample from a Participant's Reflection
PST #3 "When we were out in the preserve, although there were many insects and bugs we didn't exactly love, we were very curious to see what we would find deep into the greens of the preserve. Once we were able to get in there and see all the different types of trees and plants, we were so confused just beginning to think that we had to identify twenty selected plants and trees from the so many there were right beside one another to decide on. There were many different unidentifiable smells in just about every other station that drove me crazy wanting to know where they were coming from. Curiosity also led me to touch various leafs, trunks, and branches that didn't require much more than an arm stretch and a sense of feeling. I felt many different textures that varied from plant, to tree, to plant. Although it took a lot from me to actually get into the preserve, I overcame my foolishness and went on into the preserve. I wasn't open to new ideas in the beginning but I ended up going in and not having a problem exploring through the preserve. I had some internal tension that then became a relief to know that it wasn't all the bad as I foresaw. I felt accomplished by thinking scientifically to make observations and recordings, and I recognized the importance of being open to new ideas. Working in groups helped to locate and identify the correct station plant, but with more than one mind working and several pairs of eyes searching for the correct object led to a lot of skepticism. We would constantly ask each other if we were sure and doubted in at least twelve of the twenty stations if a group member's identification was accurate or not. Since we had the guides

printed we worked together to come to a conclusion for every station. Data, evidence, descriptions, and sketches of the leaves on the trees or plants really helped us identify the right ones. As teachers we must let our students be curious, encourage them to be open to new ideas, and be skeptical. Children's curiosity can lead to very extensive answers and discussions that can lead to success from that student and others. Being open to new ideas can lead to discoveries and accomplishments that one might have never imagined. Many may even develop a new interest by willing to consider new ideas. Skepticism will always leave many in doubt, but many times the uncertainty will lead to an accurate answer that might have been inaccurate before the doubts."

Is the Learning Experience in the Course Enhancing Growth in Habits of Mind?

Our response to this question is overall yes. We would like to study the candidates along their journey in the program to find out the particular impact of SCE 4310 on the journey. We think documenting HoM in the longitudinal system of the online commercial assessment system Taskstream, used by the college, would be a benefit to all students enrolled in the program, and this would help instructors of SCE 4310 have a more complete understanding of HoM exhibited by individuals who are challenged with demanding curriculum and teaching schedules and responsibilities with school-based field hours and constant interaction with students and teachers in different school setting each semester. We picture in the future the candidates enrolled in back-to-back content and methods of science courses that will help many candidates to construct knowledge, skills, thinking, and habits of mind, so that we would expect many of the candidates will be able to demonstrate HoM in a professional setting in this more systems approach to monitoring the candidates in the entire program. Establishing a system, where personal histories of individuals in relation to the domains of the four levels of outcomes and in respect to dimensions of growth for each knowledge, skill and disposition would have promise as part of the plan of establishing two science sequenced courses. The longitudinal information would be helpful for advising, teaching, and working together with more understanding of each individual.

Vision

Based on the history of SCE 4310 at FIU, our recent research explorations, and identifying our outcomes for SCE 4310, as a backward design (Wiggins & McTighe, 1998), we have been testing out different approaches to include in our (new) two sequenced content and methods courses. Our vision of Teaching Pre-service Elementary Teachers Content and Methods of Science is buoyed by the emergence of FIU as a national leader in STEM educational reform and newly developed opportunities available from BSCS and NSTA. We are teaching lessons with focus on pre-service teachers' conceptual change development and assessment (Driver et al., 1994; Diranna, 2012; Etheridge & Rudnitsky, 2003); scientific inquiry including approaches such as the CER Framework (Zembal-Saul, McNeil, & Hershberger, 2012; BSCS, 2010); issues in our environment and authentic science-based practices (Schepige et al., 2010; Cronin-Jones, 2000; Heimlich et al., 2004; Sarkar & Frazier, 2010; Sobel, 2004); and the fabric of multicultural (Gollnick & Chinn, 1990); language (Fathman, Quinn, & Kessler, 1992; Rosenthal, 1996; Teemant, Bernhardt, & Rodriguez-Munoz, 1996) gender (Rosser, 1990), urban (Barton, 2007); and local issues (Soto, Parker, & O'Brien, 1997) which make our university a dynamic and attractive community for students, faculty, and everyone who makes a large institution within a diverse community thrive. Since 2008, the heart of our College of Education, impacting its programs, courses, and students, has included dispositions, as Habits of Mind, as evidenced by classroom practices of diverse disciplines presented in this book. Our pre-service teachers have begun to identify many of the challenges in teaching and learning the complex and expanding knowledge-bases of modern science, one activity and investigation at a time in SCE 4310. With our help and leadership, pre-service teachers are taking further steps into the unknown via becoming more aware, and they are beginning to value dispositions as HoM, as well as the complexity and beauty of teaching and learning science. They have envisioned and begun to conceptualize the Four Levels of Educational Outcomes (Costa & Kallick, 2008) both within the framework of SCE 4310, but more importantly within the ideals and knowledge bases that consist with the COE's Conceptual Framework. We know this because of their discourse, reflection in writing and completing complex tasks, inventory responses, and our regular observations of the work accomplished with satisfaction of results instead of their bemoaning the nature of difficult tasks. With the COE conceptual framework as a moral and democratic guide, along with Costa and Kallick's outcome model, we have observed favorable progress in the effort and accomplishments of many of our candidates. With combining the Conceptual Framework (CF) and Educational Outcomes model, it has been possible for some of our pre-service teachers to visualize an urban school district using a nested objectives model (Skerritt, Hand, & Edlund, 2008) that parallel's the COE and course framework of complexity and multiple textures and dimensions, but is navigable because the candidates are able to learn via active thinking and engagement to develop their thinking skills, sciencing skills, content knowledge and PCK, and demanding cognitive tasks as part of one vision. We aim to expand our efforts and capacity, while mentoring, coaching, and teaching candidates so that they are able to enjoy benefits of actively engaging in more science experiences aligned with the CF and the models shared in this chapter. We look forward to the new arrangement and the challenges of getting more candidates further along the continuum of internalization of HoM. We believe that adding a second content and methods of science course will facilitate our candidates to build more knowledge, skills, and dispositions, however we vision adding three new courses in STEM education as a component of lower division quality education for our future teachers in elementary school classrooms. Our expectations are high, after some disappointments in the past, that our university and partners both internally and externally in the local schools will work toward the goal of providing longitudinal science and science education experiences of high quality to our future elementary teachers. We will continue to monitor and study the processes of development in the science content and methods courses. Our vision is to find out more about what approaches are the most useful in enhancing the complex array of teaching knowledge, skills and dispositions.

APPENDIX 12.1

FIU COE BS Elementary Education 1-6 (ESOL Endorsement) Program. Candidate Cadre Model: BLOCK I (PHASE 1): Philosophical/Ethical Issues (Established 1996)
Unit Questions: What is the purpose of education? (SCE 4310, major focus) How should teaching be approached? (SCE 4310, major focus) Is it an ethical enterprise? (SCE 4310, subordinate focus) Learning Goal: To think analytically (SCE 4310, major focus) and to be disposed to moral/ethical standards (SCE 4310, subordinate focus)

   BLOCK I: SCE 4310 Class Framework (Established 1998)

1. Content Knowledge	2. Nature of Science Knowledge	3. Knowledge of Children's Knowledge	4. Pedagogical Knowledge
A. What are driving questions we could ask?	A. What are the major theories in the domain that conflict? What is the evidence to support each?	A. What do students know about topic?	What learning strategies lead to better science learning?
B. What are critical concepts in the domain?	B. How has the understanding of concepts in the domain changed over time?	B. What are students interested in related to domain?	What leads to better equity?
C. What science practices, procedures, instruments, and forms are engaged to study domain?	C. What prompted these changes (e.g., new evidence, new technologies)?	C. Are there developmental issues about learning the domain (e.g., degree of abstraction)?	C. Ho0w can technology help with learning this material?
D. What are important "facts" to learn in domain?	D. What are current hot issues in the domain?	D. What else do we know about how children learn that can guide teaching of domain concepts?	D. What lessons, curriculum, and resources are there related to the domain? What are pros and cons of each?

1. Content Knowledge	2. Nature of Science Knowledge	3. Knowledge of Children's Knowledge	4. Pedagogical Knowledge
E. What larger science themes (unifying concepts in the NSES) are related to domain	E. What are scientific attitudes & processes? How are these linked to the domain?	E. What are community's beliefs and understanding about domain?	E. What are the best ways to assess student learning (process, product & attitude)?
F. How are process skills linked to domain?	F. What science products (including facts, laws, and theories) are related to domain?	F. What language or cultural issues make learning about domain difficult?	F. With what other subjects could this be integrated?
G. What are social ramifications of issues connected to domain?			G. What professional education resources can assist us with studying the domain?

*Modified and adapted from Raizen, S. A., & Michaelsohn, A. M. (Eds.). (1994). *The future of science in elementary schools*, San Francisco, CA: Jossey-Bass, Inc.

Appendix 12.2

The FIU COE BS Elementary Education 1-6 (ESOL Endorsement) Program: Six Phase Standards-based Development Model for the Education of Pre-service Elementary Teachers' Science Experiences (Established 1998 – 2003)

Phase 1a: (Lower Division) - Freshman & Sophomore Years

Science Education Focus: Preparation in Content Knowledge

General/Core science course electives 2-3 education courses (program prerequisites)

EDF 1005 Introduction to Education

EDG 2701 Teaching Diverse Populations EME 2040 Educational Technology

Phase 1b: First Semester, Junior Year

Science Education Focus: Introduction Four Strand Framework in SCE 4310 (primary focus- Content Knowledge & Nature of Science Knowledge Strands

Major assignments: Project-based science investigation & artifacts, field observations, & reflective journal

Portfolio entry: (1) Linked to Unit Outcomes - FEAP #4 Critical Thinker and/or FEAP #8 Knowledge of Subject Matter

Phase 2: authentic data Second Semester Junior Year

Profession Development Activity

Science Education Focus: Content Knowledge & Nature of Science Knowledge Strands

Major assignment: Project-based science investigation featuring open ended inquiry and analysis of

Portfolio entry: FEAP #4 Critical Thinker and/or FEAP #8 Knowledge of Subject Matter

Phase 3: Third Semester, Junior Year

Professional Development Activity

Science Education Focus: All Four Strands

Major Assignment: Optional/Self-selected activity/experiences

Portfolio entry: (1)

Phase 4a: First Semester, Senior Year

Professional Development Activity

Science Education Focus: Pedagogical Knowledge Strand

Major Assignments: Create, teach, and assess two small and/or large group science lessons in a

4b: Second Semester, Senior Year

Science Education Focus: Application of Four Strand Framework (all strands) Major Assignment: *Student teacher*-plan, create, manage, teach, and assess science instruction & learning

Portfolio Development:

Related to FEAPs 1-12Phase

local school

Portfolio entries: (2)
Related to FEAPs 1-12

Add, modify, develop entries built on Understandings, Skills, and Dispositions applicable to one's conceptual framework acquired over time/see FEAPs 1-12

Appendix 12.3

SCE 4310 Online Syllabus Linking Development of one's Understanding, Skills, and Dispositions to Self-assessment and Creation of Meaningful, Personal Portfolio Items (Class Web page, established, fall 2000)

I. *PURPOSE OF COURSE*

SCE 4310 is the elementary education content and methods course designed to provide the knowledge and experiences necessary for pre-service teachers to be disposed toward teaching science in their classrooms. It provides for the development of knowledge, skills, and dispositions necessary to prepare students to assume the role of teachers of science in elementary school. Such a course is recommended by the National Science Teachers Association (NSTA) in its Standards for the Preparation and Certification of Elementary Teachers of Science (July, 1992), and the New Standards and Pre-service Indicators (NSTA, 1998). These NSTA guidelines are supported by: 1) the "Standards for the Professional Development of Teachers of Science" reported in the National Science Education Standards (1996), 2) the Florida Department of Education, Florida Curriculum Framework (1996), and 3) the Florida Education Standards Commission Educator Accomplished Practices (1997a, 1997b). In addition, SCE 4310 and subsequent sequence of science professional development experiences (link here to Description of Science Professional Development Activities by Phase and Sequence) have been developed to include the Model Standards for Beginning Teachers of Science (Interstate New Teacher Assessment and Support Consortium: Science Sub-Committee, January, 1998). This course and subsequent science professional development experiences are required in the bachelor's degree program in Elementary Education and meet the State of Florida requirements for certification (Elementary Education, 1-6). After completing successfully SCE 4310, students enroll in a sequence of science professional development experiences during Phases II - V (or BLOCK II - IVB) of the elementary education program (link here to Current Detailed Descriptions and Specific Assignments in Phases 2 - 4a (BLOCKS II, III, IVa) of Elementary Education Program). Note that SCE 4310 is occasionally taken by Special Education and other education majors as a program elective.

II. *OBJECTIVES*

Upon completion of this course, participants will have the understandings, skills, and dispositions listed below. Some of the understandings, skills, and dispositions, are components (i.e., building blocks) of the Performance Standards for Teachers of English for Speakers of Other Languages (ESOL). At the completion of SCE 4310, the pre-service teacher will have shown development of parts of some of the specific ESOL Performance Standards, indicated by the numbers in the parentheses. (A great resource for Teaching Content through ESOL which includes the Performance Standards for TESOL.) Note in the linked document Performance Standards 1-4 correspond to bullets 1-4, and Standards 5-25 correspond to bullets 6-26. In addition, next to each number in the parentheses, an m indicates that this particular ESOL Performance Standard is a major focus in the course, while an s indicates a subordinate emphasis. Since many of the Standards refer to applications and use of essential strategies in classrooms, performance assessment of these occurs primarily in Blocks III through V (i.e., Phases 3 through 4b) of the program. (Link to the Florida Consent Decree document.)

To facilitate development of the understandings, skills, and dispositions listed below, a course framework has been developed (click here to see Class Four Strand Framework) The framework consists of four (4) major strands of knowledge (i.e., Content Knowledge, Nature of Science Knowledge, Pedagogical- Content Knowledge, and Knowledge of Children's Knowledge). Components of the understandings in the specific science theme include: 1. Content Knowledge a) critical concepts in the domain (e.g., weather, soils, Florida Everglades), b) science practices, procedures, instruments, and forms that are engaged to study domain, c) important "facts" to learn in the domain, d) larger science themes related to domain, e) how process skills are linked to domain, f) the social ramifications of issues connected to the domain, and g) authentic problems linked to the domain; 2. Nature of Science Knowledge a) the major theories in the domain that conflict, and the evidence to support each, b) how understanding of concepts in the domain have changed over time, c) what prompted any changes, d) the current hot issues in the domain, and e) what scientific attitudes and processes are linked to the domain; 3. Pedagogical-content Knowledge a) what classroom learning techniques lead to better science learning, b) what leads to better equity, c) how do these work when we try them, d) what lessons, curriculum, and resources are there related to the domain, and what are the pros and cons of each, e) what are the best ways to assess student learning, and f) with what other subjects could this knowledge be integrated; 4. Knowledge of Children's Knowledge a) what do students know about the topic, b) what are students interested in related to the domain, c) are there developmental issues about learning the domain, d) what else do we know about how children learn that can guide the teaching of domain concepts, e) the community's beliefs and understandings about the domain, and f) language issues that make learning about the domain difficult.

References

Abell, S. K., & Bryan, L. A. (1997). Reconceptualizing the elementary science methods course using a reflection orientation. *Journal of Science Teacher Education, 8,* 153-166.

Alacaci, C., O'Brien, G. E., Lewis, S. L., & Jiang, Z. (2002). Integrating mathematics and science in a pre-service elementary teacher education program, In S. McGraw (Ed.). *Integrated mathematics: Choices and challenges.* Reston, VA: National Council of Teachers of Mathematics, 117-129.

American Association for the Advancement of Science. (1989). *Science for all Americans.* Washington, DC: Author.

American Association for the Advancement of Science. (1993, 2009). *Benchmarks for science literacy: Project 2061,* Retrieved from http://www.project2061.org/bsl/online/index

American Association for the Advancement of Science. (1993, 2009). *Chapter 12: Habits of mind, in benchmarks for science literacy: Project 2061,* Retrieved f   rom http://www.project2061.org/bsl/online/index.php?chapter=12

Andersen, H. O. & Gabel, D. (1981). Science preparation of the elementary teacher at Indiana University. *School Science and Mathematics 81*(1), 61-69.

Anderson, et al. (2011, January 14). Changing the culture of science education at research universities. *Science, 331,* 152-153.

Ansbury, K. R. & Morgan, E. R. (2007). BSCS 5E Instructional Model, In *More picture perfect science lessons: Using children's books to guide inquiry, K-4.* pp. 29-34. Arlington, VA: The National Science Teachers Association.

Appleton, K. (2007). Elementary science teaching, In Abell. S. K., & Lederman, N. G., (Eds.). *Handbook of Research on Science Education.* Mahwah, NJ: Lawrence Erlbaum Associates, Publishers, 493-535.

Appleton, K. (2006). Science pedagogical content knowledge and elementary school teachers, In Appleton, K. (Ed.), *Elementary science teacher education: International perspectives on contemporary issues and practice* Mahwah, NJ: Lawrence Erlbaum Associates, Publishers, 31-54

Banchi, H. & Bell, R. (2008). The many levels of inquiry. *Science and Children.* 45(2), 26-29.

Barman, C. R., & Shedd, J. D. (1992). Program designed to introduce K-6 teachers to the learning cycle teaching approach. *Journal of Science Teacher Education,* 3, 58-64.

Barton, A. C. (2007). Science learning in urban settings, In Abell, S. K., & Lederman, N. G. (Eds.), *Handbook of research on science education.* Mahwah, NJ: Lawrence Erlbaum Associates Publishers, 319-344.

Bell, R., Smetana, L. & Binns, I. (2005). Simplifying inquiry instruction. *The Science Teacher, 72(7), 30-33.*

Briscoe, C., Peters, J. M., & O'Brien, G. E. (1993). An elementary science program emphasizing teacher's pedagogical knowledge within a constructivist epistemologic rubric, in Rubba, P. A., Campbell, L. M., & Dana, T. M. (Eds.). *1993 AETS yearbook: Excellence in educating teachers of science,* Columbus, OH: ERIC Clearinghouse for Science, Mathematics, and Environmental Education, 1-20.

Brunsell, E. (Ed.) (2008). The nature of science and science inquiry, In Brunsell, E., (Ed.). *Readings in science methods, K-8.* pp. 1-12. Arlington, VA: The National Science Teachers Association.

Biological Sciences Curriculum Study (BSCS). (2010). *ViSTA Project Online Modules.* Boulder, CO. Online at: http://online.bscs.org/

Bybee, R. W. (1997). *Achieving scientific literacy: From purposes to practices.* Portsmouth, NH: Heinemann.

Bybee, R. W. (2002). *Learning science and the science of learning.* Arlington, VA: National Science Teachers Association Press.

Bybee, R. W., Powell, J. C., & Trowbridge, L. W. (2008). *Teaching secondary school science: Strategies for developing scientific literacy, ninth edition.* Upper Saddle, NJ: Pearson Merrill Prentice Hall.

Campbell, R. L. (1978). Effects of teacher training in the individualized science materials on achievement of first graders. *Science Education, 62*(4), 523-527.

Campbell, R. L. (1979). A comparative study of the effectiveness of process skill instruction on reading comprehension of pre-service and in-service elementary teachers. *Journal of Research in Science Teaching, 16*(2), 123-127.

Campbell, R. L. (1981). Intellectual development, achievement, and self-concept of elementary minority school children. *School Science and Mathematics 81*(3), 200-204.

Campbell, R. L., & Okey, J. R. (1977). Influencing the planning of teachers with instruction in science process skills. *Journal of Research in Science Teaching, 14*(3), 231-234.

Cochran, K. F., & Jones, L. L. (2003). The subject matter knowledge of pre-service science teachers. B. J. Fraser and K. G. Tobin (Eds.). *International handbook of science education,* 707-717. Kluwer Academic Publishers. Dordrecht, The Netherlands.

Cochran-Smith, M., & Zeichner, K. (2005). *Studying teacher education: The report of the AERA panel on research and teacher education.* Mahwah, NJ: Lawrence Erlbaum Associates.

Collins, A., & Stevens, A. L. (1982). Goals and strategies of inquiry teachers, In Glaser, R. (Ed). *Advances in instructional psychology* (Vol. 2., pp. 65-119). Hillside, NJ: Lawrence Erlbaum.

Costa, A. L., & Kallick, B. (2008). Habits of mind in the curriculum, In Costa, A. L., & Kallick, B. (Eds.). *Learning and leading with habits of mind: 16 essential characteristics for success.* Alexandria, VA: Association of Supervision and Curriculum Development, 42-58.

Costa, A., & Garmston, R. (1998). Maturing outcomes. *Encounter: Education for Meaning and Social Justice, 11*(1), 10-18.

Costa, A. L., & Kallick, B. (2000). *Habits of mind: Activating and engaging.* Alexandria, VA: Association of Supervision and Curriculum Development.

Cronin-Jones, L. L. (2000). The effectiveness of schoolyards as sites for elementary science instruction. *School Science and Mathematics, 100*(4), 203-211.

Dana, T. M., & Tippins, D. J. (2003). *Portfolios, reflection and educating prospective teachers of science, In* Fraser, B. J., & Tobin, K. G. (Eds.). International handbook of science education, Kluwer Academic Publishers. Dordrecht, The Netherlands, 719-732.

DeRose, J. V., Lockard, J. D., & Paldy, L. G. (1979). The teacher is the key: A report on three NSF studies. NSTA.

Dewey, J. (1910). Science as subject matter and as method. *Science, 31*(787), 121-127.

Diranna, K. (2012, May 17). Web seminar: Conceptual flow: Bridging the gap between standards, instructional materials, and student learning. Archived web seminar, National Science Teachers Association, Online from https://sas.elluminate.com/site/external/jwsdetect/playback.jnlp?psid=2012-05-17.1450.M.C1D4AB3AF0045A371AEDADF46F7318.vcr

Driver, R., Squires, A., Rushworth, P., & Wood-Robinson, V. (1994). *Making sense of secondary science: Research into children's ideas,* London, England: Routledge.

Duit, R., & Treagust, D. F. (2003). Learning in science – from behaviourism towards social constructivism and beyond, In Fraser, B. J., & Tobin, K. G. (Eds.). *International Handbook of Science Education,* Part One, Dordrecht: Kluwer Academic Publishers, 3-26.

Eick, C. J., & Stewart, B. (2010). Dispositions supporting elementary interns in the teaching of reformed-based science materials. *Journal of Science Teacher Education,* published online: 05 January 2010.

Etheridge, S., & Rudnitsky, A. (2003). *Introducing students to scientific inquiry.* Boston: Allyn and Bacon.

Everett, S. & Moyer, R. (2007). Inquirize your lesson. *Science and Children, 44*(07), 54-57.

Fathman, A. K., Quinn, M. E., & Kessler, C. (1992, summer). *Teaching science to English learners, grades 4-8,* Washington, D.C.: National Clearinghouse for Bilingual Education.

Feinman-Nemser, S. (1990). Teacher preparation: Structural and conceptual alternatives. In W.R. Houston, M. Huberman, and J. Sikula (Eds.). *Handbook of research in teacher education* (pp. 212-233). New York: MacMillan.

Gage, N. L. (1978). *The scientific basis of the art of teaching.* New York, NY: Longman

FIU COE. (2012). Available online: College of Education Data. http://coeweb3.fiu.edu/

FIU, (2012). STEM initiative and university enrollment. News available online: ttp://news.fiu.edu/2012/02/fiu-joins-stem-education-national-dialogue-at-100kin1-00kin10-partner-summit/36229

FIU COE. (2011, August). College of Education Elementary K-6 (with ESOL Endorsement) Self Report Study: online at http://education.fiu.edu/accreditation/programreviews/dep_tl.html

Flick, L. B. (2006). Being an elementary science teacher educator, In Appleton, K. (Ed.). *Elementary science teacher education: International perspectives on contemporary issues and practice. Mahwah, NJ:* Lawrence Erlbaum Associates, Inc., 15-29.

Florida Department of Education. (2009). *2010 Florida Comprehensive Achievement Test–Grade 5 Science, FCAT Sample Questions.* Tallahassee, FL: [online]: http://www.fldoe.org

Glaser, R. (1988). Cognitive science and education. *Cognitive Science Journal, 115,* 22 - 44.

Gollnick, D. M., & Chinn, P. C. (1990). *Multicultural education in a pluralistic society,* New York: Merrill.

Hanuscin, D. L., & Lee, M. H. (2008, Spring). Using the Learning Cycle as a model for teaching the learning cycle to pre-service elementary teachers. *Journal of Elementary Science Education, 20*(2), 51-66.

Heimlich, J. E., Braus, J., Olivolo, B., McKeown-Ice, R., & Barringger-Smith, L. (2004). Environmental education and preservice teacher preparation: A national study. *The Journal of Environmental Education, 35*(2), 17-21.

Howey, K. R., & Zimpher, N. L. (1989). Profiles of preservice teacher education: Inquiry into the nature of programs. Albany, NY: State University of New York Press.

Interstate New Teacher Assessment and Support Consortium (INTASC). (1992). Model standards for beginning teacher licensing and development: A resource for state dialogue. Interstate New Teacher Assessment and Support Consortium. (n.d.) http://ccsso.org/intascst.html

Koch, J. (1997). *Science stories: teachers and children as science learners*, Boston: Houghton Mifflin Company.

Krajcik, J., Czerniak, C., & Berger, C. (2003). *Teaching Science in Elementary and Middle Classrooms: A Project-Based Approach* Boston: McGraw-Hill College.

Lawson, A. E. (2004, January). *Preserving our intellectual history: The history and development of the learning cycle.* Paper presented at the Annual Meeting of the Association for the Education of Teachers of science, Nashville, TN.

Lawson, A. E. (2010). *Teaching inquiry science in middle and secondary schools.* Los Angeles, CA: Sage.

Lederman, N. G. (2007). Nature of science: Past, present, and future, In Abell. S. K., & Lederman, N. G., editors. *Handbook of Research on Science Education.* Mahwah, NJ: Lawrence Erlbaum Associates, Publishers, 831-880.

Lee, O., & Luykx, A. (2007). Science education and student diversity: Race/ethnicity, language, culture, and socioeconomic status, In In Abell, S. K., & Lederman, N. G. (Eds.), *Handbook of research on science education.* Mahwah, NJ: Lawrence Erlbaum Associates Publishers, 171-198.

Lee, O., Lewis, S., Adamson, K., Maerton-Rivera, J. & Secada, W. (2007). Urban elementary school teachers' knowledge and practices in teaching science to English Language Learners. *Science Education Published online 27 December 2007.*

Lewis, S. P., Alacaci, C., O'Brien, G. E., & Jiang, Z. (2002). Preservice elementary teachers' use of mathematics in a project-based science approach. *School Science and Mathematics* 102(4), 172-179.

Lindgren, J., & Bleicher, R. E. (2005). Learning the learning cycle: The differential effect on elementary preservice teachers. *School Science and Mathematics, 105,* 61-73.

Loucks-Horsley, S. et al. (1990). *Elementary school science for the 90's,* Alexandria, VA: ASCD.

Moscovici, H., & Osisioma, I. (2008, fall). Designing the best urban, preservice elementary science methods course: dilemmas and considerations. *Journal of Elementary Science Education, 20*(4), 15-28.

National Academies Press (NAP). (1998). Teaching About Evolution and the Nature of Science. [online]: www.nap.edu/readingroom/books/evolution98

National Research Council (1996). *National science education standards,* Washington, D.C.: National Academy Press.

National Science Teachers Association (NSTA). (2011). *NSTA Standards for Science Teacher Preparation.* (Online) http://NSTA.org

National Science Teachers Association (NSTA). (2003). *NSTA Standards for Science Teacher Preparation, Recommendations for Elementary and Middle Level General Science Teachers* (Online) http://NSTA.org

National Science Teachers Association (NSTA). (1987, July) *NSTA Standards for Science Teacher Preparation. Washington, DC: NSTA.*

Norman, D. A. (1978). Notes toward a theory of complex learning. In A.M Lesgold, Pellegrino, J. W., Fokkema, S. D., & Glaser, R. (Eds.), *Cognitive psychology and instruction* (pp. 39-48). New York: Plenum.

Novak, J. D., & Gowin, D. B. (1984). *Learning how to learn,* Cambridge, England: Cambridge University Press.

O'Brien, G. E., Lewis, S. P., & Williams, C. C. (1999, January). Implementing a new pre-service elementary teachers' science course and program framework. Austin, TX: Paper presented at the Annual AETS Conference.

O'Brien, G. E., Jiang, Z., Moseley, B., Alacaci, C., Lewis, S., McClintock, E., Park, D., & Chebbi, T. (2002, Spring). "What makes it go?" A look at the design and implementation of an interdisciplinary mathematics and science workshop for inservice and preservice elementary teachers. *Journal for the Art of Teaching* 9(1), 85-97.

O'Brien, G. E. (1991a). Some recommended ways for including multicultural education in a pre-service science methods course. *Science Education International*, 2(1), 25-26.

O'Brien, G. E. (1991b). Computer-based learning. *Science and Children*, 28(6), 40-41.

O'Brien, G. E., & Korth, W. W. (1991a). Videotaping: A tool for enhancing the teacher's understanding of cognitive science and teacher self-development. *Journal of Science Teacher Education,* 2, 90-93.

O'Brien, G. E., & Peters, J. M. (1994). Effect of four instructional strategies on integrated science process skill achievement of preservice elementary teachers having different cognitive development levels. *Journal of Elementary Science Education*, 6(1), 30-45.

Odum, A. L., & Settlage, Jr., J. (1996). Teachers' Understandings of the learning cycle as assessed with a two-tier test. *Journal of Science Teacher Education, 7(2),* 123-142.

Oregon Department of Education. (1989, March). *Contributions of Piaget to science education - science curriculum concept paper*, Salem, OR: 1-12.

Penick, J. E., & Meinhard-Pellens, R. (Eds.). (1984). *Focus on Excellence* Science/Technolgy/Society, Volume 1, Number 5. Washington, DC: NSTA.

Pfeiffer, W. & Jenkins, S. (2003). Wiggly worms at work. Wialliamsport, PA: Harper Collins Press.

Pizzini, E. L. (Ed.) (1991, February). Search solve create share (SSCS) implementation handbook, Iowa City, IA: The University of Iowa.

Pizzini, E.L., Shepardson, D.P. & Abell, S.K. (1989). A rationale for and the development of a problem solving model of instruction in science education. *Science Education*, 73, 523-534.

Reilly, D. H. (1989). A knowledge base for education: Cognitive science. *Journal of Teacher education, 40,* May - June, 9-13.

Rumelhart, D. E., & Norman, D. A. (1978). Accretion, tuning and re-structuring: Three models of learning. In Cotton, J. W., & Klatzky, R. L. (Eds.), *Sematic factors in cognition* (pp. 37-53). Hillsdale, NJ: Erlbaum.

Rosenthal, J. W. (1996). *Teaching science to language minority students*, Clevedon, England: Multilingual Matters, Ltd.

Roychoudhury, A., & Rice, D. (2009). Discourse of making sense of data: Implications for elementary teachers' science education. *Journal of Science Teacher Education, 21,* 181-203. published online: 19 December 2009.

Sadler, T. (2006). Promoting discourse and argumentation in science teacher education. *Journal of Science Teacher Education (17)*(4), 323-346.

Sarkar, S., & Frazier, R. (2010). Place-based inquiry: Advancing environmental education in science teacher preparation. In Bodzin, A. M., Klein, B. S., & Weaver, S. (Eds.). ASTE Series in Science Education: *The inclusion of environmental education in science teacher education.* Dordrecht: Springer, 159-172.

Schepige, A. C., Morrell, P. D., Smith-Walters, C., Sadler, K. C., Munck, M., & Rainboth, D. (2010). Using Environmental Education Project Curricula with Elementary Preservice Teachers. In Bodzin, A. M., Klein, B. S., & Weaver, S. (Eds.). ASTE Series in Science Education: *The inclusion of environmental education in science teacher education.* Dordrecht: Springer, 281-296.

Settlage, J., & Southerland, S. A. (2007). *Teaching science to every child: using culture as a starting point.* New York: Routledge, Taylor & Francis Group.

Shulman, L. S. (1986). Those who understand: Knowledge growth in teaching. Educational Researcher, 15(2), 4- 14.

Skerritt, N., Hard, E., & Edlund. (2008). Integrating the habits of mind: A district perspective, in Costa, A. L., & Kallick, B. (Eds.). *Learning and leading with habits of mind: 16 essential characteristics for success.* Alexandria, VA: Association of Supervision and Curriculum Development, 362-377.

Sobel, D. (2004). *Place-based education: Connecting classrooms & communities.* Great Barrington, MA: The Orion Society.

Soto, P. M., Parker, J. H., & O'Brien, G. E. (1997). Our forest, their forest-A program that stimulates long-term learning and community action, in Totten, S., & Pedersen, J. E. (Eds.). *Social issues and service at the middle level,* Boston, MA: Allyn and Bacon, 319- 339.

Teemant, A., Bernhardt, E., & Rodriguez-Munoz, M. (1996, Summer). Collaborating with content area teachers: What we need to share. *TESOL Journal,* 5(4), 16-20.

The College of Education., Conceptual Framework of the College of Education. (n.d.)., http://education.fiu.edu/docs/Conceptual%20Framework%2006-19-09.pdf

Thornton, H. (2006). Dispositions in action: Do dispositions make a difference in practice? *Teacher Education Quarterly, 33*(2), 53-68.

Victor, E., & Kellough, R. D. (2000). *Science for elementary and middle school,* 9th ed. Upper Saddle River, NJ: Merrill Prentice Hall.

Von Glasersfeld, E. (1989). Cognition, construction of knowledge, and teaching. *Synthese, 80*(1), 121-140.

Vygotsky, L. S. (1978). *Mind in society: The development of higher psychological processes,* M. Cole, V. John- Steiner, S. Scribner, & E. Souberman (Eds.). Cambridge, MA: Harvard University Press.

Wiggins, G. and McTighe, J. (1998). *Understanding by design.* Alexandria, VA: ASCD.

Yager, R. E. (1987). Assess all five domains of science. *Science and Children,* 24(2), 36 - 40.

Yager, R. E., & Penick, J. E. (1990). Science teacher education. In Houston, W. R. (Ed.). *Handbook of Research on teacher education: A project of the Association of Teacher Educators.* New York: MacMillian Publishing Company, 657-673.

Zembal-Saul, C., McNeil, K. L., & Hershberger, K. (2012). *What's your evidence? Engaging k-5 students in constructing explanations in science.* Boston, MA: Pearson.

CHAPTER THIRTEEN

Reflections

By

George E. O'Brien
Lynne D. Miller
Erskine S. Dottin

Historical Context

As noted in this book's introduction, education scholars have identified different conceptual orientations with regard to teaching and learning in teacher preparation. These scholars have referred to these different conceptual orientations as academic, practical, technological, personal, and critical social (Feiman-Nemser, 1990; Gage & Winne, 1975; Joyce, 1975). In the 1970s and 1980s, the early years of teacher preparation in the College of Education at Florida International University, the focus, at the Unit level, was more on a technological conceptual orientation to accommodate performance or competency-based outcomes and field-based professional training. At the same time, courses taught by individual faculty members may have been framed by one or more of the aforementioned conceptual orientations. The chapters in this book point to the growth of the college and to portraits of teaching and learning, by faculty, that are more consistent with new constructivist paradigms of teaching and learning. For example, the authors of the chapter "Using an Historical Lens and Reflection to Establish Our Vision of Teaching Pre-Service Elementary Teachers Content and Methods of Science" note that in 1988 when one author, George E. O'Brien, arrived at FIU, the undergraduate science course SCE 4310 could be said to be more oriented to a technological orientation with a very focused implementation of science process skill development.

The chapters present a portrait of the kinds of teaching behaviors that relate to the idea of meta-cognition and the methods used by the chapter authors to model their thinking about their own thinking. These current research and theoretical constructs were non-existent during the infancy days of the college, 1972-1996. Constructivism was in its infancy during the 1970s and did not become the dominant learning paradigm until the 1980s. Change occurred within the college in light of developments in the field of teacher education.

College's Collective Commitment to Work from the Base of a Conceptual Framework

The major catalyst for change in the college was its being denied national accreditation by the National Council for Accreditation of Teacher Education (NCATE) in 1993-1994. To secure national accreditation meant the college having to attend to a critical component of the NCATE Standards, having a conceptual framework that provides philosophical direction for programs and operations. More importantly, the philosophy in that conceptual framework is supposed to lead to coherent learning outcomes for learners: the knowledge, skills and dispositions they should acquire. The co-editors of this book were instrumental in helping the college commit to working from a conceptual framework (see Dottin, E. S. 2001, *The Development of a Conceptual Framework: The Stimulation for Coherence and Continuous Improvement in Teacher Education.* University Press of America).

To work from a conceptual framework, however, also meant that attention had to be given to nurturing and assessing candidates' dispositions-a construct entirely new to teacher education programs. The collective effort in the college on a conceptual framework, and embryonic work on dispositions, led in 1996 to its receipt of national accreditation and to be the recipient of an award from the American Association of Colleges for Teacher Education.

Working Towards Common Ends and Cohesiveness to Work of the College

One of the seven habits of highly effective people is that they begin with the end in mind. They use personal vision, correct principles, and their deep sense of personal meaning to accomplish tasks in a positive and effective way. They live life based on self-chosen values and are guided by their personal mission statement (Covey, 2004). This lesson from Covey (2004) about a salient ingredient in personal change may be gleaned clearly from the chapters in this book. The chapter authors all demonstrate the relevance of grounding their pedagogy in an aim, a common end to which their pedagogical efforts are directed. It is their attention to this common end – a particular conceptual orientation – that guides how they structure their learning environments to call forth habits of mind, that is, key dispositions that are consistent with, and emerge from, that conceptual orientation. A key lesson that one may deduce from the chapters is that it is possible for faculty members in colleges of education to live the philosophical ideas in their conceptual framework(s) as a means to enhancing teaching and learning for themselves and students in their respective units.

The pedagogical strategies that are described in the chapters point clearly to the realization that the authors were not pursuing the common end in their college's conceptual framework by just following a prescriptive mandate. As such, one senses in the chapters, the authors' moral agency as manifested in their choosing the purpose toward which their teaching and learning is directed. In fact, the majority of the authors' sense of connecting purpose and actions in the teacher education program is strengthened by their sense of community drawn from their being a member of a Faculty Learning Community. This is echoed by some authors explicitly and reaffirms John Dewey's idea of community as an enduring form of association in which the members of the community stand from the beginning in relations to one another and in which members get direction for their conduct by thinking of the whole group and their place in it, rather than by an adjustment of egoism and altruism (Dewey, 1960, p. 164).

From the chapters, one senses the chapter authors who are members of the Faculty Learning Community having a kind of like-mindedness that ensures their participation in a common understanding of what they are trying to achieve in their teaching and learning, and, as a result, they regulate their learning environments in view of that like-mindedness. There seems to be a tacit expectation from each of the chapter authors, who are members of the Learning Community in the College, wanting to know what the other is about and wanting to keep the other(s) informed as to his or her own purpose and progress in achieving the common end. In fact, while not described to any extent in the chapters, we, the co-editors' experiences in the Faculty Learning Community attest to community members working to visualize both the methods and the outcomes of the intent of the College of Education's Conceptual Framework. This occurred through the Faculty Learning Community meetings across a two-year span: through members engaging in active learning, for example, learning about and using learning protocols like MYST (see chapter by Joyce C. Fine); through members getting to know and trust each other, that is by learning each other's personal histories and gaining more confidence and trust in each other over time; and, through community members putting the ideas they were learning in the community, as well as related community activities, such as workshops and conferences, into practice, in many cases for the first time in their respective courses (see the chapter by George E. O'Brien and Kathleen Sparrow).

It is clear from the chapters that some authors are exploring a model of teacher as learner, modeling in effect the process of the professor's disposition to be truthful and moral, thus exposing him or herself to candidates' criticisms, since many teacher education candidates have often been most comfortable with professors who espouse the teacher/professor as expert, "sage on the stage." Some of the authors clearly demonstrate risk taking in their modeling the teacher as learner (for examples, see the chapters by Teresa Lucas, Aixa Perez-Prado, and George E. O'Brien and Kathleen Sparrow).

Working toward common learning outcomes of knowledge, skills and dispositions, for all graduates, helped some of the chapter authors to gravitate to visualization models where they could readily visualize their respective courses as integrating/nesting together/blending together learning objectives across these knowledge bases of knowledge, skills and dispositions. For example, one sees this in the use of Costa and Kallick's model of nested objectives in the chapter by Angela Salmon and Debra Mayes Pane. On the other hand, some authors come to realize that knowledge, skills and dispositions are not separate and unrelated entities as is seen in the chapter by Joyce C. Fine and Lynne D. Miller.

Dispositions that are Applicable Across Programs (Initial and Advanced) and may be Developed by Faculty Whose Work Stems from Different Philosophies

Further analysis of the chapters reveals pedagogical diversity in delivery of courses and programs in the College of Education. More importantly, one may trace that diversity to differently held Conceptual Orientations in teacher education. Another insight that may be gleaned from the chapters is that a faculty may have diversity of pedagogical thought, but if that faculty is guided by a common aim as delineated in a conceptual framework, then faculty members do not have to fear uniformity, but they can use different means to achieve the articulated common. Coherency emerges and is not gained at the expense of the personal and professional perspectives of each faculty member. Nurturing and assessing dispositions as habits of mind from this perspective leads to dispositions that are first grounded in the pursuit of a common aim, and, as a result, these dispositions may apply to both initial and advanced level programs.

The coherence about teaching and learning about dispositions that emerges in these chapters facilitates a model for enhancing growth in dispositions that may be useful for other teacher education programs. The approach to growth in dispositions as habits of mind may be conceptualized from entry to the program (through developmental levels of awareness, seeing value, internalization), to exiting the program, and to transfer in the world of practice (on the job).

Entry to Program	Awareness	Seeing Value	Internalization	Exit from Program	On the job
	Develop capacity to articulate meanings of dispositions (habits of mind)	Learn to see and apply connections between habits of mind and content acquisition	Habits of mind serve as internal compass to guide pedagogical actions in clinical practice		Habits of mind guide professional conduct
Pre-assessment (Scale)	Self-reports	Qualitative and quantitative measures	Qualitative and quantitative measures	Post-assessment (Scale & surveys)	Performance assessment

Insights from Chapters about Reflective Intelligence

Finally, the chapters provide a learning path to reflective intelligence: experience, reflect, apply, and transfer. One sees clearly in the chapters a tacit thread of John Dewey's concept of "plasticity" – learning from experience and retaining from one experience something used in coping with difficulties in another situation (Dewey, 1916/1944). The chapters show that to learn from experience, that is, to act on the world, undergo the consequences, and make connections between the act and its consequences (learn), requires the cultivation of certain dispositions (that is, habits of mind) or as called by Dewey (1916/1944) "moral traits." Such habits of mind "characterize a [teacher and learner] who is extending and deepening interest in learning from all of his [her] contacts in the world" (Hansen, 2002, p. 269).

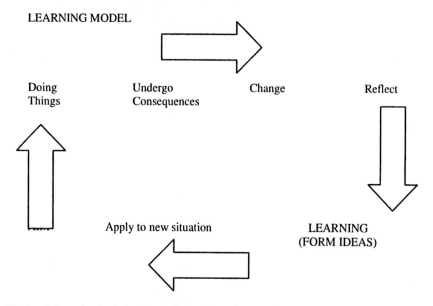

LEARNING MODEL

Doing Things

Undergo Consequences

Change

Reflect

Apply to new situation

LEARNING (FORM IDEAS)

The book's major insight about dispositions is that dispositions as habits of mind must be seen as expressions of moral growth. Furthermore, one sees in the chapters the idea that educative environments must be structured to enhance the acquisition and/or demonstration of habits of mind. But, to structure "educative" environments requires three vital ingredients (Dewey, 1916/1944): (1) one must work toward common ends, or in other words, have an aim that facilitates acting with meaning; (2) one must effect a sharing of purpose through communication; and (3) one must foster a sense of community based on the things community members have in common.

References

Covey, S. (2004). *The 7 habits of highly effective people: Powerful lessons in personal change.* London: Simon & Schuster.

Dewey, J. (1960). *Theory of the moral life.* New York: Holt, Rinehart & Winston.

Dewey, J. (1916/1944). *Democracy and education: An introduction to the philosophy of education.* New York, NY: The Free Press.

Dottin, E. S. (2001). *The development of a conceptual framework: The stimulation for coherence and continuous improvement in teacher education.* University Press of America).

Feinman-Nemser, S. (1990). Teacher preparation: Structural and conceptual alternatives. In W.R. Houston, M. Huberman, and J. Sikula (Eds.). *Handbook of research in teacher education* (pp. 212-233). New York: MacMillan.

Gage, N. L., & Winne, P. H. (1975). Performance-Based teacher education. In K. Ryan (Ed.), *Teacher education* (74th yearbook of the National Society for the Study of Education, Part II., pp. 146-172). Chicago: University of Chicago Press.

Hansen, D. (2002, autumn). Dewey's conception of an environment for teaching and learning. *Curriculum Inquiry, 32*(3), 267-280.

Joyce, B. (1975). Conceptions of man and their implications for teacher education. In K. Ryan (Ed.), *Teacher education* (74th yearbook of the National Society for the Study of Education, Part II., pp. 111-145). Chicago: University of Chicago Press.

White, P. (1996). *Civic virtues and public schooling: Educating citizens for a democratic society.* New York, NY: Teachers College Press.

CONTRIBUTORS' BIOGRAPHICAL SKETCH

Charmaine DeFrancesco is the Chairperson of the Department of Teaching and Learning in the College of Education, Florida International University. She is a Hall of Fame Athlete from Northern Illinois University and received the "NJCAA Basketball Coach of the Year Award" in 1984. She earned her Master of Arts degree in Teaching and Administration from Northern Colorado University, and focused on learning and performance strategies during her doctoral studies at Florida State University. Her scholarly interests include a focus on individuals and groups often absent from the sport limelight.

Erskine S. Dottin earned his bachelor's and master's degrees from the University of West Florida, and his doctorate from Miami University of Ohio. He is currently a faculty member in the Department of Leadership and Professional Studies in the College of Education, Florida International University. His research interests are in the areas of humanistic education, the use of case methods and dispositions in teacher education.

Maria L. Fernandez, PhD, graduated from the University of Georgia and is presently Associate Chair of the Department of Teaching and Learning and Program Leader for Mathematics Education at Florida International University. Her scholarship is primarily within the areas of creating and investigating approaches for the professional development of prospective and practicing teachers of mathematics, and developing and exploring approaches for improving the mathematics teaching and learning of diverse learners. She was the original creator and researcher of Microteaching Lesson Study, an innovative approach for teaching prospective teachers that draws on and integrates features of lesson study and microteaching.

Joyce C. Fine is Program Leader of the Reading, Language Arts Program in the College of Education, Florida International University. She earned her bachelor's degree from Goucher College and her master's and doctoral degrees from Florida International University. Her research interests include reading and writing strategies and assessment, adolescent literacy development, assessment and intervention of literacy development, history of literacy instruction and curriculum development.

Barbara Johnson is currently the principal of Charles David Wyche, Jr. Elementary School in Miami, Florida. She received her bachelor's and master's degrees from East Carolina University and acquired her specialist and doctorate degrees from Nova Southeastern University. Her areas of interest include helping children and adults become consciously disciplined so they may practice using the habits of mind to build more intelligent behaviors.

Esther F. Joseph is a Doctoral Student in Curriculum and Instruction in Secondary Mathematics Education at Florida International University. Esther has taught Math for Miami Dade Public Schools and has also taught undergraduate mathematics education courses at FIU. Esther is currently researching Mathematics educator recruitment efforts in the Learning Assistant Program. Esther has presented her findings at local conferences and has published a co-authored paper. Esther's motto is that 'Tough times never last but tough people do', in the future she hopes to inspire her students to succeed and believe that their environment does not determine their destiny.

Teresa Lucas earned her bachelor's and master's degrees from the University of Illinois and her doctoral degree from Florida State University. She is Interim Program Leader for Modern Language Education, and teaches the ESL endorsement courses for undergraduate students and courses for graduate students in Foreign Language Education, TESOL Track. Her research interests include bilingual language development, application of visible thinking strategies in higher education, and learning communities.

Lynne D. Miller is the Program Leader for the undergraduate Elementary Education Program in the College of Education, Florida International University. She earned her bachelor's degree from the University of California, Santa Barbara; her master's degree from California State University, Northridge, and her doctorate from the University of Arizona. Her scholarly interest is to foster the development of knowledge, understanding and professional growth through research and scholarly activity related to literacy and teacher education.

Roxanne V. Molina, PhD, graduated from Florida International University and is currently a Program Professor at Nova Southeastern University. Her research interests include the professional development of preservice and practicing teachers of mathematics, and developing and investigating approaches to mathematics teaching that incorporate technology. In conjunction with Dr. Fernandez, she has helped expand the research related to Microteaching Lesson Study.

Leslie Nisbet is a PhD student at Florida International University who is planning on defending her research proposal in Fall 2012. Leslie has assisted with math course curricular development and has taught undergraduate mathematics education courses. Leslie has presented research findings from work conducted in collaboration with FIU colleagues, which investigated the use of contextual problems as a strategy to reduce mathematics anxiety. She presented her findings at multiple local, state, national and international conferences, and has published a co-authored paper.

George E. O'Brien is the Director of the Master's of Science, Curriculum and Instruction Program in the College of Education, Florida International University. He earned his bachelor's degree from the University of Massachusetts- Lowell, his master's from Teachers College, Columbia University, and his doctorate from the University of Iowa. His research interests include pre-service and in-service science teacher education, project-based science, educational outreach and learning community development, environmental education, and interdisciplinary approaches in teaching science.

Debra Mayes Pane is the Founding President at Eradicating the School-to-Prison Pipeline Foundation, Inc. (ESToPP), and has served as an Adjunct Instructor in the College of Education, Florida International University, and as Part-Time Executive Director at Miami-Dade County Public Schools Educational Alternative Outreach Program. She earned her bachelor's degree from Sam Houston University, and her master's and doctoral degrees from Florida International University. Her research interests include culturally responsive pedagogy, culturally responsive classroom management, empowering education, transformative teacher education, and transformative literacy.

Aixa Perez-Prado is an Instructor in the Department of Teaching and Learning in the College of Education, Florida International University. She is currently ESOL Coordinator in the college and her duties include faculty development and work with the Office of Academic Affairs towards accreditation. She has an interest in incorporating new technologies into the classroom that are interactive and offer students access to the global community of learners. She earned her bachelor's degree from State University of New York, Buffalo, her master's from Monterey Institute of International Studies, TESOL, and her doctorate from Florida State University.

Helen Robbins is a Reading Education Instructor in the Department of Teaching and Learning in the College of Education, Florida International University. She earned her bachelor's degree from New Jersey State College, and her master's and doctoral degrees from Florida International University. She has taught in the Miami-Dade County Public Schools, and teaches undergraduate reading education courses at Florida International University.

Angela Salmon is the Program Leader of the Early Childhood Education Program in the Department of Teaching and Learning in the College of Education, Florida International University. She earned her bachelor's degree from Catholic University of Ecuador, and her master's and doctorate degrees from the University of Cincinnati. Her long-standing partnership with Project Zero at Harvard Graduate School of Education has evolved into numerous research initiatives and professional development opportunities. She is founder and leader of the Visible Thinking South Florida Initiative. Her research interests include the interplay between cognition and language and literacy development, children's theory of mind, teachers' discourse in the classroom, music and thinking and the development of communities of practice.

Patsy Self Trand is an Instructor in Reading Education in the Department of Teaching and Learning, College of Education, Florida International University. She earned her bachelor's degree from Hampton University, her master's from the University of Missouri, and her doctorate from the University of Virginia. She was the Faculty Administrator for the Reading and Learning Lab at FIU for more than 20 years. Her research interests include literacy-critical thinking for college and secondary readers and teaching elementary students to read or to read better.

Gwyn W. Senokossoff is a faculty member in Reading Education in the Department of Teaching and Learning in the College of Education, Florida International University. She earned her bachelor's, master's, and doctorate degrees from the University of South Florida. She teaches graduate courses in Reading, and her research interests include early intervention in reading, literacy coaching, reflective teaching and professional development in literacy that encourages teacher change.

Kathleen G. Sparrow is an Adjunct Instructor at Florida International University and an Online Advisor for the National Science Teachers Association (NSTA) Learning Center. She earned her bachelor's degree from Miami University (Oxford, OH), and her master's and doctorate degrees from The University of Akron. She served as the Science Supervisor for Akron, Ohio Public Schools after teaching middle and high school science classes in Akron. She received the National Science Supervisors Award in 2000. She has served as president of National Science Education Leadership Association, as a regional director for SECO (Ohio's state science organization) and on the NSTA Board of Directors .

Maria Alvarez Tsalikis is an Instructor in the Department of Teaching and Learning in the College of Education, Florida International University. She earned her master's and doctorate from Florida International University. She has taught in public schools in Miami-Dade County, Florida, and teaches both undergraduate and graduate courses in Reading at FIU.

Mickey Weiner earned her bachelor's degree from the University of Wisconsin-Madison and her master's and doctorate degrees from Florida International

University. She has been a teacher in the Miami Dade County Public Schools for 28 years. She is National Board Certified and is currently working in the areas of curriculum support at Charles David Wyche, Jr. Elementary School in Miami, Florida. She enjoys collaborative partnerships between universities and elementary schools and is interested in learning new ways to practice habits of mind.

Lynn Yribarren is an Instructor in the Department of Teaching and Learning in the College of Education, Florida International University. She earned her bachelor's degree from Edinboro State University, and her master's and doctorate from Florida International University. She teaches undergraduate courses in Reading.